Journeys

An Anthology of Adult Student Writing

2011

Chau Yang, Saint Paul

Mission

The mission of the Minnesota Literacy Council is to share the power of learning through education, community building, and advocacy. Through this mission, MLC:

- Helps adults become self-sufficient citizens through improved literacy.
- Helps at-risk children and families gain literacy skills to increase school success.
- Strengthens communities by raising literacy levels and encouraging volunteerism.
- Raises awareness of literacy needs and services throughout the state.

Acknowledgements

The Minnesota Literacy Council extends our heartfelt thanks to Elizabeth Bance, Stephen Burgdorf, Katharine Engdahl and Sara Sparrowgrove who have donated their time and talent to the planning, design, editing, and production of this book. Special thanks also to MLC staff Guy Haglund, Allison Runchey, Melissa Martinson and Cathy Grady for helping make Journeys a success. Finally, we are deeply grateful for the generous donation of $500 from Todd and Mimi Burke through the Burke Family Fund in memory of Todd's late mother.

The Minnesota Literacy Council
www.theMLC.org
651-645-2277
Hotline: 800-222-1990
700 Raymond Avenue, Suite 180
Saint Paul, Minnesota 55114-1404

Table of Contents

Cover Art by Abdir Ahman Samatar, Rochester • Back Cover Art by Vue Xiong, Saint Paul

Introduction

Dear Reader,

The following pages are filled with stories by Minnesotans whose voices are rarely heard. Some are immigrants or refugees writing in their second or third language. Others are sharing their writing for the first time after years of frustration over their low literacy skills. All of them are improving their lives through education – often along with huge work and family responsibilities.

We are grateful these writers have taken the time to share their thoughts and experiences with us in *Journeys*, the Minnesota Literacy Council's annual journal of original writing and artwork, now in its 22nd year. The authors represent adult literacy students across the state who are enrolled in reading, English as a Second Language, GED, and basic skills classes. Each one has worked hard over the past year with the help of their teachers and volunteer tutors to be able to share their experiences with you through the written word.

Year after year, we call upon learners to submit writing and art for *Journeys* because we believe it speaks to our mission of sharing the power of learning. It provides a forum for the creative expression of adult learners, a text of authentic learner stories for teachers to use in the classroom, and an acknowledgement of the contributions adult education gives to the larger Minnesota community.

When *Journeys* was born more than two decades ago as a thin stack of stapled pages, we never could have imagined how it appears today: a bound literary journal with nearly 600 writing and drawing submissions. We owe its growth and success to the dedication of volunteers. The 22nd annual anthology would not have been possible without our four interns, Elizabeth Bance, Stephen Burgdorf, Katharine Engdahl and Sara Sparrowgrove, who donated hundreds of hours of their time to producing this book.

Thank you for supporting us by purchasing *Journeys*. I hope you enjoy it.

Eric Nesheim
Executive Director

Ming Hai Zheng, Cloquet

Lucy Brown, Hugo

I Am...

Glad for the Animals of the U.S.A.
Oo Thundarah, Saint Paul

My name is Oo Thun Darah. I am from a Thailand refugee camp, but I am originally from the Karen State of Burma. I came to the United States on April 29, 2008. At that time, I didn't know anything about America. I was scared to go outside because the people here showed their hands and said hello to me. I didn't know how to say anything back to them. I only worried about that.

One day, my friend took me to Phalen Lake. I saw many birds and many squirrels playing in the trees. I felt happy to see them and to smell fresh air. I wondered why were they not scared of the humans? "Why are they tame with humans?" I asked my friend. He said, "All the animals here are free. Nobody can hunt them. If you hunt them here, you could get in trouble. If you want to hunt, you need to have a license. You can hunt them many places where the government allows."

That is what I dreamed before when I lived in my country. I thought about the animals. I wanted them to be free. But that was only my dream. The reason why I thought that, was because I had to run from bad situations many times with my people. So I didn't want them to run away from us, like we had to run away from the military. When we began to settle down in the jungle, we heard many kinds of birds singing and many kinds of animals calling in the mountains.

After one year, I didn't hear the birds sing or the call from the animals on the mountains. I felt sorry about that. Sometimes, I thought to myself, about how we ran away from soldiers and now the animals run away from us. Maybe they thought we were a bad situation for them to. We were not fair with them. But we are the humans. We need to sympathize with them. If I were a person who has the power, I would give them freedom.

That is what I dreamed before. It never happened like my thoughts, but it really did happen in America. I am really glad for the animals here, but I will always feel sad for the animals in my country.

Oo Thun Darah has been a student at Lao Family English School in St. Paul since July of 2008. Earlier in his life he lived in Burma, where he was born in 1967. He became a Buddhist monk because of his interest in peaceful existence for all creatures, as evidenced in his Journeys story. He is deeply concerned with suffering, whether that of a human being or any other living thing.

Story About My Life
Nhia Thor, Saint Paul

I was born in Xiengkhouang, Laos. When I was a child, I liked to run, play with my neighbor kids and I loved to draw. I was a good drawer in school. I came to the United States of America in 2008 from my native country of Laos. I came to this country through marrying an American citizen. My muscular, handsome husband is Gary. We were married in June 2009. I don`t have any children yet and I don`t plan to have any children until I finish school. I live in Saint Paul, Minnesota. I like my place and my neighbors because they are nice but I don`t like some of the neighbors' teenage kids because they smoke and they wear baggy clothes and their pants hang way below their butts. That makes them walk like ducks. Every day, I go to work and go to school. I like to go running around Lake Phalen and go bowling and I like to dance. I love to learn and I believe in education. I`m learning English and I want to improve my English skills. My goal is to finish college and have a good paying job so I can help my family and relatives back home in Laos.

Nhia Thor is 22 years old and is originally from Laos.

When I Came to America
Anisa Hersi, Rochester

My name is Anisa Ishak. I was born in Mogadishu, Somalia. I will never forget how badly I wanted to come to the United States when I was 16 years old. That was my big dream. The truth was that my sister lived in Arizona, but she never told me how hard the life she lived was. She was always sending money and things to support us. When I came, she paid for everything for me plus rent. She didn't tell me how hard she worked, but two weeks later I saw my sister worked four jobs. She never had enough time to sleep. She took many medicines and she destroyed herself because of us.

First I thought to go to school, but that day my decision was to apply for jobs, and I forgot about school. My first job I applied for was Saint Mary's Hospital housekeeping. Four days later they called me, and said come to the interview. When I went there I met a woman and a man and they asked me many questions. Mostly I didn't understand because I never went to school for English. I only know how to read and write my language, Somali. I remember the last question she asked me was what time are you available to begin work, and I didn't understand. I will never forget that day. Anytime I see Saint Mary's Hospital, I remember I have never had a good job since I came to the United States. I am a very hard worker, but my luck has never sent me a good job.

Seven months later we moved Minneapolis and my wonderful sister got married. When we came to Minnesota my sister found Hawthorne Education Center and she said to me, "You have to go to school because without education, life is very hard." So I started Hawthorne Education Center, and I am very happy because I can read, write, and understand now. My life is better than before and I say to every teacher in Hawthorne thanks because they are wonderful teachers. I will study and one day have my chance.

Anisa Hersi is originally from Somalia.

My Story
Fardowsa Ahmed, Minneapolis

My name is Fardowsa. I am from Somalia. I live in Minneapolis, Minnesota. When I was younger my country was fighting. Then my family and I went to Kenya. I missed a lot of my friends. Some died. That day was sad for me. After two years I came to America. I started a new life. I married and I had six children. My children were born in the United States.

Fardowsa Ahmed is originally from Somalia.

I Want to Be a Hard Worker
Myint Maung, Saint Paul

I was born in Burma on January 1, 1986 and in 1993 I started school. When I was a child, I liked to draw a picture. In 1997 I moved to Thailand Refugee Camp. From 1998-2003, I studied in school again. When I lived in Thailand, I worked on a Thai fishing boat. On 18 September 2006, I came to the United States of America with my family. I lived in Austin, Texas. In 2007, I moved to Saint Paul, Minnesota. In March 2007, I started Leap School for some months. On May 15, 2008, I had first my job in Worthington. I don't like this place because there is so much snow. I have 3 sisters and 3 brothers. They are all married. I am single now. I live in Saint Paul. Now I come to Hmong-American Partnership School since 2009. I want to learn more English. Now I am working at Dakota Premium Food.

Myint Maung is originally from Burma.

How My Life Changed
Lourdes T., Brooklyn Park

I am from Mexico. I came here in 1998. I was 23 years old when I arrived with my sister in Minnesota. Here I got married. I have three children now, but I miss my own country, the culture, and holidays such as the 12th of December, which is Virgin Maria Day, and Christmas. I hope to go back to my country soon, but sometimes I feel scared because the violence is high in Mexico. But my dream is to return to my own country one day.

Lourdes T. is originally from Mexico.

My Life
Gia, Lake Elmo

My name is Gia Yang. I have been in the United States for about 8 years. I am originally from Laos, the country of a million elephants. I came from a good family.

I have four brothers and three sisters. All of them still live in Laos, except my sister and me. I came from a poor family. Back in Laos I did not go to school. I was a farm girl who helped around the house and the garden. I did not receive any formal education. My dad died when I was five years old. After my dad died our family was even poorer. My mom then remarried a new man. Some of my brothers and sisters went to live with my mom and my new step dad. I was six years old and I was chosen to stay with my uncle from my original dad's side. Since my uncle had many of his own kids I was still not able to go school.

In January 2002, I met my sweetheart during the Hmong New Year in Laos. I fell in love and became his fiancée. In July of 2002, I came to America. I then married my husband. We now have five kids together. We have three boys and two lovely girls.

Now, I am finally able to go to school in America. I am so happy with my life now. My life feels complete.

Untitled
Anonymous, Saint Louis Park

I am from Ethiopia. I remember the first day I came to the United States. I arrived in New York on February 14, 2007 at the airport and at the hotel. The problem was the weather. It was too bad. I stayed for three days in New York. My family, my father, two brothers, three sisters, and I came to the United States together. My older brother was in Minnesota and after three days, I came to live with him and relaxed. The United States of America has different weather and a different culture than my country.

Autobiography
Yayneabeba Weldeyes, Eagan

I am from Ethiopia, my mom and dad took in my brother and my brother baby and me. My first job in my country was teaching science for grades five to eight. I was very, very interested in helping students. I graduated in my country. My job was interesting and my life. I came nine months later to the United States of America and it was very beautiful but everything is not the same. I feel I miss my family. I am very, very love with my mom and dad but my life changed and respected me. I won the visa lottery in 2009 and the process was finished in 2010 and then I was very happy at that time. I moved to Atlanta, Georgia and then Charlotte, North Carolina. My cousin had no job and so Charlotte was hard because I had no job, hard because in my country we don't speak English but I try to learn to say everything. In my country, we only learn English but don't speak it and that is not enough for me because my problem is to speak English. America is very, very overwhelming. I learn and I work but my family life is changed. I help God, I am not married, and I am single. In the future, I will get married. I live in Saint Paul, MN. I love this country and I like snow. It is beautiful. I am not working but I try to apply for a job. I like American malls. I go every day, that's fun for me and so is swimming. I watch TV and talk to my friends. I go to church, this is very happy. I am studying at Hmong-American Partnership in America. I am a very special person in spoken English but I am very, very interested in school. I appreciate my teacher because I am speaking English. My future is to go to college and then I will get a job. I have many plans but help me God everything's fine and my friends are happy. THANKS.

Yayneabeba Weldeyes is 22 years old and is originally from Ethiopia.

My First Life in America
Anonymous, Minneapolis

When I first came to the United States I had a lot of problems. I was one of the first Sudanese refugees who were resettled in America. There was nobody who could help translate English for me. So to get around to places became difficult for me. One of my biggest problems was transportation to stores, school, hospital, and other appointments. One day I wanted to go to the hospital. I got confused. I took wrong bus, I found myself in different direction. I got lost, and I

didn't know what to do. At last, the bus driver decided to call the police station, so I was taken to the police station. I was questioned. I didn't know how to speak, so they had to call the Center for New Americans. Then one volunteer checked my name in the list of new Americans and I was helped. It took one day.

Now I am better because I can speak little bit of English, and at least I can move around by myself. I know all nearby roads. There are a lot of the Sudanese refugees. I am happy.

Untitled
Muhibo Mohamed, Minneapolis

My name is Muhibo. I came from Somalia. I remember my country many times. When I was a child, I had more freedom to go outside to play. When I had free time, I wasn't scared of anything because my country at that time was very safe. I finished high school, and after that, I started work. When I worked one year, I was married. I had my oldest child, Sahra, then my country started civil war. Than I came to the United States. I was excited, but I saw a different culture. My children grow up in North America

The Four Seasons
Anonymous, Blaine

I like all four seasons. All seasons in Minnesota and in my country, Moldova, are the same. All seasons are important and wonderful. In the wintertime everywhere is wearing all white colors.

Most people like to celebrate New Year's and Christmas Day in the wintertime. In the springtime, grass, flowers, and trees grow and have new leaves. The springtime is enjoyed by the people who are farmers.

In the summertime, it is very hot. I like to go fishing after a rain and take pictures with my family. I like to go with my friends to the lakes on the weekends. In the fall time, I like it when the leaves change their green colors to red colors or other colors. I like fall season because after rain, my husband and I go to the forest to find mushrooms.

My favorite season is summertime, because often my family and my friends meet in the park and go to the lakes. I like the summer season because in July is my birthday. So, do you like the summer season the most?

My Story in Thailand and in the United States
Phainee Yang, Saint Paul

My name is Phainee. I came from Thailand. I have been living in the United States for four years. I'm married and I have four children. I would like to tell about my life in my old home country when I was a child and when I moved to the United States.

When I was a child, my family was very poor. My parents couldn't afford their children, so my three younger brothers and I had to go to live with a monk. The monk took care of everything for us. The monk really loved us like his children, and he helped the other people who were poor who lived in the village. The monk was 73 years old and he died when the people who lived in the village were beginning to come to the United States. When Hmong people began to move to the United States in 2004, Hmong were almost gone from the village. I still waited for my turn to move to the United States. I had to wait until December 31, 2006, when I heard that I could move to the United States with my two children and with other families. I came to the United States on January 1, 2007. When I came to the United States I didn't know anything about living here. I couldn't speak English and I couldn't drive. Everything was difficult for me, but now it is better than before. I can speak English and I can drive. I can do anything here by myself. I really like to learn English, and now I'm learning English at Lao Family School. I will continue to learn more English because it is a way to support my life to live in the United States.

Phainee Yang is originally from Thailand.

Coming to America
Asho Bidare, Saint Paul

I am from Somalia. I moved to Nairobi, Kenya in 1998 with my family and I have 4 brothers and one sister. When I was young, I really wanted to go to school in Kenya but my mom didn't let me. Then my family moved to Minnesota in 2001. My uncle helped find a deaf school here and I was so happy when I went to school for the first time since I never went to school in Somalia. My family is happy living here. My home is very dangerous in Somalia and there is no education or jobs for deaf people. When I was a kid, I played soccer in Somalia. I liked playing soccer with my friends who are hearing and I was the only deaf person. I really miss a lot of my old friends from Somalia. Because I was leaving to Minnesota, I never saw snow before. I tried to grab it with my hand. It was cold and it hurt! Then my brother gave me gloves.

What's in a Name?
Esperanza, Minneapolis

Esperanza is my name. I don't know why my parents chose that name for me. I will try to make a phone call and ask to my mother why she chose the name.

When I was child, I was the only one who had that name in the whole small city. When I was in the school, the students mocked my name. Then I started to not like my name. When I was a teenager, the boys started to call me a spy. Then I started to like it.

When I moved to the United States, one time a women asked me if I know what is the meaning of my name. I told her I don't know. Then she said it means "hope" and she told me, "Your name is beautiful."

Esperanza is originally from Ecuador.

The Short-Term Story of My Life
Courtney Mason, Minneapolis

I was born on September 26, 1990 in the afternoon at Cook County Hospital. I lived with my mom, brother and stepfather on the 13th floor in Robert Taylor's Building. When I was five years old my mom moved in with my grandparents on 73rd and Kingston, then my grandparents moved to 72nd and Jeffery when I was six years old. I guess I got so attached to my grandparents, I wanted to live with them for some reason. My mother wanted to leave Chicago and live in St. Paul, Minnesota, but I chose to not leave Chicago and need to make new friends.

Two months passed and I really started to miss my mother and brother, so on Easter Day my grandparents and me drove to Minnesota. When I got there, I was surprised that my mom was pregnant. We stayed in Minnesota for three days after Easter. When we left I was kind of sad, the school I went to was Bradwell. When I graduated, I went to Hale's Franciscan High School. I got kicked out for cursing at the teacher, but I was kind of glad because it was an all boy's school. I got in trouble for a week. I couldn't go outside or watch T.V. but after a week passed I went to a school that was two blocks away from me. My last year there I got a job at Finest Shoe Repair on 71st Jeffery. I was eighteen at the time. That's the short term story of my life.

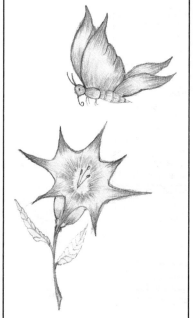

Vue Xiong,   *Saint Paul*

My Job
Selie P. White, Minneapolis

Hi, my name is Selie P. White. I am writing about my job and how I help others at work and all. So here are some things about myself: I started working at Recovery Resource Center at 1900 Chicago Ave. S. on November 7, 2010.

I work with individuals in a treatment program being a support to the women and men by mentoring them. I am willing and able to devote my time to others. I am a trustworthy, patient, honest, and supportive person to people in the program. I talk with people every day in Recovery asking them, "How can I help?" I get enthusiastic about helping people develop themselves and talk about their pain and how to get through it that day. Also I encourage them to get through treatment: Follow the rules, go to meetings, get a sponsor, work a 12-step program, and get a God to talk to.

Untitled
Abdulqadir Dini, Minneapolis

My name is Abdulqadir Dini. I came to the United States June 12, 2007. When I came to the United States I was very happy, because I started a job and I also started to learn English. When I worked six months, I bought a car. After that, I achieved my driver's license. I was very happy when I got my driver's license. I work six days a week and I go to school four days a week. I'm excited to live back home and also I'm excited to live to the United States of America.

My Story
Ahmed Warsame, Saint Cloud

My name is Ahmed. I was born in Somalia. I am married. I have four kids. They live with my wife in Yemen. My father and brothers live in the United Kingdom. When I was in Somalia we lived a good life because my father was working. During the Civil War in Somalia we went to Yemen with the whole family to get a better life than in my country. I got a small job in Yemen. I stayed there for ten years.

I came to the United States nine years ago. I came to Saint Cloud with my friends. We rent an apartment with two bedrooms. Now I work in a big company. It is called Electrolux in Saint Cloud. I start work at 3:30 p.m. till midnight. In the morning, I go to school to learn English (reading, writing, and speaking). Now I live a good life and I am a citizen. One day I want to bring my family into the United States.

My Native Country
Sergei, Coon Rapids

My name is Sergei. I am from Belarus. My country is in Central Europe. There are 10 million people. People in my country are very friendly. When we have free time, we like to go to the forest and the lake. The weather in my country is different. It is cold in winter. It is rainy in fall and spring. The best time to visit my country is summer, because it is warm

Typical food in Belarus is potatoes and pork. Typical jobs that people have are construction. A problem that my country has is no money and no good jobs. One thing that is better in my native country than in the United States is bread. One thing that is better in the United States than in my country is freedom.

What I miss most about my native country is my father. One interesting thing about my native country is one dollar equals 3.000 rubles. This is very expensive.

What's in a Name?
Rosa Anita Cardenas, Minneapolis

My name is Rosa. I think my name is popular in the world. I always think the meaning is like a flower because when the people ask me my name they always tell me it is like a flower. I am so glad about my name.

When I asked my mom about my name she told me she gave me that name because my grandfathers

looked on the calendar for my name. They gave the name for me. Also my mom and father like that name for me. Now they call me Rosanita. I feel so happy with my name.

Rosa Anita Cardenas is originally from Ecuador.

Untitled
Lan Thanh, Minneapolis

My name is Lan Thanh. I'm Vietnamese. I came to the United States in 1997 and lived in Minneapolis, Minnesota. I came here with my husband and two children: one nine year old boy and one seven year old daughter. I have no relatives here, only my in-laws. In Vietnam, my husband was a dentist and I was a homemaker. Now, I have lived in Minnesota for 13 years. I like to live in the United States because I live in a big, free country, and everyone has equal rights.

Lan Thanh is originally from Vietnam.

Dear Teacher
Muhubo Ahmed, Minneapolis

My name is Muhubo Ahmed and I am from Somalia. I came here four years ago to the United States with my daughter. Now I live with my son, and my daughter goes to high school. In my free time, I like to read and write English, read the Quran, visit my friends, and talk on my cell phone. I enjoy relaxing at home, cleaning my house, and washing clothes. On TV, I like to watch the weather. I thank you, and I am excited to learn English. I appreciate it. Sincerely yours, Muhubo Ahmed.

Coming to the United States
Liubovi S., Blaine

I came to the United States on March 26, 2008 from Moldova. The reason I came here is my parents and my brother live here. I wished to see my parents and brother because I didn't see them for 6 years. On my first day in the United States, I saw beautiful houses. On my first day, I felt happy because so many friends were coming and we had fun. My children did not go to sleep. The best thing about living here is my children go to a new school. I am very happy because my children speak English. I like everything. I brought my books, pictures, clothes, and toys for my children with me. I planned to come to the United States for one year and 6 months. I didn't miss my country because I like to be here. I wouldn't like to go back to my country and live there. I like my new life in the United States.

What's in a Name?
Javana, Minneapolis

My name is Ananias and means "compassion of God." My name is not common. In my life, I have not heard any people who has the name Ananias. I think my name is special because nobody has it. I'm a special guy.

When I was born my mom decided to call me Juan but my dad decided to put Ananias because my dad heard it in the church.

Javana is originally from Mexico City, Mexico.

My Story
Elizabeth Tot, Saint Cloud

My name is Elizabeth Tot. I was born in 1960. My country is Sudan. When I was growing up in my village, it is called Maiwut. When I was fifteen years old, my father and mother died. At this same time, I got into trouble because I lived alone. I did not go to school.

When I was 18 years old I got married. I had six children. My husband was a soldier in Sudan. My family we were eight people. I had a best friend. Her name was Elizabeth, like me.

Now I live in the Saint Cloud area. I like Saint Cloud because I go to school and to work. My work is the Skylight Gardens. Now I live with my two children, one is 16 years old and the other one is 19 years old. They are in high school.

Also, I work in our church. I am a Pastor in First Presbyterian Church. Last Saturday, September 18th, 2010, I was ordained. I am the first woman ordained in the Presbyterian Church of the South Sudan.

Thank you for listening to my story.

My Life
Hana Duki, Eagan

I am from Ethiopia. I came to the United States five years ago. I am married and have two daughters. They are beautiful. I want the best for them. I am happy because I am attending school with my children. It makes me feel happy and proud.

I work hard and help my husband support our family. We bought the American dream house. It has four bedrooms, a three-stall garage, a big backyard, and nice neighbors.

Hana Duki is originally from Ethiopia.

What's in a Name?
Agustín R., Minneapolis

My name is Agustín. I really like my name. It is not the most common name in my country, but many men have this name. Some people told me you have wonderful name. It means "majestic" or "having impressive beauty or dignity."

My parents decided on Agustín. I think they took it from a calendar. I did not know the meaning before, but right now I know it. I feel so glad to know it. When I found out what majestic means, I felt happy because it is interesting to know it for the future. The computer really helps us.

Agustín R. is originally from Mexico.

My Life
Mu Shee Po, Saint Paul

My name is Mu Shee Po. I'm married. I have four children: three sons and one daughter. My family came to the United States 2 years and 5 months ago. When I lived in Thailand, the people talked about freedom in America, so I wanted to come to the United States. My family was very happy to come here. We got to go to another country. My son and daughter got to see a lot of things. Sometimes my family is very happy to be here. Sometimes my family gets upset because we don't have enough money to pay the rent. Sometimes I am homesick for Burma and Thailand. But I like being here because I hope my sons and daughter will get a good education.

My mother died when I was 15 months old. My brothers and my sister are all older than me. We moved to Mae La Camp when I was 9 years old. When we got there, my father went to the mountains to cut trees and bamboo to make our house. Our house was very big. We had two bedrooms and one big kitchen, one bathroom, and one restroom.

Mae La Camp in Thailand is a very small place. It is a very beautiful place. There are many flowers and many mountains. When we lived there, sometimes we went to visit our friends in a different part of the camp in the mountains.

I need to speak English in my life because I don't speak it very well. I want to speak English every day. I want to do everything well in my life.

Mu Shee Po is originally from Burma.

Moving to Minnesota
Myriam Wolfson, Minneapolis

My name is Myriam and I am from Uruguay. I have been here in the United States almost seven years. When I first came, I didn't speak any English and I remember how sad I felt when people met me and asked me questions, and I couldn't answer them. In the beginning, it was very hard. Then one day a friend told me about ESL (English as a Second Language) class. My life changed when I started to speak English because now I can communicate with the teachers in my kid's school, with the others parents in the school, and I can find a good job. Every day I try to improve my English. Sometimes I think to myself how incredible it is that I live here in Minnesota. I never expected to end up here, and I never knew that there is a place in the world called "Minnesota." We can make many plans but at the end, God decides. And God decided to send me here.

Now I am more used to living here. It is still difficult for me, especially in the winter. The reason it is hard for me is that in Uruguay the winter is not as cold. Summer in Minnesota is enjoyable.

My Story
Addis Taddese, Saint Louis Park

My name is Addis. I am from Ethiopia. I have two brothers and one sister. My family and I lived in Ethiopia in the city of Nazareth. I went to school in Nazareth from elementary through high school. I came to the United States in January 2008 with the DV lottery. I am lucky. After two months, I started work. I am happy in the United States. I have a job and I work from 6 am to 2 pm. My job is at Caribou Coffee. I live in St. Louis Park.

Addis Taddese is originally from Ethiopia.

Part of My Life
Gabriel, Roseville

My name is Gabriel and I am from El Salvador. When I was a child, every day I went to school. I started when I was 10 years old. I started working because my father was poor. He didn't have any money to put me in the school. I was working and a student.

When I was 18 years old, my father and my mother helped me come to the U.S.A. Two years later, when I was working in America I helped my three sisters and my brother come to the U.S.A. too. I was happy with my family. This is my history.

Gabriel is originally from El Salvador

My Story
Diep Tran, Saint Cloud

My name is Diep Tran from Vietnam. I came to the United States of America in 1997 after my husband sponsored me.

I am living in Saint Cloud, Minnesota. My new life started here and everything is very hard for me because English is my second language. My husband helped me go to school and also to apply for work at the Stearns Company after changing from Coleman Company since February 1998. I tried to learn to drive a car but I was very worried. My husband took care of me for everything. I help my family with all the meals at home.

In September, 2009, I was laid off. I went to ESL school. In class I learn very well. The teacher shows me everything about the English language. I learned, in my mother country a long time ago about cooking. Now I can cook all Vietnam meals very well, but sometimes I can cook some American food with some of my friends. It's good food, too! I think if Coleman Company calls me back to work again, I will go to work.

Now every day I continue to learn at ESL Class. America is a land of freedom and many chances to build good in my life. Everyone in America will become a United States citizen. Good for them! I am already a citizen of America.

My Family in the United States
Lan Khuu, Minneapolis

My name is Lan Khuu. I am Vietnamese. I arrived in the United States in 1997, when I was 33 years old. I came here with my husband and two children, a nine-year old and a seven-year old girl. My brother in-law sponsored my family as immigrants. When I got to Minnesota, my family lived in an apartment and it was on the twelfth floor of the building. I had no my relatives in the U.S. but many in-laws. The first year I was here, it is difficult for me, because I spoke no English and I grew up in a tropical climate, but in Minnesota it was very cold, windy and the streets were slippery when it snowed in the winter, so I was afraid of the cold. I worried the most about my English. So, my plan was to go to school to learn English as soon as possible. Because to learn a second language, it's best to do it when we are young and I did that. Now I have lived in Minneapolis for almost 14 years and my children are grown up. They are in college and my family is living together in our own house. I thank God for giving my family a life in a big, free and civilized country, where everyone has equal rights. My children's life will be better than in my country but we are still homesick for our house in Vietnam.

Lan Khuu is originally from Vietnam.

At the Buddhist Temple
Lang Nguyen, Saint Paul

My name is Lang Nguyen. I'm from Vietnam and I am a Buddhist. I am 63 years old. On Friday at 4:00 p.m., I went to the Buddhist temple with my friends. We stayed there until Saturday at 7:00 p.m. We had four women cook tofu, broccoli, cauliflower, cabbage, tomatoes, mushrooms, celery, and pumpkin soup. About forty-five people ate breakfast and lunch. When we finished cooking, we went to pray one time for a half hour. Then we did deep breathing for about 15 minutes. After that we went to learn about the history of the Buddhist religion. Then we rested for about 15 minutes. After we ate, we prayed again and then did the breathing and learned more about the Buddhism. Many times, I am sick but when I go to the temple, I feel very better.

Lang Nguyen is 63 years old and is originally from Vietnam.

My First Time in the U.S.A.
Abdulkadir Omar, Minnetonka

I am from Somalia. The first time I came to the U.S.A., I lived in Columbus, Ohio. I was confused and because of this, I didn't get a job for eight months. That's why I moved to Minnesota. I have been studying at ESL classes. Also I looked for a job, and I found one in Minnesota. After that, I met many friends and I decided to get married. Now I have five children: four boys, and one girl. I like to learn English to help my kids and family.

My Name Is Khadra
Khadra, Minneapolis

A difficult time in my life was when I came United States 10 years ago by myself.

I was scared, lonely and unhappy because I had no family, no friends, no place to live, no job and it was hard to understand the people. Language is very important in a foreign country. Imagine a new place and a new culture. For me it is too hard learn what am I going to do and sometimes I cry. I called my family and they told me to take it easy. Every day I miss my family back home but I will visit them soon than my mother see my children.

Khadra is originally from Somalia.

A Story for My Grandchildren
Miguel Torres, Rice

My name is Miguel. I am from Mexico. I was born in Guanajuato, which is the name of the state. Guanajuato is about seven hours driving from Mexico City. I have six brothers and four sisters. I am the second born in my family.

I came to the United States in 1978 I married twice. From my first marriage, I have two sons. Their names are Miguel and Daniel. Then from my second marriage, I have one son. His name is Felipe.

When I was 27, I came to the United States. First, I went to California. I was working in the fields in Bakersfield. I was picking tomatoes, peaches and nectarines. Then I worked on a tree farm. I was picking oranges, lemons, peaches, and nectarines. That was hard work and dangerous. This was because I was climbing up on the trees, twenty feet high, so if I fell down I could get hurt. There were about 85 of us who worked from 5:30 a.m. to 12:00 p.m. After work every day, we played baseball and soccer. Those years were some of the best of my life.

Now I live in Rice, Minnesota. I have lived in the same place for twenty years. I like where I live. I'll have been coaching softball for sixteen years. I coach three teams. Two teams are from first grade to seventh grade, the other team is seventh grade to tenth grade.

In July of 2008, I lost my job working for Stearns, Inc. where I had been working for sixteen years. Now I am looking for a job. I have been going to school for two years. My dream in the future is that someday I can get a diploma. Right now, my English is coming along much better than before. This is my life story.

My Life
Kiin Yusuf, Minneapolis

My name is Kiin. I was born in Mogadishu, Somalia in 1975. When I was 15 years old, my country started a civil war. I was living with my mother, father, brothers and sisters. We came to Nairobi, Kenya in 1991. I married and I had four children in Kenya in 1993 to 2001. I came to the U.S.A. in 2002, alone. I left my children with my mother. They lived in Nairobi, Kenya.

When I came, I started in a warehouse. I sent money every month. I sent a visa for my children and they came two years ago. Again, I sent a visa for my mother. She came one year ago. All my children went to school. Two of them go high school and two go to middle school. One, she goes to Head Start. I feel happy because I live with my children. I say "Thank you, God and America and God bless you America."

So I'm happy but I don't have a job and I don't like welfare money. I want to get my income to support my children. I want to get my GED because I learned four years of nursing before I came here. I want to learn more English grammar and vocabulary so I can go back to nursing.

My First Impressions
Galina, Minnetonka

I want to tell about myself and my family. I have seven children: five daughters and two sons. One daughter is adopted. We arrived in America one year ago. One American church has been generous. They have shown great love and care for us. They have given us a place to live until we find out own home.

One of our main difficulties has been not knowing the English language. I understand how important it is to know and understand the language of this country in which I live. I study the English language. I go to adult ESL classes.

My first English teacher was Mr. Dan. He is a young, vigorous man who helped me to take the first steps in studying English. With him, we learned to speak English for the first time. We used the most simple phrases and used elementary syntax. He very patiently taught reading skills and corrected our mistakes and our pronunciation.

My Life
Farhiya Yusuf, Minneapolis

Hello, my name is Farhiya. I was born in Mogadishu and have a mother, father, and seven brothers. I don't have a sister, so I am the only girl in my family. I spent most of my life in Somalia. I finished high school, and I was planning to go college, but unfortunately, that didn't happen. A civil war interrupted my beautiful life I was planning.

So in1991, I came to Kenya as a refugee. I lived in a refugee camp that I was thinking was my worst nightmare because the life was so hard, but I got a lot of experience. In the refugee camp, I met a good friend, and that friend came to the U.S. before me. That friend is my husband. When I came to Minnesota, I felt safe and calm, but at the same time, I felt sad because my whole family was separate. That is okay now. I have my husband and two beautiful children, but still I am planning to go college.

Farhiya Yusuf is originally from Somalia.

The Different Places We Moved
María Godínez, Minneapolis

My name is María Godínez. I was born in Mexico. I lived in Mexico for eighteen years. While in Mexico, I got married. Then my husband and I moved to Texas. My first daughter was born in Texas. Our stay lasted three months, and then we moved to the state of New Jersey. Next, we moved to Georgia, and I didn't like it there because there were no jobs available. Finally, we moved to our current state, Minnesota. I like this state because it has many job opportunities and education for all ages. My second daughter was born in Minnesota. After that, we moved back to Mexico, but we couldn't adapt again to our old lives. Then, we returned to Minnesota. Right now, I work in hotel and I come to night school. Before starting to work at the hotel, my third daughter was born. In my spare time, I take care of my daughter.

María Godínez is 35 years old and is originally from Guanajuato, Mexico.

My Life in the U.S.
Anonymous, Saint Louis Park

I come from Cambodia. I came to Minnesota in 2008. I came here to live with my husband. I like Minnesota but I don't like the winter in Minnesota. It is so cold. My life is hard right now because I keep looking for a GED, a job, and a driver's license. I think when I get everything I need, I will have a good life.

I have a wonderful family-in-law; they always help me and teach me well. I want to say thanks to my husband and his family. They are so sweet, lovely and friendly.

Home Is the Best
Abdullahi Jama, Minneapolis

My name is Abdullahi Jama. I was born in Kenya, Africa. It was all one day that I decided to go out of my country to see the world around me, to go across the seas and oceans, but I couldn't expect the choice of my mind was to take me to United States of America.

I landed in Chicago at 2:00 in the morning. Traveling miles and miles in the sky, I was so tired only wishing to see my feet on the ground once again, but to my surprise, when the plane that was carrying me was above Chicago area, my eyes could see through the darkness of the night; buildings covered by sand! What happened? Is this Sub-Sahara land in the United States? But after getting my feet on land, I realized it's the snow I used to hear of! On the ground were scattered ice cubes, which later people told me it sometimes rains ice cubes.

The end of my journey was Minnesota, but after a couple of days of my stay in the United States, the worst snow in 20 years happened. I was so excited to see, walk, and drive in the snow! My friend was also happy to take the adventure and quench my enthusiasm and I found myself on the road. I could see quite a number of accidents— cars falling from the road, getting stuck in the snow, and people seeking help and asking for ride. I did not know that we were out to help and we gave many people a ride.

After few days of my stay, everything was boring. I missed my land, my people, and my family so much, I wished never to come to the United States. I remembered the proverb, which says, "East to west, home is the best."

Abdullahi Jama is 25 years old and is originally from Kenya.

My Dreams for Life
Rosa García, Richfield

My name is Rosa G. García. I am from San Juan Quiotepec, Mexico. San Juan is located in the mountains where it is cool all year round. There I grew up and finished high school. We grow corn, sugar cane, some fruits, and a few vegetables there. When I married my husband and I decided to move to the United States, it was hard for me to come here because I left my mother alone. Also, we miss the culture and traditions of my country, but there we didn't have good opportunities.

That is why we decided to move here to get a better life for us and our children. This country is beautiful because here everybody has an opportunity to progress. I especially like Minnesota because I can see all four seasons.

I have a lot of goals. The first one is learning English to help my children and other people like me. I would also like to be a nurse or health care worker, and one day travel with my family and see many places. Lastly, I want to grow old together with my husband, Gabriel. Step by step I can gain my goals. Now we need to live day by day and be happy with the life we have. Also, I would like to say thanks to my tutor, Mary S. She does very hard work with me, and God bless.

Rosa García is originally from San Juan Quiotepec, Oaxaca.

A Young Woman from Somalia
Sofia Gure, Saint Cloud

This is me, Sofia. I was born in Somalia in a small village called Dobley in 1987, just before the Civil War. I have five brothers and four sisters. I was the youngest of our family. When I was three years old the great civil war had started and people started fleeing from the country. I remember one day my mother went to work. My brother and sister were away from home. I was the only child at home and suddenly I heard a gunshot, so I ran towards the gun shots and found myself in the middle of a battle! Luckily, one man who was in the fight grabbed me from behind and took me to a nearby building and told me to stay there. I finally returned home safe. That was the beginning of difficult days and months.

Now I finally arrived in the United States, it is another chapter of my story. I came here July 25, 2005. We came together, three brothers and my husband. My Mom lives in Africa. I miss my Mom, but my Dad is dead since 1992. When I came here I was alone the first night. I came to the United States and I didn't know anybody. I was not sleeping. I was looking for my home and I didn't see anything!

One day I saw a man who was from Somalia. I asked to use his telephone and he gave it to me. I called my cousin who lived in South Dakota. I said that I didn't want to live here and he said, "What is wrong with you?" I said that that I am scared and he said, "Do you want to be here with me?" I said, "Yes, OK." After that, I moved to South Dakota. At that time I was pregnant. Now I have three beautiful children and I live in Saint Cloud. I like Saint Cloud because I have lots of friends. But I don't like Saint Cloud because there are no jobs. Maybe someday things will change and all will be well.

Asha Ali, Owatonna

My Happy Day
Houa Yang, Minneapolis

Hi, my name is Houa Yang. I came from Thailand to Minnesota six years ago. One sport I love is bow hunting. I began to hunt in 2008. I was very excited my first time hunting in southern Minnesota. I saw many American people who were very friendly and very nice. If I saw American people they were very polite and very respectful to me when I saw them. We talked and shared our experience with each other.

On October 2009, I went to hunt in southern Minnesota. I locked my keys inside the car by accident. I just prayed for someone to pass my way. My dream came true. I saw an American person who went to hunt also. His name was Tom. He saved my life when he took me to the camp. Now I still remember him, and I didn't forget that day. He is always in my heart.

On October 23, 2010, I went to hunt in southern Minnesota like last year with my brother Chai. After hunting, we came back to the car. I always tell myself "don't forget your keys." I am very careful about it because I don't want to forget them again. During our ride back to the camp, I thought I saw someone waiting beside the road. I asked my brother. I didn't see very well because it was very dark outside. My brother said he saw like me, too, so I stopped my car and took her with us. While we drove to the camp, she said her name is Lynn and she's from Plymouth, about two and a half hours from here. She said she locked her keys inside the house. She was waiting for her husband to come and bring another set of keys to open the house, she said. It's so cold at night, so I took her to the coffee shop in Lanesboro. During our drive to Lanesboro, I told her I did one time like you. After I locked my keys inside the car, another took me to the camp and she laughed. She said I saved her life and hopes someday she has a chance to save another life like me. She said thank you for saving her life. I'm so proud to help her.

Houa Yang is originally from Thailand.

The Story of Hong Pham
Hong Pham, Waite Park

My name is Hong Pham. I am from Saigon, Vietnam. I came to the United States on September 22nd, 1992. In my family there are six people: husband, two sons, and one daughter. We live together. My mom and dad died in my country long ago. I have one brother and five sisters. They live in Vietnam right now. I miss them a lot, but I have a computer and the internet. I can e-mail them every week. Sometimes I call them when I have free time.

Now my own family and I live in Waite Park, Minnesota. My home has a very big yard. My husband and I planted a lot of trees: apple, cherry, palm trees and a lot of flowers, different colors. I like summer because I can go anywhere if I want to, and have picnics outside some days. And I can go to see my family, like visiting my son who lives in Iowa.

When I first came to the United States of America, about one month afterward I went to work. Because I needed money for my children to go to school, for renting an apartment, for food, clothes, and other things. We needed money for living our lives. I worked at Coleman Company for about 17 years. Last year my company moved to a different state. I was laid off.

Now I go to ESL English language classes. The program is called, "Hands across the World." I like to learn English because I want to know something new for my life. Some customs are different from my country and now I can learn a lot of them through my classmates.

Some of my dreams are to visit places like Las Vegas, Nevada, Disneyland or Disney World, Washington D.C., and New York City. I hope to live in Florida because I like the weather near the ocean and it is warm. I like to listen to lovely music and watch TV. I watch CNN news before I go to sleep at night.

This is my story.

My Life in Minnesota
Olga K., Saint Louis Park

My name is Olga. I came from Siberia, Russia in year 2010. I like Minnesota's winter, because it more warm than Siberia's winter. Many Americans think that the cities of Siberia have bears. This is not true. Bears live far away in the deep taiga. In Minnesota live a lot of animals, I really like it.

I met a lot of interesting people in Minnesota. There are a lot of open, honest, and friendly people. Slowly I am getting used to a new culture and learn more about this wonderful country. I really like the laws, the roads and kind attitude to people here. People are free and have a lot of opportunities here.

In English school I'm studying English. In Russian school I teach Russian language for children. These children came from Russia. They have adopted American parents. These children are happy and contented. I am sincerely grateful to the Americans who adopt children from around the world and make these children happy by giving them a warm and caring family.

Olga K. is originally from Russia.

My Story
Joweriya Issa, Minneapolis

I am from Somalia. I was born in Mogadishu, but I grew up in Bosaso, Somalia. Before in 1990 and before the war occurred, our country had a peace and life was good. The education was free including higher education. I used to be happy in that time enjoying life with family and relatives. In 1990, the civil war started in our country, which lasted in bad result and caused us to leave our country in 1997. I departed Somalia and went to Yemen. I faced a lot of problems back there in Yemen. The language was different and I couldn't speak Arabic but fortunately my sister lived there for five years. So she helped me to go beyond most of the problems, but the most thing that upset me was the lack of work. Finally, I got a lottery and it was in 2002. I came to U.S., specifically Minnesota. It was wintertime and you can feel how the cold winter was awkward to somebody new. In addition, there were language obstacles with people. Friends helped me by translating and showing me that I can do most of the things by myself or without help. I like the government of United States. They help the refugees from my country and other countries. We can do whatever we like to do in United States.

Joweriya Issa is originally from Somalia.

My First Time Winter in Minneapolis
Safiya, Minnetonka

When I saw snow for the first time I was very excited. One day I had a doctor's appointment in downtown Minneapolis. I took a bus and I got lost that day. It was a bad day in my life. Then I walked around, around and around for 2 or 3 hours, but I didn't know I had a snow allergy. After all of that walking, around my body itched.

About Myself
Hashim Mohamed, Minneapolis

When I came here, I did not speak English and I started at level zero. I had a hard time understanding and speaking to the teacher. I studied hard to improve my English on the school's website. I bought the Rosetta Stone CD set and I used it to practice every day after school. I am still struggling with English, but I understand and speak much better now. I am getting better at reading, but I am still struggling with conversations. I will study harder to improve my English so I can work on getting a GED. After I get the GED, I would like to go to college to further advance my studies and get a better job to help support my family. I would like to study something in the computer field. I enjoy working with computers. I would like to have my own business in the future.

I enjoy spending time with my family and taking walks in the beautiful summer nights. In Sudan, the weather is mostly warm, unlike here in Minnesota. Sudan does not have snow. When I first came to the United States, I did not like the winter in Minnesota. I did not think I would be able to live in this environment, but after the first winter passed, spring and summer came. I loved the weather and I said to myself maybe it is not too bad to live here. My wife and her family also lived here for 11 years and they love Minnesota. They keep telling me that I will love it too after I spend some time here. Mostly, I enjoy my time in Minnesota. When winter comes and the temperature gets so low and we get so much snow like we have had this year, I question myself and say maybe I need to move somewhere else where the weather is a lot warmer. When we had the big snowstorm earlier in December, I could not believe the amount of snow on the ground. I had to do a lot of shoveling and it was too hard. I had a lot of back pain. I also struggled with moving my car from the street so the city workers could plow the street. Overall, I enjoy living in Minnesota but sometimes, especially in winter I tell myself that I need to move out of here.

Hashim Mohamed is originally from Sudan.

Wow, Minnesota!
Tadesse G. Bushu, Minneapolis

My first night in Minnesota was December 1, 2009. At midnight, I saw by the reflection of the outside light, something flying around. I said to myself, "Where do all these gnats come from? The country is very clean, no dirt." In the morning, I got up, went down the stairs and opened the door and I saw the ground was carpeted with white things. I touched and I felt cold; at the same times, I tasted, whether it was salt or sugar, but it was none of them. I said, "Are you snow?" The next day my son sent me to the grocery to shop for what I wanted. I went to the grocery and I looked at everything. I got some canned food with lower prices, and I took it home. At night when my son came back from his job, I showed him what I had bought. He looked at it and laughed and laughed. He said, "How many dogs have you here, Tadesse?"

My son went to his country never to come back to America. I moved to my wife's apartment to live with her. She was operated on in one of her eyes, and the eye became blind. She had no job, no Medicare. She then went back to her country leaving me in the unit. After one month, the manager told me to fill out a new lease and vacate my wife's apartment. I filled out the new lease, and waited. I left everything in and left the apartment. Sitting at the bus stop, I started thinking, "Where shall I go until I get public housing? My son is not here, and I don't know anybody." Walking on the ice, I fell down and hurt my left leg. I had no medical care. I said, "I am sick and tired of everything," and I became full of stress. In the daytime, I roamed the town and read books in the library, and got foodstuff from Home of Charity. At night, I slept at the Salvation Army with people I can't define. After five months of living without a home, I got a house from MPHA and food support from Hennepin County. I thank both of them; they saved my life with the help of God.
"Faith is taking the first step, even when you don't see the whole staircase." - *Martin Luther King, Jr.*

Tadesse G. Bushu is 69 years old and is originally from Addis Ababa, Ethiopia.

How I Escaped Somalia
Malyun, Eden Prairie

I was born and raised in Somalia. I would like to share with you an account of my journey, of how I escaped from Somalia's bloody civil war and came to the U.S. It is still fresh in my memory.

When I woke up one fine Sunday morning in the suburbs of Mogadishu (Sunday is a working day in Somalia), I prepared myself to go to college like a normal, routine day. The weather was so appealing; it was a perfect Sunday. The sky was blue and there was not a single cloud in the sky. I thought, "What a great day." In some parts of the city, there was some armed robbery, burglary and some gunshots, especially in the nighttime, but that was all. Right after I got to my college, I noticed something was different about this day. I could hear some gunshots from all corners of the city. Then I decided not to stay longer. I found a group of young people who had similar intentions in mind. They had an SUV car and we went to Kenya.

Malyun is originally from Somalia.

Minnesota Is Different but Good
U-sa Kruse, Rogers

I like to live in Minnesota. The weather is very cold in the winter but I like the summer, fall, and spring. In winter, it is too difficult to go out and do things outside. In the other seasons, I'm outside a lot of the time.

I like to live in Thailand too. The weather is very hot but not in November, December, and January, and these are my favorite months. This is the time we harvest rice and I can be outside most of the time.

In conclusion, I like to live here when the cold season ends and in Thailand when the cold season starts. I'm a two-country person.

U-sa Kruse is originally from Thailand.

My Life in the United States
Roberto Cotorra, Eagan

I'm from Mexico but I have lived in Minnesota for eight years. I now live in Eagan. I am a very happy person. I work at Keystone. It is a car parts warehouse. I receive car parts that come from others states and countries like China, Taiwan, and Japan. I work with three coworkers. I have worked at Keystone for ten months and like it very much. I like my job for many reasons. My coworkers are great people. They helped me learn my job. They taught me to use the computer and drive the forklift. They are good teachers. I also like my hours. I like to work the 2nd shift. It gives me time to spend with my family during the day. Sometimes I can work overtime on Saturdays and make more money. This makes my supervisor happy to, because all of the work gets done.

My family is wonderful. I have two little boys and a great wife. My wife is a wonderful person. She keeps the house in order when I'm working. I love weekends because I can play with my little boys all day for two days. They have much energy and they want to run all the time. In the winter, they want to play in the snow and make snowmen and go sledding. They are very happy when it is snowing. I give thanks for all that I have in my life.

There is only one thing that I want to change in my life. I want to learn English to continue to do well at my job and to help my children grow up in the United States. I want them to have better lives than I had growing up.

Roberto Cotorra is originally from Mexico.

What's in a Name
Carmen C., Minneapolis

My name is Carmen. I am happy with my name, but my name is not popular in the world. I didn't know what my name means, but now I know Carmen means garden. So I like my name and I think my name is going with me. My parents chose my name. They told me in my town nobody had this name and that's why they gave it to me.

Carmen C. is originally from Ecuador.

Waiting for Some Signs
Chery Hlar, Saint Paul

My name is Chery Hlar. I was born in Burma. I lived there until I was 13 years old. I have two brothers. My father died when I was nine years old. He was sick for four or five years before he died. When he died, I was nine years old, my younger brother was seven, and my baby brother was five months old. After my father died, I walked for two hours every day to the city to sell flowers and fish. I bought rice with the money I got. I walked for two hours to get home every day. I brought the rice home so my family could eat dinner.

Sometimes I was afraid because we were very poor. Once, we went to a monastery. I asked the monk, "Why don't you have a celebration for the New Year?" He said, "Because we don't have anything." I thought, "Oh, okay, this is my life." I understood. They were poorer.

I moved to Thailand by myself when I was 13. I worked at a restaurant in Bangkok and I lived with my boss's family. I lived in Thailand for 19 years. I moved to the United States of America on Sunday, October 29, 2009. My mother came to the United States in January 2008 with my stepfather.

In my life, in the United States, I have four children all girls. I have been in Minnesota for a while. I study English. I would like to help people. I told my children. "When you are girls, you must know something about helping people." I am a student at V.S.S. I live in Saint Paul, Minnesota.

How do you control your mind if you are so angry? I think if I am so angry, I will do meditation. How will you try to improve your life? In my life, I will try again and again.

May I discuss this with you, because I can't speak English very well, although I am learning. Everything changed for me because I don't understand English. It's difficult for me. Every day I miss Thailand. I trust one day I will have success. Maybe me or my children also.

Chery Hlar is 32 years old and is originally from Burma.

Jodi Sperandio, Buffalo

I Am from Vietnam
Mary Nguyen, Minneapolis

My name is Mary Nguyen. I am from Vietnam, and I speak Vietnamese. I didn't come from a refugee camp. In my country, I was a seamstress. I came to the United States in 2004, and I have lived in Minneapolis with my family. I am old and I don't have a job. I want to be a housewife, a mother, and a grandmother. Now I am also a student. Sometimes I am sick and go to school another day. I am sorry, teachers, please understand an old student. I am still trying to learn more.

Journey of My Life
Lia Yang, Saint Paul

My name is Lia Yang. I am 58 years old. I came to America in 2007. What I like about America is freedom. There is nothing I don't like about America. In America I'm learning and speaking English. I have eight kids in America. I want to be a citizen in the United States. I don't want to go back to my own country. I miss my family in my old country.

Lia Yang is 58 years old and is originally from Laos.

Find My Future in the U.S.A.
Blong Yang, Saint Paul

I am from Laos. I grew up there and I finished high school 2003-2004. I went to college in 2005 and I studied two years. I moved to the United States of America so now I like to learn the English language. My favorite animals are fish and dogs.

So now I am living in the United States with my family. My family has ten people. I am very happy with this country. I am married. My wife's name is Veng Phang. She is 20 years old. She is a beautiful girl and her work is taking care of children. I have a daughter, my daughter's name is Huab Cuaj.

My first job was medical machine assembly. I like cooking, playing music for fun

and studying English, because English is the language of the world. Do you know language is money and you can use it to go to many countries? So I am studying English for my future. Yes. If I can speak English and spell well I can make a lot of money for my future. My dream is to be a good teacher and a good man in the world.

Blong Yang is 23 years old and is originally from Laos.

Journey of My Life
So Yang, Saint Paul

My name is So Yang. I am 20 years old. I came to America in 2010. I like everything. There is nothing I don't like about America. I learn the ABC's in America. No, I don't have any kids. I want to learn English. I want to go visit my own country one day again. I miss my family in my country.

So Yang is 20 years old and is originally from Laos.

Story About My Life
Cheng Ly, Saint Paul

I speak Hmong, Lao, Thai, French, and English. I was born in the Xiangkhouang Province of Laos in 1957. When I was a baby, I lived with my parents. My parents had five children. In 1962 because of the war between America and Vietnam, I moved around my country. In 1964, I went to middle school. In 1968 because of the war between the U.S. and Vietnam I moved around again. In 1970, I went to school again and in 1975 I moved from Laos to Thailand and I lived in Thailand one year. In 1976, I was married in Thailand. In 1977, I had one child. I moved to France in 1977. I lived in France for 20 years. I worked assembly and farmed and I had seven children in France. In 1998, I moved again to America and I worked assembly in America until 2003 when the company moved. Now I study English four days a week and I am an American citizen.

Cheng Ly is originally from Laos

Untitled
Mauricio Ortiz Diaz, Austin

Hi, my name is Mauricio. I'm a person that has many goals in my life. My country is Guatemala. I am really happy to have been born in this beautiful place.

Now I live in the United States. I left my family to have a better future. I miss them. I want to see them. I miss walking on the driveway. I used to go out every day.

In the United States, I have met people from different countries.

I like to take English class. I hope someday to learn perfectly this language. The teacher has a class that is really interesting. She is a good person and friendly.

Mauricio Ortiz Diaz is originally from Guatemala.

Story About My Life
Pa Seng Her, Saint Paul

I am going to talk about my life.

I am from Laos. I was born in 1959 in Xiangkhouang. In my country, I was a student. In 1975, I moved to Thailand because of the war. I had to run out of the country. I lived in Thailand for 2 years, and then I moved to France in 1977. In France, I worked for 2 years, and then I married in 1979. In 1980, I had my first son. By 1989, I had five children: two sons and three daughters.

In 2004, I was divorced. In 2006, I visited the United States. I moved to the United States in 2007 and I remarried. My new wife has eight children: one son and seven daughters. My family lives in Saint Paul, Minnesota. I still have five children in France. I had to leave my children in France.

Pa Seng Her is 52 years old and is originally from Laos.

My Life in America
Mao Xiong, Saint Paul

My name is Mao Xiong. I am 50 years old. I came to America in 2005. What I like about America is freedom. There is nothing I don't like about America. I learn how to drive. I have five kids in America here. I want to become a citizen. I want to visit my country. I miss my brother that lives in Laos.

Mao Xiong is 50 years old and is originally from Laos.

My Short Story
Aniso Mohamed, Minneapolis

My country is Somalia, and I came here from a refugee camp in Kenya. In my native country, I was a shopkeeper; I sold clothing. Now I want to be a teacher of English because I like it a lot. I speak two languages: Somali and English. I have been in the United States for five years, living in Minneapolis. I am here in America with my husband and my two children.

My Life in Burma
Than Shwe, Saint Paul

My name is Than Shwe. I was born in Burma. I had a mom and dad, two daughters and four sisters. My mom got a job taking care of animals in 1976 and Mom passed away because the Burmese shot her so they could take the animals. We lived with my daughter for ten years because in 1983 we moved to Thailand for ten years. I got married in 1984. I had five children. I came to the U.S. with my family four years ago.

Than Shwe is 45 years old and is originally from Burma.

Journey of My Life
Neng Yia Yang, Saint Paul

My name is Neng Yia Yang. I am 57 years old. I came to America in 2007. I like everything, but Minnesota is too cold. I learn how to write in America. I have nine kids. I want to go back and visit my old country, which is Laos, some day. I miss working in America since I don't have a job.

Neng Yia Yang is 57 years old and is originally from Laos.

My Family

My Sister
Khoua Yang, Minneapolis

My sister had ovarian cancer. The doctor wanted my sister to be treated with chemo, it would prevent the cancer to spread further; she would have a better chance to live. During the chemo treatment, my sister was tired, lost all her hair, and couldn't eat anything else except honeydew melon; it was the only food that kept her stomach full. My sister was healthy for a couple months, and we were happy. The cancer came back and it already spread to most of the parts of her body. There wasn't another method to cure the cancer than the chemo; she had only 3 months to live.

With the bad news, I felt numb, empty, hurt, and helpless. I couldn't cry, but it hurt. There were no tears on my eyes. I stared at my sister with my two dry eyes. My other sister and my brother cried hard. I was telling myself that it was unheard of what the doctor said, but a part of me said that it was beyond the shadow of a doubt. I had a sinking feeling that my heart was going to be stopped beating. I just sat tight, felt blue, and alone. In my mind, my sister's life was at stake. When my husband and I were on our way home, I started to cry as hard as a baby wanted his belly to be filled.

Day in and day out, I could see my sister's light burned out. Even though she tried hard to get by, the cancer still knocked her out. Seeing her pale face, I had a sinking feeling that one day her beautiful face would vanish into thin air. Even though she was very sick, she always kept a smile on her face. Day in and day out the cancer finally knocked her out and left the distress behind her.

Now her beautiful face vanished into thin air and left a hole in my heart. I missed her so much. After she died, I was sorrow, lost, and felt a part of me died with her. She was my sister, my mom, and my best friend. She will always remain in my heart and I will cherish her memory for the rest of my life until it is my turn to join her. We will be together again in a beautiful paradise.

Khoua Vang was born in Laos. She has nine siblings and is the baby in her family. Her parents passed away when she was little. She was raised by her older siblings. They cherished, loved, cared, and protected her. Without her wonderful siblings' care, she thinks she would have died in the war between Vietnam and Laos. She has lived in the United States for about 20 years. She has five grown children. Since she moved to the United States she never had the opportunity to go school. She is now very happy to be in school improving her English skills and hopes that one day she can read, write, and speak fluently.

The Best Day of My Family
Anicha Peare, Burnsville

My name is Anicha. I'm from Thailand. I have one sister and four brothers. Everybody is married. We have a big family. We get together two times a year. My father and mother passed away twenty years ago. On April 4th every year, we pray for mom and dad. We have foods, fruits, hot tea, etc. After we pray, we enjoy eating, talking, and remembering when we were young.

Anicha Peare is 49 years old and is originally from Thailand.

The Values of Life
Fonda Johnson, Minneapolis

I'm very proud of my mother. She has raised four children, and three grandkids. As long as I can remember my mother has always worked very hard. She made sure we were safe and always had a roof over our heads and food to eat.

As we started growing up and were able to work, she filled out the paper work for us to work in the summer. At a very young age she showed us how to save all of our money and buy school clothes at the end of summer. I am so glad she taught us responsibility early. That has played a big role in my life today. I've been working for 25 years. I have a good work history because of what she taught us. I wasn't able to finish high school because of some of my actions and not being focused on school. After a period of time I matured.

Because of some of the values that are instilled in me, people judge me for the way I dress and care for myself. I was taught to care for myself in a respectful way and be helpful to others. And well-dressed people receive respect. It is instilled in me. It has made me a better person.

Fonda Johnson is 48 years old and is originally from Minneapolis, Minnesota.

An Important Object
Chanh Tran, Plymouth

I have a very nice tea set from my dad. I keep it in a china closet.

In 1999 my parents went to China and they bought a lot of china tea sets. They gave one to every kid for a present. The tea set has one tea pot and six little tea cups. The tea set has a lot of flowers and many colors. It is very beautiful.

Now that my dad has passed away all of us still keep the tea pots. Every time I use the tea pot I feel sentimental.

The tea pot is very small but makes me feel very warm when I use it to drink tea.

Dad, I love you.

Chanh Tran is originally from Vietnam.

My Life
Rosa Girón, Arlington

Hello, my name is Rosa Girón and I am 31 years old. I arrived in the United States ten years ago. The United States is a place filled with opportunities and a place where I have come to mature as a person. I have a normal life. I have an eight-year-old son named Carlos who is currently in second grade. I have a friend in Honduras and hopefully – soon – I will be wed to him. I sometimes miss the traditions of my motherland, especially when it comes to holiday season. Even though I have most of my family living in the United States, we aren't all together. I miss not having my family together.

Untitled
Zemaor, Minneapolis

When I came from my country in Central America (Honduras), to United States my first time was in December 19, 1999. My daughter was three years old. We came with my husband. I never thought how the U.S. was. We went to the house of my husband's son and stayed here for three months only. We went back to Honduras. Four years later I had a green card and could not travel to the United States, but one year more I came alone for one month. After five years, I came alone so I would not lose my opportunity to live here. Now my daughter is 14 years old and she is in school and I have been living six months in Minnesota. I want to live here.

Zemaor is originally from Honduras.

My Family and My Dream
Bertha, Woodbury

I am proud to say that I have a happy family. I have a lovely, caring and hardworking husband. We married ten years ago in Mexico. We are so busy with our three kids: one girl (8) and two boys three and two years old, respectively. We really enjoy our busy life. My husband works third shift, which is hard and I have a part-time job. We work out our schedules to make sure our children get the best from us. Our daughter is in third grade and the boys and I go to the same school where they take preschool classes while I'm in my ESL class.

Every morning I help my daughter get ready for school. I drop her off at school and drive back home to do some house cleaning, cooking and getting ready to go to our school.

Later, when we all come back home it's time to set up the table and enjoy a delicious dinner. This is the best part of the day for all of us. It's always the same, you will hear my husband or me saying to our little son "please remain seated" or "stop eating from your brother's plate, you have your own food." I really enjoy these moments because I know they are unique and will never come back.

After dinner, I help my daughter with homework while my husband plays with the boys. My daughter also takes piano and ballet classes and every Wednesday and Saturday we go to church so she can get ready for her First Communion this year. I want my kids to have nice memories of their hardworking parents instead of remembering us as people who were usually sitting on the couch watching reality shows or watching somebody else's success on TV.

This year, I have a professional goal and that is to get a masters degree in international business. I wish next year I could write that, "Yes, I did it." Nobody knows when the last day of our life will be, so I think we all should do everything possible to reach our goals.

I only got to know one of my grandmothers—my mom's mother—and I have beautiful memories of her that I share with my daughter. She often asks me to tell her more and more stories about my grandma and my childhood in Mexico. My daughter says she wishes she could get to know my grandma, so that's also what I wish that my great grandchildren will say "I wish I could get to know great-grandma Bertha."

Bertha is originally from Mexico.

I Remember My Mother
Arlinda Gjiriti, Minneapolis

My mother was special for me. She was a very quiet person and never angry. I was very close to her. She was my body and my mind. Everywhere she told me to be careful, to not do something wrong. When I became engaged, she sometimes felt bad, because I needed to go to my husband's work. I remember when she told me one day, "You forget me," because I used to go everywhere with her. Next year when I was still engaged, she died, and I was very sad. It has been 10 years since she died. She died without me. And now here in Minnesota, I'm very sad. I remember each day, each time, for each detail when she lived. However, I believe that she lives in me now and forever. I miss and love her so much. She is everywhere in my heart.

Arlinda Gjiriti is originally from Albania.

Friends to Brothers
Dia'Monte Black, Saint Paul

Friends.

Not many people can say that they have one real friend but I can say that I have six. We tell the truth to each other, no matter how harsh or mean it is. I feel like they do it because they are my friends and they wouldn't want us to find out in more hurtful ways. My friends are more than friends. We're family. We're at each other's houses all the time, just hanging out playing basketball. We have been friends since 2005. We've done it all: argued, fought, had kids and finished school. I think that we're going to be friends to the end!

My Second Mother
Imelda Gutiérrez, Shakopee

I was a child when I lived in Guadalajara, Jalisco, Mexico. I was 10 years old when I had my first communion. My godmother's name was Hortencia Landeros. I was happy she was my godmother. She was nice to me. She was my second mother she gave me a lot of attention. She had three boys and I helped in her house in the afternoons. At my house my parents were always fighting. I didn't like to see this. I went to my Hortencia's house. She always fed me, she was a wonderful godmother. When she was pregnant, she wanted a girl. When the doctor told her it was a girl she cried and was overjoyed. It was blissful for her. When I went shopping with her she saw some shoes and asked me if I liked these shoes. She bought them for me, I was pleased with her. She asked when my birthday was. I told her it is on May 8. Hortencia asked if my mother celebrated my special day. I told her my mother did not celebrate my birthday with a cake, piñata, or party because my parents never paid attention to me or had enough money. My godmother celebrated my birthday for the first time when I was 11. I was very glad!

When I was 18 years old, my godmother was sick. I was unhappy for her. Her little girl was unhappy because she did not see her mother anymore. She was 5 years old. I told Hortencia I was working. She was happy for me. One day, when I was at home, I saw my godmother knock on her friend's door. I went to help. My godmother was crying because she was in pain. I was sad. I found somebody with a car to take my godmother to the hospital. She said not to worry or cry.

The friend who drove my godmother to the hospital drove as fast as she could, but Hortencia died before they reached the hospital. When her family told me she was lifeless, I was very sad. At the funeral, I looked at her face and said I will never forget you. You will always have a special place in my heart because you are my second mother. I love you so much.

In memory of Hortencia Landeros. She died June 17, 1998.

Imelda Gutiérrez is 30 years years old and is originally from Guadalajara, Jalisco, Mexico.

My Special Moments
Yolanda Pena, Shakopee

My first special moment was when I had my daughter. I remember that special day when I held my daughter in my arms. I was very happy. It changed my life, because I no longer thought only about myself. After she was born, I thought less about myself. After she was born, I thought more about her because she was my first beautiful, innocent experience. That day I learned how to take care of her every moment. Sometimes it was difficult because she cried and I did not know what she wanted. Sometimes I gave her milk and I changed her diaper, but she still cried. Sometimes I gave her medicine and she stopped. Then I learned that she cried just for sleep.

When my daughter was two years old, my son was born. He was my second wonderful experience. When he was born my daughter was very jealous. She thought I did not love her, but three months later she understood when she watched me give the same attention to both. I was very busy because my children were babies. Sometimes they wanted milk, sleep, and their diapers changed at the same time! Also they cried a lot.

Now they are growing up and every year is a little less difficult. My third special moment is my happiness watching my children grow day by day.

Yolanda Pena is originally from Veracruz, Mexico.

My Big Surprise
Miriam Rivera, Shakopee

We planned to have two children. We had two beautiful daughters. My first daughter is Yahayra. She is 8 years old. She is intelligent and does well at school. She competed with other students at a spelling bee. My husband and I went to school and saw my daughter. We were happy to see my daughter compete. My second daughter is Deyanira. She is 4 years old. She is very smart too. She always wants to do what her sister does. She loves books. Some books she has memorized and she makes believe she is reading to us. She wants us to think she knows how to read just like her sister. But really, she is repeating what she memorized. Now she has learned to add and subtract. She is very good. She is also very friendly. She smiles a lot with everybody, and sometimes she is funny. If she does something wrong, she becomes very sad, but she is a good girl. We love our daughters.

Four years later, I thought something was wrong with me. I went to the doctor at the mobile clinic. The nurse checked me and gave me a pregnancy test. The test was positive. The doctor came and told me everything was fine. To find out I was pregnant was a big surprise! I was very happy that there was nothing wrong with me. I could now relax. I then enjoyed my time before the baby was born.

After 8 months, my water broke. I was very scared. My husband was working. I had to call him and I called my sister-in-law to take care of my two daughters. My husband came and we rushed to the hospital. We got there at 9 a.m. Thirteen hours later my baby was born. We now have another beautiful girl. Her name is Gisselle. She was premature, but now she is healthy. I always say thanks to God for these three pretty girls. We are very happy and our family is complete now.

Miriam Rivera is originally from Mexico.

This Is My Favorite Memory
Cecilia López, Hudson, Wisconsin

I think my favorite memory from my childhood is my 8th birthday. My grandma arrived at my house with a pink dress and white shoes for me, because we were celebrating my 8th birthday.

"I am glad you come," I said. Then my grandma gave me a gift. I said "It's beautiful!"

The most important gift for me was the arrival of grandma. I was happy because my grandma lives in another city (in Morelos) and I live in Veracruz. It takes 6-7 hours to drive to Veracruz from Morelos. She hardly ever came to visit my house. This was the first birthday that she had ever spent with me. Because my grandma was with me, this was a very special day.

Cecilia López is originally from Mexico.

My Successful Mom
Monika Villeda, Saint Paul Park

My mom's name is Estefana Villeda. She was born in Xilitla in the state of San Luis Potosi, Mexico, on August 3, 1954. In this state she went to elementary school for three years, but she had to leave her studies because her mom died of cancer. So she started to take care of her responsibilities of cooking the meals, washing and other necessities of the home. When she turned thirteen years old, her problems with her father started, because he decided to get married. His new wife didn't like her so she preferred to run away. She started working with a nice teacher in her own town, but she didn't make enough money so she got an opportunity to travel to Mexico City and she worked for six months. Then she wanted to visited more cities so she moved to Puebla. She lived there for a year and then she went back to Xilitla where she studied and worked for three months until her father heard from people in town that she was back and he would like to take her back home and try to have a nice relation with her stepmom. It was very hard for her and she thought about looking for other ways to travel to another city and start again. This is how she moved to Reynosa, Tamaulipas at the age of seventeen years. She proposed new goals on how to keep studying and got a good job that helped her save more money. She wanted to bring her little sister there because she was having a bad time over at her father's house and she wanted her to have the opportunity for a better future and be someone in life. So, this way with lots of dreams and much courage and purpose she was successful. When she was twenty-one she finished her elementary school and took two years more at the academy to study secretarial work. She kept working hard to get what she wanted. My mom is a strong woman and very powerful and brave. She is the best example I have to be successful. I have admiration for her forever. Right now my mom is fifty-seven years old but her age is not a problem to keep learning. She is still studying, but now to learn English and she does it here in Saint Paul, Minnesota. I love you, Ma!

Monika Villeda is 30 years old and is originally from Reynosa Tamaulipas, Mexico.

How My Life Changed
Fabiola Vázquez, Austin

In 1998, I came to the United States. At that time, my plans were to stay here for about three years. I wanted to work to save some money and offer to my family something better than the life we lived in Mexico. There we had a different life than here. Especially in towns where many people came from, there are no jobs. People live from day to day. They raise their children crawling on the dirt. In effect, my life changed from the moment I arrived in this country. At the beginning, I couldn't understand the language. I got pregnant but I worked until my first daughter was born. I couldn't work anymore and I couldn't go back to Mexico after three years how we had planned with my husband. I left my sad parents there for who I wanted to go back someday. I talked to them by phone very often. They used to ask "When are you going to come back?" My answer was soon, someday I'll be there. They didn't really trust me that I was going to go back there. So instead of me going in 2005, they came to see me. My parents were here for only one month.

They didn't like the weather here, it was too cold. That was the last time I saw them. My dad had diabetes and that illness was taking his life, he was losing his eyesight. In 2009, he really needed surgery. It was successful. He could see well again. Suddenly my mother died. Her death surprised everybody. I couldn't go to see her. After her death, I wished to die also to go with her but I thought of my four children. They still needed me. Six months later my father's health became worse. I went to see him. A week later he died too. In the same year I lost my parents. I'm never going to see them again. Of course, my life changed. Nobody is ever ready to say good-bye to the people who we love and left there. Anyhow, all of us will go someday. We live different but the price we pay is so high.

Untitled
Illiana Mestizo, Waite Park

I remember when I was little my mom would force me to go with her to church. Because I was little I didn't want to go, it was boring for me and I would just fall asleep. I learned a lot from my religion, but I felt like I was forced to do something I didn't want to do.

One day when I was a little bigger, I told my mom I didn't want to go with her all the time. I told her I will only go on Sundays to church, because God doesn't like to force people to go to church. He wants you to go because you feel from your heart to go. My mom got upset because I didn't want to go. I still went with her on weekdays to please her because I felt bad. But one day she understood that I can only go to church with her on Sundays, so I felt much better and happier because I was not forcing myself to go to church.

Now that I live here and away from my mom I miss the days we used to spend together even it if was at church. I don't go that much to church here, but I try my best to go on Sundays because it makes me feel better and more peaceful. I try to take my kids because I want to teach them that it's good to dedicate one day of the week for God, and to thank Him for all the good things we have.

My Family
Soon Sellen, Farmington

I was born in Seoul, Korea in 1953. I came to the United States in 1983. I have four siblings, two brothers and two sisters. One of my sisters wants to come to the United States, but she is sick. Also, I have two children. They are in college. My first son is very tall and thin. My second son is short and chubby.

Soon Sellen is originally from Korea.

My Life
Katherine Daley, Minneapolis

I grew up in the city of Minneapolis and I said that I would not have one kid, because all of my friends when I grew up had kids. In 2003, I met my kids' father. I live with my mother and stepdad and have stayed with them ever since I was little. My mother is a very strong person. She was with me the whole time when I had my twins. They were one pound apiece. She was there all through the program I had. I live in a five-bedroom house on the north side of Minneapolis with my family and I have a black cat and two puppies. The house is fenced in and people are nice in my neighborhood. I have two brothers, one is married to my sister-in-law and they have two boys and two cats, I think. My other brother stays in a group home. I am struggling to take care of my kids and my mother and stepfather. My kids are growing healthier, but my parents are sick.

Untitled
Anonymous, Saint Cloud

I didn't consider myself superstitious; however, there were certain things I believed in which brought peace and comfort to my heart. While I was preparing for my marriage, my mother gave me and my husband white robes and towels which she thought were the perfect gift for any newly wedded couple. The color white had a very nice meaning that a couple would start their marriage from a blank. My mother and I didn't see eye to eye on so many superstitions which she considered good luck. She believed that a newborn should be wrapped tight so he or she would have strong body bones. Another superstition she believed in was praying in the baby's ear so the baby would be protected from evil eyes. When my first child was born, he had white clothes, white sheets, white towels, white blankets, and even a white hat. The thing was, before I had my child, I thought any color would fit in. But when I had him, the only color that would match an angel was clean, pure white. Then I started believing that white was so pure and was the best color for any new beginning. I would finally admit that my mother and I had something in common.

My Gift from Up Above
Lana Nielsen, Minneapolis

I'm a stay-at-home mom of two. My husband works a full time job and so do I. I'm up and going by 6:30 am, seven days a week. I also went back to school. My job is never done. The day is not over until the kids are in bed and the house is clean. Each and every moment is a gift. Every step and milestone, I get to see. I love being a stay-at-home mom. I wouldn't miss it for the world.

A Difficult Time in My Life
Dora Hurtado, Saint James

As a human being I think we all go to hard times in life, but I think the hardest time that I remember was when my lovely sister died. We were very close and I never knew the feeling of losing someone you love. When the doctor told my sister that she had cancer and that it was very bad, that she had only a few months to live, it was many different emotions combined. It was fear, sadness, disappointment, confusion, a lot of things that went through my mind. I think when something like that happens with someone you really love you realize that life is short and that you don't own you're life and that we should all appreciate the day we live in, because nobody knows what will happen tomorrow. For me that is the hardest time in my life when lost my sister.

Dora Hurtado is 37 years old and is originally from Mexico.

A Little Bit About My Life
Jimmy Sanmartín, Minneapolis

I was born in 1983, in South America, Ecuador. Ecuador is a small country geographically but huge in generosity, kindness, and honesty. I come from a small town called Gualleturo. This is where my parents were born as well. I have a big family and most of my family members are still alive.

My father married my mom when he was forty years old and she was twenty. They had twelve children. After thirty years of happy marriage, my father passed away at the age of seventy years. He was a very responsible man; he took care of us as well as he could. My parents obtained some properties while they were married. My family and I have worked on these properties, raising animals and cultivating some crops.

I think I'm blessed to have this family, and I would do anything to keep them happy and together, especially my mom who raised me since I was 8 years old, when my father died. This was my life in Ecuador; now I'm living in Minneapolis, Minnesota. I like the life I have and I like enjoying every day of my life.

About My Sister
D. S., Minneapolis

When we were in Sierra Leone in May, 2000. I was 25 years old. I started teaching my little sister, Margret, how to cook. She got mad at me because she doesn't like to cook. I used to tell her that one day you will need me to teach you how to cook. My sister liked to play with boys. One day, I told her that someday you will get married and have your own family. When I was sick, I asked her to cook food for me. The food

was so salty. I was mad. She said "Sister, I am sorry for what happened. Today, I will learn how to cook and clean for my own good because I am a woman. I need to know how to do all women's things so I can cook and clean for my family. Sister D, thank you for what you have done for me in my life. May God bless you and your family." Now she is married and she is a cook now. One day she call me at her house to come see her. She cooked. The food was so good. She was always happy about me for what I have done for her.

A Little Thing About Me
María De Los Angeles, Austin

I came to United States on December 23, 2003. When I came to United States, my life was difficult. I could not speak English. I was married and I had three children. When I was pregnant, my husband said, "You have two babies." I said, "You are crazy." When I went to the doctor, the doctor said, "You have two babies." I said, "Two?" My husband was very excited. He asked the doctor, "Are there two boys or two girls?" The doctor said, "You have one boy and one girl." We looked each other in the eyes and we cried. We were very excited. Our family was very happy and excited. I think that my family is perfect and beautiful.

My First Baby
Anonymous, Saint Louis Park

It was the year 2004 and I was pregnant. I had back pain and stomach cramps early that day. I called the nurse's station. The nurse told me that I have to stay home until the pain got worse or the water broke and then come to the hospital. A little while later my water broke and I went to the hospital. I waited in the delivery room. The pain was very hard, I couldn't say how hard it was. I did ask for some help! The doctor ordered an epidural for me. They gave me the medicine. That medicine helped me, I didn't feel anything. I slept for 18 hours. My doctor decided that they had to do something before it was too late, because my baby wasn't moving. The doctor told me that he had two choices. One choice he had was to pull out the baby, the other choice was surgery. My husband and I were shocked. We don't have a choice, we took the first option that would work. I have had my baby. What happened was that the umbilical cord was wrapped around my baby's neck. It was so hard without my family here.

Share Your Special Gifts
Rebeca & Anthony S., Somerset

One day after school, my thirteen-year-old son was telling me about an art contest which all the schools in the St. Croix area were participating in. To participate, you needed to submit a drawing suggesting that drugs, alcohol and cigarettes are unhealthy for you. At school, the teacher told my son that whoever wins first place will win a $400.00 savings bond and there will be eleven second places which will get $50.00 bonds.

Joni Sperandio, Buffalo

The participants that win the contest will have their drawing in a special school calendar displaying their artwork. My son was very excited to hear that kind of news, so he asked me if he could participate. "Of course, I said. You'll be one of the finalists." He just smiled. A couple days past by and I asked him how his drawing was coming. He said it was almost done. I couldn't see his work because he had to keep that at school. One day before the deadline I asked him again but he didn't sound too sure. I asked him what happened.

"I don't think it's good enough," he said. It's dumb." I reassured him that all his drawings were special.

"Mom you should see some of the drawings other kids did they are very good, I don't think I'll have a chance to win I'm not only competing with kids in my school but the whole county of Saint Croix too." He said sadly.

I was driving while we were having this conversation and right away I firmly took his hand and reminded him that he had special gifts.

"Anthony, one of the gifts that God gave you is the ability and creativity to draw. Please promise me you are going to use your gifts as part of your life and enjoy them every opportunity you have. Don't hide them but share them with the world. Can I pray with you so God can teach you to be brave?"

"OK," he said.

So we prayed. A few days later we received a letter, Anthony's drawing was selected and he received a $50.00 bond. The whole family was invited to a special ceremony in Hudson to celebrate one of my son's special gifts.

"I'm so proud of you Anthony."

"Thank you mom for believing in me."

Rebeca & Anthony S. are originally from Guadalajara, Mexico.

Christmas Break
Alexandra Bondeson, Willernie

My Christmas break was very happy because I spent time with my daughter and my husband. We watched movies, went to shopping and put ornaments on the house. My daughter enjoyed everything, but the best part was when we put the Christmas tree up because she just wanted Santa Claus to come to give gifts to her but I was a little sad because it made me remember me my older daughter. It's sad story to know why she is not here with me. Her name is Laura. She's ten years old. She has brown skin and black hair. She is in the sixth grade. She is smart and she likes swimming. She is in Colombia, not here with me where she is supposed to be. Laura came to my home when she was born. Her mom took her to my mom to take care of.

We loved her. The baby was so cute. Her mom left and the baby stayed in my house. Her mom didn't come to see her very often because she was a drug addict and she just preferred parties so we didn't care, we supported the baby. I worked for her and I supported her. The most part was that later she began to call me mom. She knew I was her mom because I stayed with her most of her life and that made me very happy. I will be her for all my life…

Alexandra Bondeson is originally from Colombia.

Remembering My Mom
Paw Pleh, Saint Paul

I remember my mom. Her name is Lah Po. She was born in 1954 in Burma. She was the second oldest child among eight children. She married Saw Htoo in 1983. She gave birth to two daughters and one son. One day when my dad was working on their farm he was faced with the Burmese soldiers who caught him and forced him to labor in the battle field carrying mortars, shells, and other army supplies. Later they killed my dad. Sadly my mom faced poverty with her three children. In 1988, because of the political situation in the country we all moved to a Thailand Karen Refugee Camp. When that camp got burned we moved to another camp. Later we moved to the U.S. but she stayed in the camp.

She was a mom who loved God, loved neighbor, and her children. She was a valued mother who we never forgot and we miss her. In February 2009, she came to the U.S. and was reunited with her children and grandchildren with happiness. She was a hard worker. She loved going to school and learning the English language and working as a cleaner in the evening hours. She helped cook and take care of the grandchildren. In July 23, 2010 she noticed she had

stomach pains. She went to see her doctor and they gave her an ultrasound. When the results came back they found cancer. This was a shock to all of the family. She was treated a couple weeks in the hospital. But the cancer was incurable and finally her life was taken back to heaven. She was sleeping peacefully in Christ on August 13, 2010. The valued words of mother to all her children are, "Love your God and worship Him, read the Bible and pray to God and give the offering at church."

Paw Pleh is originally from Burma.

My Daughter
Rahma, Saint Louis Park

I came from Somalia in 2004 to the United States. When I came to the United States my daughter was 8 years old. She started school as a second grader. There were nice principals and teachers. My daughter didn't like lunch. The teachers didn't know that. After that, she got a teacher to help her eat. After a couple of weeks, she learned how to eat. Now my daughter is 15 years old. I will never forget her principals, teachers, and school. I like to live in the United States. It is my second country forever.

Making Decisions
Kathleen Loyd, Minneapolis

A difficult decision I had to make was if I wanted to work or go to school because my income does not cover all of my bills. So, I picked school because in order to get a good job you must have some kind of education. My bills will get paid with help from my dear mother. I also choose to go to school because I don't have child care or anybody to watch my children and with my mental health it does not allow me to work. I've had jobs before but the problem is I can't keep one. So, here I am in class trying to educate myself so that I can get my G.E.D. It's going very good so far. I am here by 9:30 and out of school by 11:45. Then when I am out, I still have the rest of the morning to take care of business or appointments. Now it's a new year and I feel better about myself. Everything is going great. I have three birthdays coming up: Charles, January 26; Bessie, February 11; Keith, February 25. Now, this is going to be another difficult decision. Where are they going to want their party? Charles will be 12 and he doesn't like parties, he just wants a game or two. Bessie will most likely want a sleep over or a hotel party. Keith wants to go roller-skating. He and Bessie got roller skates for Christmas. So they should be all good. So these are some of my difficult decision that I have to make with the help of my kids. I have three very smart and bright kids.

My Good Family
Anonymous, Brooklyn Park

I have a very good family. We get together often. We are friends, sisters, and brothers. We have fun. We cook and eat together. My family helps each other with problems. For example, if someone needs a little money or groceries, we help.

A Strong Emotion
See Thao, Saint Paul

My aunt came from Laos to visit America in Minnesota, but only in the spring season. I believe that she missed the very cold weather in Minnesota. She has three sons living in the United States. Two are in Minnesota, the other is living in California. After her husband died, she was very sad. So her sons bought her a ticket and she came here to see us. She is my mom's sister. When my aunt came to visit here, she came to my house. My mom was watching my kids. My aunt came and stayed with my mom for a day. I came home from work, and I heard them talking to each other about how they missed their homeland and my mom wanted to go with her back to their country. As they were talking about missing their homeland, my mom's tears fell down on her cheeks. They hugged each other and cried like crazy for a while. As I saw that happen,

I was very sad by myself. And I had a strong emotion right there. I had a feeling of how bad people feel when they were broken apart from their family and their homeland to make a new life in America.

See Thao is originally from Laos.

A Journey
Dalia Gregorio Castro, Rochester

When I was 14 years old, I took a journey with my aunt for one week. We slept and prayed at the camp. The camp was Mountain Maria and it is in the mountains. Then we went to the Basilica of Guadalupe. This is the church's name because more than 450 years ago, Lady of Guadalupe appeared in that place. I was excited to be in that place.

When we traveled, I was happy because it was the first time I slept outside from my home. We took the bus especially for that trip. We arrived at the camp and old people built our tent. Each tent was for 10 people and we slept in it. Those nights were very cold, and I remember I brought one blanket with me, and it was hard to sleep.

The next day we went to pray at a place where there were some trees. That day the sun was very hot. One person was in front, he was the orator. Many people were praying and they had their eyes closed. One person touched their heads and many of them fell down. After that, we came back to our tent to take a rest. During the night some of the people were still praying.

After the camp, we went to the Basilica of Guadalupe and I saw the picture of Lady of Guadalupe on the wall close to the sanctuary. I was excited to be there because it was the first time I was in that place. We approached to take some pictures in front of the church. I want to go there again because it is a beautiful place.

I am thankful to my aunt for inviting me to travel. I was excited to sleep outside of my home, to visit the church of the Basilica of Guadalupe, and to pray with other people in the camp.

Dalia Gregorio Castro is originally from Puebla, Mexico.

Letter to My Mom
Anonymous, Austin

Mom, it is a blessing to me you are my mom. When dad died, you got the difficult task of raising seven children and making it look easy. You had just lost the love of your life but you knew that despite your own sorrow you had to think of your children first. You continued living positively so that each one of us could do the same. You gave the time to teach us the fundamental values of life that were so important so we could go our own way. As time went on, your children became adults of free mind with purposes. You became our greatest fan expressed to anyone who will listen to you. Now we are raising our own children and making our own decisions, and facing personal challenges. There is not a day that passes without your influence and your legacy. Thanks, mom, for your wonderful integrity, strength, and poise and thank you especially for showing me how to be a great woman as well. I learned from your example. Mom, you are and will remain for my siblings and me our most essential example to follow. I am grateful for your strength, your unconditional love, and your many sacrifices especially after the death of my dad. I thank God for giving me the most wonderful mom in the world. All I can wish is that my three sons find in me the inspiration that I found in you, Mom. You have all my love and admiration.

My Always-Loved Grandmother
Mariela Landi Bautista, Minneapolis

My grandmother is the most important person in my life. She took care of my brother, my sisters, and me when my parents had to come to the Unites States to give us a better life. I was only 1 year old when they left. Since, the day they left my beloved grandma took care of me. At night she hugged me when I felt lonely, and together we prayed for my parents' goodness. She loved me no matter what. I still remembered how she used to dress me up in a small blue skirt with a white blouse and some fancy shoes. I looked precious. It was funny when she brushed my hair I barely had hair, but

I don't know how but she used to make a hairstyle out of it. We used to have many animals such as, chickens and hamsters. Grandma used to take me out to the yard to help her out with the animals I had lots of fun. I had a sister a year older than me and together we were trouble. Grandma used to be after us all day because we used to fight. She would put both of us in a corner until we apologize to each other. After that Grandma would say, "Hug your sister and tell her that your sorry and that you love her." That was nice because that made me feel relief. As I got older, I wanted to retrieve Grandma for all her sacrifices. I was the best student in my class. I would never misbehave in the classroom and I was polite and charming with all the students and teacher. She taught me that respect and honesty were essential in life. Her advices made me a better person and encourage me to be better in school. Today, I don't have my Grandmother Zoilita by my side. I miss her so much because she was unique. I would always love her and admire her for her generosity and kindness. Thank you, Grandma. I would always keep you inside my heart.

Mariela Landi Bautista is 21 years old and is originally from Ecuador.

I Miss My Mom and Youngest Brother
Mimi, Roseville

My family had eight people. When I was 13 years old, my father died. My youngest brother was three years old. He didn't know anything. I felt sorry for him. My mom took care of all the children. She took us five children to school. Everything was expensive. She was hard working and very tired. She was a good cook. We loved her so much. In 1989, I moved to a Thailand refugee camp. I met my husband and I had three children. In 1996 my second brother died. In 2006, older brother moved to Australia. I left the refugee camp and my mom and youngest brother stayed in the refugee camp. I miss them every day. My mom said they would come to the U.S. right away but in April 2010, my mom died so my dream was ruined. Right now, my youngest brother lives alone in Thailand.

One day, I hope he really comes to the U.S. When he comes my family and the U.S. will welcome him.

My Daughter
Yesica Avila Salazar, Minneapolis

One day I had my daughter and I will never forget when she was born on June 3, 2010. Her name is Yoselyn Bricia Castro-Avila. I was at the hospital on June 2 at night with a lot of pain. I was at the hospital for a week and I had a C-Section. At the hospital, I had my husband and my whole family except for my brother, my sister- in-law and my brother-in-law, but I had my best friend there. I got to the hospital with my older sister who drove. When I got out of the hospital, I had to stay with my mom for one month because I needed help with my daughter. After I could come to Minneapolis with my daughter and my husband to live together. After I had my daughter I became pregnant again, and I'm not sure how many months I am. Now my husband and I want to have a boy. But the thing is that my mom told me, it will be another girl because sometimes she is right.

Yesica Avila Salazar is 20 years old and is originally from Los Angeles, California.

Forgotten Faces but Not Feelings
Anonymous, Minneapolis

My relationship with my parents has changed so much since I have been living here. When I was in my country, I used to see them, hear their voices, touch them, and smell them when they hugged me. Then everything was gone, as if a wind came from the ocean and took everything I had, leaving me to walk empty-handed. I have children who make me happy, yet I am afraid that maybe this will happen to me one day again.

Now I live only the dream, my thoughts telling me that I am still connected with them. But I feel like my love for them is not very strong because there is a huge space between us. We continue to communicate by phone, but I have not seen them for 29 years. I am so far away from my mother, sisters, and my brothers. Far from my eyes, they cannot be seen but they are here in my heart. I do not remember their faces.

If I won a million dollars, I would make them happy by going to see them, building a big house for them, and spending time with them. I miss their presence, affection, touch and all the little things, such as sharing my clothes with my sisters.

My First Child
Velez, Brooklyn Park

It was a day of the week, that my girlfriend called me to invite me to Mystic Lake Casino. I went there before and I got a coupon for the hotel. I said, "yes lets go I have a coupon and let stay over there for a night." She said, "OK." When we got there, she told me that she had good news for me.

I said, "What is it?" She said, "I'm pregnant!" I got in shook up for a little bit then I had no words to say because I wasn't ready for that. I got so sad but we stayed there anyway until the next day I dropped her off on her house. Then I went home. I was at my house for a couple hours and I decided to go out of the state—something that I wasn't supposed to do. The state I choose was New York, however, as soon as I got to New York I started to realize what I have done. I passed another day without talking to my girlfriend but it helps me to think exactly what I did and what I was going to do from now on.

The next day I decided to come back to Minnesota. I married my girlfriend. And now I'm here with two beautiful children, a girl and a boy. I love them more than my life.

Velez is originally from Ecuador.

My Life
Sergey Gavalov, Saint Cloud

My name is Sergey. I am from Ukraine and I was born in 1971. Before I arrived in the U.S.A., I lived in a beautiful place, Crimea, near the Black Sea. I have two beautiful daughters, nine and seventeen years old. My younger daughter, Katy, is a very interesting girl who likes animals and likes playing games in the garden near our home. She likes to give medicine to the animals and care for them.

My oldest daughter, Mariya, is a very good girl and student. She studies agriculture at the University. She likes to make pictures and photos. Her photos are amazing. When Mariya was small, she very much liked to play with dolls and talk to them. There were no less than thirty different ones! When she came to play with her girlfriends and her dolls, they played for hours and hours and pretended that they lived in a kingdom and all of them were princesses and that many princes lived near to them. They would dance a waltz and could proceed all daylong! In addition, she very much liked a cartoon film, *The Little Mermaid*. She looked at it every day of the year. Sometimes we had to hide it so not to repeat it over and over again!

My Parents
Michael Gei Khaw, Saint Paul

My parents are Mi Gei Shign and Mrs. Om Hning. They lived in Mindat Myo, Chin state in Burma. They helped other people and our neighbors. My father and my younger brother died at the same time in 1999 when I was gone to school in Mindat. I was confused and sad. So I didn't like to go to school. My mother was working a long time but not enough money for our family. My mother told me that I must pass the university. So I tried my best. In 2005 I have finished the university. She was very happy. Her face was very shining and very beautiful. That was a day I can never forget.

One day we were going to the church on Easter Sunday at midnight in 2007. The Burmese Army took me and all my friends. They taking out our identifi-

cation. They kept us in a hole for 4 weeks. On Friday, they needed to buy food and light bulbs. Three soldiers and I were going shopping. I carried a lot of goods. I saw my friend and she told me to run. I was running home. I took my school card and some money. My mother was crying. That is the last time I saw my mother. I went to Malaysia. Right now I am living in the United States. I miss my mother but I can't see my mother. So I am very sad.

My History of My Life
Anonymous, Minneapolis

When I was nineteen years old, I had a daughter. When my daughter was three months old, my father died. That was so bad for me because my father helped all of us. After that, I had to work. I also had to leave my daughter with my mother because I needed to work in another city. After I worked one or two months I came back to see my daughter. I needed to work very hard to make some money to help my little sister go to school. I made a decision to come to the U.S. I had to leave my daughter with my mother to come to the U. S. but I miss my daughter and my family and I hope to see them soon.

My Trip to Peru
J. Ivan Ruiz-Ayala, Minneapolis

From the January 6 to January 12, 2011, I went to Lima, Peru, to visit my relatives. I changed from the winter of Minneapolis, Minnesota, to the beautiful summer.

Oh my goodness, everything was beautiful, starting with our food. After that, I went to visit the traditional places like museums, beaches, and my father who had ninety years. I said "had" because incredibly he died today. Just one week after I came back to USA, he went to see God. He was in the hospital for a couple of years and, talking with a brother, he was telling me that it was not just that he lived so many years ill. He survived my mother for twenty years. Now they will be together at the cemetery. I say thank you to God for permitting me to stay with him for one week before his death. When I was at the hospital visiting him, he was still good; he recognized me.

What can I say about my trip to Peru? I visited one brother and one sister. He is a mechanical engineer and she is a teacher, married to an economist. The rest of the four came to the U.S. Two of us live here in Minnesota, one in California, and one in Texas. Before I came back to the U.S., my elder brother in Lima organized a meeting with all the family: his spouse, elder son and two daughters, my sister and her daughter. Her husband was in another city and her second daughter was studying engineering in Finland.

J. Ivan Ruiz-Ayala is originally from Ayacucho, Peru.

My Parents' Loving Is Number One
Deevang, Hugo

There are many kinds of love, such as love from friends, love from a special person that you love, and love form parents. I don't know that what do the other people think about these kinds of love? And what kind of love is the most important for them? But for me loving from my parents is the most important.

In this world I think nobody love me more then they, their loving is represented by pure water full of good intentions, and unable to find in other people. When I got married or separated from my parents as I am right now, I knew exactly that nobody loves and cares me equal to my parents.

Now every single day, I usually imagine if I could turn back my head or that time, I would stay with them for a longer time and do the best thing for them until the last minutes before I left to go get married. The happiest time of my life is the time when I was living with my family. We gave assistance to each other, we smiled all the time, and we were full of joy. The time that I spent with my family was deficient. For these reasons the loving that I gave to them is endless, I would remind anybody if you love someone, especially your parents and you siblings please tell and show your loving to them, do the best for them before

everything is too late! Finally you will not regret anything that you have done.

I hold my parents and all of my siblings in my memory, I imagine their faces all the time since I was sleeping, I keep their loving in my heart, I promise myself that the rest of my life I will spend with them and take care of my parents like when I was a little girl and they took care of me.

Deevang is originally from Laos.

Gifts
Abdul Raheem Akeed, Columbia Heights

The best gift for me was from my dad. When I graduated from high school, I remember he gave me a small piece of gold. It was my favorite gift because I can keep this piece of gold for my whole life. My mom, I gave her on her birthday every year a gift. We gave her a gift from my brothers and my dad. Her favorite gift was a gold necklace, and when we gave it to her she said, "This is the best year in my life." When I was in middle school, I had a rooster. I played with him most of the time. When he grew up a little bit, he ran a lot in our house. When I was in the school, my mom, she cut his neck and she cooked him for lunch time. When I came back to the house I asked my mom about him. She said, "He is in front of you." I was very sad about him.

Abdul Raheem Akeed is originally from Iraq.

My Childhood Vacations
Patricia Sagredo, Saint Paul

When I was a child, I always waited for vacations because my mother let us go with our grandmother and stay with her the entire time. Most of my cousins did the same. We all stayed with our grandmother.

My grandmother's house was very big, and had a big space to play. It had four bedrooms on the second floor. The main floor was very roomy with a big kitchen, patio, garage, and garden. Every day we woke up early and my grandma was in the kitchen making us a healthy breakfast, sometimes eggs with beans, or other times fruit, bread, and milk with chocolate.

In the afternoon, we invented funny stories about princesses and witches, and we built amazing castles and dungeons with the blankets and beds. Sometimes we enjoyed throwing water balloons or riding bicycles. By the night, we finished eating bread and milk and we went to sleep all together, like 6 or 7 kids with my grandmother in only one bed.

We never needed more than a good imagination and to choose to enjoy our vacations, but either way, these are the best memories from my childhood.

Patricia Sagredo is originally from Mexico City, Mexico.

My Family
Hilda Wilson, Columbia Heights

When it is too cold we like to go out and walk, because my children and husband they love to play in the snow. I like to make hot chocolate and popcorn, and watch a movie together. I plan to go camping with my family because it is fun and we can do things together like fishing, walking, and swimming. I like warmer weather because we can do different things like cook and eat outside with the family and friends.

Hilda Wilson is originally from Mexico.

I Live in the U.S.
Taw Naw Paw, Saint Paul

I lived in Thailand. I came to the United States with my family. There are six people in my family. I have two daughters and two sons. My children go to school. I go to school too. I study English. I'm very happy. My husband can't go to school because he goes to work to help the family. In the future, my children will go to college. I think my family is better. I hope so. One day in my life in the United States, I think we will be a happy family.

Taw Naw Paw is originally from Burma.

Immigration
Mauricio González Villafuerte, Robbinsdale

I moved to America from Mexico City when I was 17 and now 13 years later I have to go back—against my will. Coming to America illegally is wrong, but when you have intentions to do something good with your life and your circumstances do not allow you, you are forced to look for other ways to survive. In my case, I crossed the border illegally. I knew there was work and money in the North. Now all these years later, I am a witness to the constantly changing immigration laws in the United States.

I am married to a U.S. citizen and have two beautiful children who were born here. I have worked steadily for 13 years, paid taxes and not gotten into trouble. Now, in order for me to be here legally, I have to leave the country as a punishment.

The separation from my family will be hard. I do not know how my wife will manage with our two daughters, work, the house, and the bills. Monday through Thursday, I get my daughters ready for school. I take them to their classrooms, and then I go to my own class. At noon, we have lunch together for a half hour. After school, we go home or to the grocery store. While the girls are napping, I tidy up around the house, do dishes and vacuum. I worry how my wife will do all this by herself. I worry that my daughters will think that I abandoned them.

I grew up without a father. I needed him, and he was not around. I do not want my daughters to grow up like that, and I will to do anything possible to be there for them. My only hope is for a miracle law that will allow me to stay here and continue living the American Dream.

Being a husband and father is the most wonderful thing that can happen to a man. My wife has taught me the value of family and helped me be a better father than I could have been otherwise: responsible, consistent, patient, kind, persistent and even spiritual. My daughters have put color in my life. When I see their eyes and their smiles, I know that I do not want the cycle of a fatherless family repeated. I will do anything to be the father that God intended me to be.

Mauricio González Villafuerte is originally from Mexico.

My Life with My Twin Sister and My Family
Diana Miranda, Austin

I'm going to start talking about who I am. My name is Diana. I am 29 years old. I have two beautiful children, Karime and Samantha. Karime is 6 years old and Samantha is 11 months. I am married and I am a teacher. I have been married for 7 years. My husband's name is Raul, and he is 31 years old. I love my family.

Now I want to talk about how my life was before, when I was in Mexico and after I came to the United States. My life was complete when I was in Mexico because I had everything; my mom, my twin sister, and my dad. Wherever we went, we enjoyed being together. But when my sister and I were three years old, my mom and dad decided to live separately. For me it was terrible because I missed my dad. Well, my mom, my sister, and I continued our life. We lived only with my mom. I don't have too many memories of this part of my life. My sister and I saw our dad every morning when we went to school. My dad always took care of us. I love my parents. I don't care if they had problems. Now I am a mom, and I understand their problems.

My mom, my sister, and I enjoyed going to dances with friends every Saturday. We went to shop and it was very fun for us because we loved to buy clothes and shoes. We loved to be together. We were best friends. We were never alone.

My sister and I studied to be teachers. We finished at the university, and finally I met my husband. We decided to get married. The party was special for both of us. Then we talked about coming to the United States. I only said that I wanted to follow him. Wherever he went, I would go with him.

I have lived in the United States for seven years. My daughter Karime is beautiful, very intelligent and creative. She likes to paint, dance, and go to first grade. I love my Karime because she looks like me. Our second baby's name is Samantha. She loves to dance when she hears any song. She looks funny because she is tiny. She looks like my husband.

Every night I pray and thank God for my daughters. I feel happy because God has given me more than I have asked for.

Diana Miranda is 29 years old and is from Mexico.

Economic Problems
Miguel Angel Guallpa, Minneapolis

When I was a child, I thought I would never be far away from them. I grew up with all my family—my brothers, my sister, my mom, and others. But when I was 12 years old, my first brother came to the United States. After three years, the other one came too. I felt sad because I used to go everywhere with them. Just my mom and my sister stayed in my country. My two brothers moved to the U.S. because the economy in Ecuador was bad.

A few years later, I decided to come to this country also. Why? Because I had the same problem there. I tried to find a better life than I had before. And my brothers gave me helped me. Now all my brothers and sister are together. But the most important person in our life, our mom, is still in Ecuador. We miss her a lot.

I haven't seen her in about 11 years. It makes me feels so sad. But I talk to her a lot by phone. I wish someday that I can go visit her, and when that day happens, I will be the happiest person in the world.

I know many people have the same problem in every country and they will understand my feelings. I have talked with many people from other countries and they have the same problems that I have. But I wish all these people could do what they want, because money is not everything in our lives. Our family is more important. Be careful!

Miguel Angel Guallpa is 32 years old and originally from Cuenca, Ecuador.

My Life Story
Hamso Lul, Minneapolis

I came from Africa. I was born in Mogadishu on January 1, 1998 in Somalia. After three years, my country fought each other. After that, we had a difficult life. We didn't have food, water or shelter. My parents didn't have a family. Everyone ran alone, that is my parents got frustrated. After that, my family moved to Kenya because we needed somewhere to have peace. After we came in Kenya, it was different country. They have a new language, cultures, and the weather outside always is wet but it is nice because it has peace.

We are ten children plus our parents. We didn't have money or our own house. After a few months, my father tried to find a job to work at because his family needed some money. When my father got a job, he felt significant. He could solve our problems and take care of his children.

My parents are important to me. When I was young they can took care of us. They prepared us to be nice, smart children. My mother saw we learned one idea, to respect all adults and other people. Also I love my parents and I will never forget their advice they gave all my brothers and sisters because it is important. When I was a young they told not to lie to anyone, to respect old people, and to be happy. They told me to try to learn everything and get an education and I will be successful. I always remember which is right. Now when I see some children who don't listen to their parents I get really angry because it's not good.

Hamso Lul is originally from Somalia.

My Family
Viktoriya Azo, Coon Rapids

My family came to America at the end of winter 1998. It was the first time my family flew in an airplane. It was exciting and at the same time, it was quite the adventure to leave our homeland and come to a new land overseas. I was only five years old. Back in Russia, life was good. We lived in a tiny, poor village. My dad was an agronomist, he specialized in growing vegetables. My parents worked growing different crops for a living, mainly cabbage. We had about 2 acres planted with cabbage. We didn't have to pay a mortgage or high bills. All we paid was a low electricity bill. My mom baked bread in the "pechka," an oven that is also used to heat the house. On the top of the pechka there is a place to sleep. We also had some farm animals, like pigs, and chickens.

Life here is very different. There are many more possibilities and directions in education and careers. It is always harder for parents, or older adults, to adjust to the new climate, atmosphere, environment, culture, and language. For example, my dad had a great reputation in Russia. He was his own boss, made good money, and was in control of his time. Then at age 50, he had to do heavy labor at least 8 hours a day with a low hourly pay. Almost half of this money was used to pay rent, bills, gas, food, and other household expenses. As for us younger children, we learned the language fast and went to school or college to get a good career. Overall, we are very happy to be in the United States.

Most of the world thinks that "money grows on trees" in the United States. Those that actually live here know how this money is earned, and that it is not earned easily for most. In fact, in the United States, most hard, low-paying jobs are done by immigrants. It might not be easy here for some, but I think that all people who have moved here are happy to live here, and will say life in America is better for them than it was in their country. America has been blessed because this country respects and worships God. God will continue to bless this country if the people live a right moral life. God bless America and all the people!

Joni Sperandio   Buffalo

Untitled
Ray Loh Paw, Saint Paul

My name is Ray Loh Paw. I was born in Burma, January 21, 1981. I have three brothers and one sister. I'm the older daughter. We lived in a little town in Burma. When I was four years old, I took care of my sister because my parents were busy all day. My mom made many kinds of baskets and sold them in town. Then she could buy some food to bring home.

I wanted to go to school but I didn't go because we were a poor family. When I was seven I had one sister and one brother, so I was very busy all day. I felt very sadness for my future. One day I went to school with my sister and brother but I was hiding outside because I was scared of teachers. Then a teacher saw me and said, "Oh, little girl you can come to my class." So, I started school with them. I went only part time because I was busy at home. When I tested, I passed very well. Every night I dreamed about I'm a teacher and can speak English well. But when I got up I'm not a teacher and can't speak English. I was so tired and wanted to die. Later in my future I became a teacher in the Thailand refugee camp.

I came to the United States on August 24, 2010 with my family, so I'm very happy about that. I want to go to school every day to improve my English but we have many problems in our family. My sister is very sick. I know for my family I need to translate and to help them. I will try until they don't need me and can help themselves. Then I hope I can study more again and have a better future.

I Love to Visit the City
Ly Nhoua, Minneapolis

I was 8 years old. I loved to go with my grandma to the city. They was shopping over there. We went with many people, my grandma and cousin too. That day I was not feeling well enough to go. But I wanted to go shopping in the city. My grandma didn't know I was sick. My grandma woke up at 5:00 in the morning to go and I thought I could go with them too. After we ate lunch, I felt very dizzy and headachy. So we had a long way to go, and we sold some vegetables for the people in the city. That day was a hot day. After 12:00, I had a fever and I was dizzy. It was very difficult to walk. After we sold all the vegetables, we had to go shopping, and then we went home. But I was very sick, I could not walk or go any more. My grandma found a place to relax. And they had a soldier base close to there. My grandma took me to the soldier base, and they gave me some medicine and water to put on my body for one night and half a day. I was feeling bet-

ter, and I asked the nurse, "How much money did it cost?" Then they told me. It is free for me and don't worry about anything. So we said thank you to them. And we went home, and when I went there I brought something for them because they helped me before!

Ly Nhoua is originally from Laos.

My Country
Farhia Bedel, Eden Prairie

I was born in Somalia in the big capital city of Mogadishu. I miss my country and friends a lot. I started a new life in Kenya. I lived there ten years and then came to America. I have a big family now. I have five kids now. America is the best place in the world. GOD BLESS AMERICA.

Farhia Bedel is originally from Somalia.

Summer
Sokunthea Phang, Brooklyn Park

My favorite season is summer. Summer is very beautiful because there are many different colors of flowers. They grow many kinds of fruit everywhere, such as strawberries, cherries, and apples. And the weather it is very warm and makes me remember when I was living back home in Cambodia. In this country my family likes to take pictures at Como Park and go on one picnic there in summer. My daughter likes to go swimming at Lake Calhoun and Lake Minnetonka. I like summer because the weather is like Cambodia is all the time.

Sokunthea Phang is originally from Cambodia.

My Story
Alicia Daynuah, Coon Rapids

In 2003, I was 15 and living with my parents in Kenlay when the third Liberian Civil War started. One night, a group of rebels from Monrovia came to Kenlay. They started shooting innocent animals and beating up innocent people. They wanted the people of the village to open the gates. One of my uncles, Johnson, was a leader in the village. He gathered young men together and they agreed to guard the village at night.

That night, the rebels entered the village. Uncle Johnson was attacked by rebels, who beat him and took his clothes. One of the village elders volunteered to open the gate for them. The next day, other rebel groups came from Monrovia. A few hours later the leader of the rebels called my uncle, Wilson, the town chief, and told him he should tell his people to go to their homes. We were locked inside for four days with no food to eat, no water to drink, and unable to go to school.

After the four days, my parents and I left for Duoplay. After we had been walking for hours, we heard heavy noises coming towards us. We stopped to see where the noise was coming from. In few minutes we saw five to ten trucks coming toward us and shooting into the bushes. We jumped in the bushes to hide. Luckily none of the bullets hit us. We spent five days walking through the forest until we found the road to Duoplay that was far from the rebels.

We came to my father's town, Behplay, but when we got there the rebels had circled the entire town.

Vue Xiong, Saint Paul

We were confused and trapped. The Liberian border patrols told us to go into our homes for two weeks, and again we had no food or water. People were dying from hunger. My family lost so much, including my cousin David, who was killed by the rebels. We suffered through the war in Behplay until 2006, when the peacekeepers from the United Nations came to Liberia. There were no more gunshots around the town and we were happy. The people were happy and free, looking for food for their children. We thanked God for the United Nations peacekeepers.

Alicia Daynuah is 21 years old and is originally from Liberia.

Untitled
Adelfa, Austin

When I was 7 years old, I saw something happen with my grandfather. He died when he was eating soup with meat. He was sitting on the chair. When I remember it, it makes me sad, because no adults were there. Then I started to scream to my dad and my mother to come to see my grandfather. This is the story about my grandfather.

My Gift of Life
Luis Gutiérrez, Blaine

One of the nicest gifts that I have received has been life. I'm grateful to God for giving me the opportunity to have and enjoy many things. By having life you can create a family, see your kids grow up, and every day share with them. The most important thing for me in this life is my family. That's why every day I say thanks to God for this precious and wonderful gift.

Luis Gutiérrez is originally from Costa Rica.

My Secret Place
Getenet Tamerat, Fridley

When I was a child I liked to play under my bed with my brother and sister. Especially one day when we played under my bed, my brother and I were sleeping and my mother found us. She called me and my brother but nobody answered her. So my mom she was crazy. She cried and my dad came outside and they looked for us together. Finally they found us under the bed.

Getenet Tamerat is originally from Ethiopia.

My Trip to Florida
William Spence, Blaine

I went to Florida with my sister, her husband, and three children in 1985. We went to Sea World and Epcot Center. We were there for two weeks. When it was time to leave, we went to the airport. I didn't want to wear my winter coat to come back to Minnesota because Florida's weather was so nice. I saw my sister with the coats and I started crying because I didn't want to leave Florida. I hate winter now because I know how nice Florida is.

My Trip to Virginia Beach
Charlotte, Blaine

When I went to Virginia Beach on vacation at Easter in 2009, I went to see my nephew, his wife, and children. We went shopping, we saw the ocean, and went for a boat ride. I stayed two weeks at his house. We drove both ways. It was a long trip.

My Grandmother's Gift
Lydie Ilunga, Coon Rapids

I received a necklace from my grandmother the day of my 10th birthday. My mother was the last child in her family. And I am the first girl for my mother. This necklace is my family tradition. I lost this necklace when I was 15 years old. I regret that I lost this necklace. If I still had this necklace I would have given it to my first born daughter. I would have wanted her to have it to keep the tradition that my grandmother started with me.

Lydie Ilunga is originally from Democratic Republic of Congo.

My Birthday
Genet Moges, Fridley

I was ten years old and I had a lot of friends. All my cousins were my friends and we all lived together. My best friend was my auntie, and we played together and went to school together, we did everything together. She was my friend and I love her now. I was always happy on my birthday, because God always helped me the whole year and when I celebrated my birthday I always said, "Thank you, God."

Genet Moges is originally from Ethiopia.

Isabel Suazo, Shakopee

Traditions and Customs

My Favorite Tradition
Arlette García, Shakopee

In Mexico we have many different traditions. When I was a child, I celebrated a lot of these traditions. One of my favorites is Dia de los Muertos. We celebrate it on November 1st and 2nd. These traditions come from many years ago. This tradition is interesting because people think that children and people that are dead come to this world to remove the flavor of food. Families cook for them and leave water, or some kind of drink. All of this is put on a decorated table with special flowers that are only grown in this season. This decorated table is called Ofrenda para los Muertos (offering for the dead). All offerings need to have a road made with flowers and candles because this guides the dead people to the food.

I remember when my grandfather died. My grandmother and my aunts made a beautiful, big ofrenda. They decorated the offering with my grandfather's favorite foods like mole, tamales, rice, corn tortillas, bread, candies, water, beer and hot chocolate. Large roads decorated with flowers and candles began at the door and ended at the offering with a picture of my grandfather. Dia de los Muertos has many meanings, for example, some people think on November 1st all dead children come and remove the flavor of food so, they believe November 1st is for children. People also believe November 2nd is for adults and people with no family. Some families put a picture on the offering. Many offerings have candy skulls made from chocolate or sugar. Some schools make a competition of the best offering. Some businesses decorate, too. Also, families go to cemeteries to decorate the graves. When the families remove all the food from the offerings, they keep all the food and then go to the cemetery to eat this food in front of the grave. They listen to the favorite music of the dead person. Dia de los Muertos is not Halloween. Halloween is not a Mexican tradition. All people make different offerings and celebrate differently from other persons, but I like this tradition because it doesn't matter what age or religion you are. All Mexican people celebrate this tradition.

Arlette García is an ESL student at the Shakopee Family Literacy program. She is 24 years old and lives in Shakopee with her husband, Daniel, and her two daughters: Daniela, age 5, and Gabriela, age 2. She came to the United States seven years ago from Veracruz, Mexico. She is a homemaker and student.

Autumn in Our Village
Kanika Basak, Duluth

In my childhood, I lived in a village in Bengal. The scenery of the village was mind-blowing. There were paddy fields, flower gardens, mango trees, jackfruit trees, coconut trees, guava trees, banyan trees, bamboo bushes, and many ponds in the vicinity of our house. One of those ponds was full of lotus flowers (it was called lotus pond). There were many big pink, red, and blue lotuses in the pond.

In the autumn, the Bengalee's greatest festival of the year, Goddess Durga's worship is held. The worship of Goddess Durga needs 108 blue lotuses. Sheuli flower is another important part of Durga's worship. Interestingly, every year these flowers start to bloom almost from the day the worship begins. Another kind of flower blooms at this time, called kaash (beside these, other kinds of flower also bloom). When people see the buds are coming at sheuli trees and kaash plants, they are alarmed that the autumn is coming. In the autumn the sky is clear with wings of white cloud, and flowers start blooming making the arrival of the festive season.

After the rainy season, the autumn comes. There are six distinct seasons in Bengal. They are summer, rainy, autumn, pre-winter, winter, and spring. All the dust particles and smog are washed away by the rain. That's why the sky at this time remains clear and blue, and the sun shines brightly.

In the autumn, people fly kites in our country. On the 17th of September one festival (worship of god Viswakarma) is held, and on that day thousands of colorful kites are flown. The sky becomes fascinating.

In the autumn, the leaves start to fall, which I enjoy. When the leaf falls, it trembles. I like to see the falling and trembling of the leaves. I had a cat named Mini. I took him in my arms, and when the leaves fell, I rushed to catch them. I could hear the crunching of leaves under my feet with every step that I took. Sometimes a gust of wind would come and cool down the atmosphere. At this season various types of migratory birds come from Siberia; they build nests, make various sounds, become happy, and make the surroundings joyful.

During this season many kinds of vegetables and fruits are grown in rural Bengal. Various kinds of colorful flowers bloom. Butterflies and honey bees start to fly, lawns become lush green, and the village becomes a fairyland. I am amazed by nature's beauty in the autumn.

The Reunion Day
Shao Yan Fu, Burnsville

The Mid-Autumn Festival is a very special holiday in China. On that day, the moon becomes round. The Chinese people think it means reunion. The whole family should have a merry party. For example, we eat a traditional food named "moon cake," which is round and looks like the moon.

Throughout the Mid-Autumn Festival, the Chinese people remember that reunion is a very important thing in their lives because more and more people are too busy and forget their relatives now. It is really a wonderful festival.

Shao Yan Fu is 26 years old and is originally from China.

A Traditional Wedding
Belayneh Kirba, Rosemount

In my country, Ethiopia, there are more than 89 nations and nationalities. People usually get married now when they are eighteen years old. When they get married, they have a party and they eat typical foods and drinks such as enjera, wete, kitfo, tela, and tej. Moreover, in some nations and nationalities, the bride's family gives money or land, cows, and camels to the groom, but the groom gives gold and different clothes to the bride for the marriage.

Belayneh Kirba is 49 years old and is originally from Ethiopia.

The Moon Festival
Anonymous, Apple Valley

The Moon Festival is the biggest holiday in Chinese culture. The Moon Festival is at the end of summer and beginning of fall (autumn). On that day, we eat a lot of moon cakes. They are different flavors. On the Moon Festival night, every family always cooks at home. Everyone is together for family reunions. In Chinese culture, this is an important day.

Don't Forget to Remember
Miroslava Kapranov, Prior Lake

When I was a child, I loved the New Year's. My mom cooked many different dishes. We had on the table many candies, sweets, pies, and cakes. In the living room stood a big fir tree with toys. That holiday is in winter on December 31. Usually, it snows and the children play with snowballs and make a snowman. At 12 a.m. the people go out of their houses and light fireworks. The children get amazing gifts.

My family has a special tradition. Before the New Year, we draw a big picture in the windows of the living room, for example, a snow-maiden or children with gifts.

Miroslava Kapranov is 22 years old and is originally from Kyrgyzstan.

A Happy Eid
Muna Mumin, Apple Valley

It was Tuesday morning. The Eid was coming. We were preparing sweets for the Eid and buying new clothes. My family had happy thoughts. We were tired from preparing for the Eid. We all slept early that night to wake up early and have fun. In the morning, we all wore our new clothes. They were beautiful. We went to the mosque, prayed, then came back home. We were happy. We had fun. It was good to be together, talk, and have fun.

Muna Mumin is originally from Somalia.

The Tradition of Eid
Sirad Yusuf Ahmed, Burnsville

My name is Sirad. I'm from Ethiopia and I have three kids, two boys and one girl. I am married. My husband is from Somalia. We have been married for nine years. I miss the holiday Eid in my country. This holiday is very nice. The whole family is together. We eat food and play with our kids. I feel happy.

Sirad Yusuf Ahmed is originally from Ethiopia.

The Peruvian New Year
Rosa Moynihan, Apple Valley

The Peruvian New Year is the biggest holiday in Peru. On New Year's evening, some people go out for dinner and other people cook at home. They decorate their homes with the color yellow and they wear yellow clothes too. Most people think this is a special color. Everybody says many good luck wishes for the next year. Most families celebrate in their homes and make delicious food. It is beautiful to see all of the family together. Dancing children play with new toys from Christmas. You can see new bikes around the streets. Everybody cleans and paints their homes. Everybody looks for the biggest oven in the bakery. You can see the big turkeys, chickens, and pigs cooking there.

Every house puts out a puppet, and at midnight everybody burns it. It means burning the Old Year. I miss celebrating the New Year's holiday in Peru.

Rosa Moynihan is 30 years old and is originally from Peru.

Thanksgiving Day
Halima Talha, Saint Michael

On Thanksgiving Day it's the time to take a moment to give thanks for something that makes our lives comfortable. There are several things to be thankful for. We can be thankful for the gift of sight, to see our families, light, Nature, and the beautiful world. We give thanks for the gift of hearing. We can listen to others, your parent's voice, your favorite music, and any voice in the world. We take it for granted that we have the grace of speech. We can communicate with others and talk about anything. Another thing to be thankful for is the grace of walking so we can move, run, play, and dance without the help of others. We can appreciate God for health. That is the main thing because if you lose money, you can make it back, but if you lose your health or part of your body, it's hard to get it back. So you lose it forever. Always we have to be thankful for the gifts we got from God, but if we haven't been thankful, Thanksgiving Day is the best chance to do that.

Halima Talha is originally from Morocco.

New Year in Vietnam
Hien Nguyen, Brooklyn Park

My country's New Year is not like New Year around the world. We follow the moon calendar, usually in January or February in the solar calendar. Everyone in my country gets ready for the New Year a month before or at least two weeks. We have a lot of things to do for the New Year. We clean the house, buy new clothes, buy sweetmeat, buy a lot of food because everybody in the family will go home on New Year. We eat together, play some games and then we go to visit our grandparents' house. We wish the best for our grandparents to have a long life with descendants especially. Most people in my country like to wear the color red at the first day of new year because they think red is a lucky color and luck will be true for them. All the children are so happy when they have a red envelope; it has lucky money inside. And one more special thing every house has a special flower we call Ochna integerrima, and five juices (custard-apple, mango, papaya, coconut, watermelon). That is traditional South Vietnamese New Year.

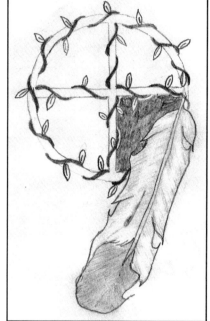

Thomas Nelson Jr.   Duluth

My Family
Shushila Ojha, Lakeville

My family is small and beautiful. My mom is my best friend. I am the oldest daughter in my family. I was born in a small town called Bhawani Bazzar. At the age of nineteen, I got married to my husband and moved to America. I have three siblings. Two of them live in Nepal and one lives in Australia. My grandpa lives in Nepal with my parents and my son also lives with them. My grandma left us while I was only eight years old. Just recently, my parents got visas to come to the United States. My son will be following them to come here for his education. I will be with them very soon!

Shushila Ojha is originally from Nepal.

The New Yam Festival in Nigeria
Florence Iketalu, Brooklyn Park

I want to write about the festival in my country Nigeria. The festival I want to talk about is the New Yam Festival. New Yam Festival is celebrated in my country once every year, mostly in August.

The New Yam Festival is when the yams are being harvested. During this time, farmers will go and dig their yams. After they have harvested them, they will hang all the yams they got in a room. This preserves them for a while. They will bring out the one they need for the New Yam Festival.

During this celebration, farmers and the rest of the people will be cooking yams. They will put the yams on fire in order to make them dry. After they are done, they will use palm oil, salt and pepper to eat them.

People will have merriments with the yams. Children will gather in the playground, beating on turtle shells, dancing, masquerading, throwing parties and so on. People will go from house to house in order to be entertained. Some elders will paint their faces, showing the tradition of the festival.

On the night of the festival, teenagers will be having parties in the village hall. They will be dancing and having fun. Children will dress in their costumes. They will be going round and round the village and having fun.

Visitors and tourists do come for the New Yam Festival. It is a very big occasion you will never forget. When I was back home, I enjoyed it. It is fun and nice to celebrate. Remain bless!

Florence Iketalu is originally from Nigeria.

My Favorite Holiday
Choe Xiong, Albertville

My favorite holiday is Christmas. I like to decorate the Christmas tree. The thing I like best during the Christmas season is when I drive on the street I see Christmas lights everywhere. This makes me feel like it's a new world. I like Christmas green and red colors. When these two colors are combined, it is a beautiful sight.

Christmas is a holiday that makes people happy because families come together. You show your family that you care and love your family by exchanging presents.

Choe Xiong is originally from Laos.

Somalia Traditional
Anonymous, Saint Louis Park

I came from Somalia and I am a mother that lives in Minnesota. I am writing about one of our country's traditions. My traditional country is beautiful and strong. We have good treats for guest, and we give full respect to the people who come to the marriage family. The main foods are milk and meat. We are farmers and we love camels so much and we like to raise them.

Superstition
Joelle Nde, Waite Park

Back in my country, I used to sell at the boutiques with my Aunt. She made me believe in one superstition. Anytime when her left palm was itchy she said, "my money is coming," and after about an hour many clients came and bought some things. It was always true. One day, I asked, "What would happen if your right palm was itchy?" She said, "I will give money to somebody. It may be for the rent or for the electricity." She also told me that the left palm is to receive and the right palm is to give. There is another superstition we use to do. When I was in the elementary school, before the day of the result of the exam, many students grabbed a leaf and threw it over their backs. If the leaf is opened, you're going to pass. If the leaf is closed, you're going to fail.

Joelle Nde is 23 years old and is originally from Cameroon.

Carnival
Elizabeth Turmero Kovacs, Edina

In Venezuela people celebrate Carnaval in February. They celebrate with music and costumes. That season is for staying with family and enjoying a good week. Carnaval, or Carnival, is seven days—one week. Most people spray water on their bodies. This is a joke. The children enjoy this season because in the street different stores have a "Carroza," which is a big float with balloons and music. On the floats the people dance and give candies to the people who are in the street. After that they go home and prepare a food, not a formal dinner, but it's a dinner with family. Every day of Carnaval is the same routine. I hope you one day will go to Carnaval in Venezuela and learn more about this culture.

Elizabeth Turmero Kovacs is originally from Venezuela.

Holy Week
Marfelin, Hopkins

Most people use the Easter Holiday in the Dominican Republic to do things: go to beaches and rivers, go to relatives and where you were born, and reflect on Catholic traditions and celebrations. The capital city is practically deserted from Thursday to Easter Sunday because during those four days, all institutions including federal and state are closed. Yet the supermarket, bars, discotheques, and some locations are open on these days. Everybody takes a vacation and most people go to the beaches and the rivers. The people who live in the capital of the Dominican Republic travel to different rural areas of my country. That is why the capital is deserted on these days.

Most Dominicans do not eat meat on Fridays and Wednesdays during lent, the 40 days prior to the Passion and Death of Jesus Christ. At the beginning of Holy Week we make popular dishes. One of them is sweet beans. This dish is served hot or cold, and we make large quantities and share with friends, other families, neighbors, or whoever you visit.

This is a great time for you to visit the Dominican Republic and to have an experience you or your family will not forget. The weather is excellent with much sunshine, the people are friendly, and we have the best beaches in the world.

Marfelin is originally from Dominican Republic.

Women's Day Celebration
Andja, Blaine

Women's Day in Croatia is celebrated on March 8. On this day, women do not go to work, because companies pay for them. Every man buys flowers and special food for every woman. Some men who love women go dancing. This is a tradition in my country. Men buy special food for women. Every woman needs to be twenty years old or more. If a man loves a woman he buys special flowers to give to her. Flowers and presents. My daughter was born on this day. She needs two gifts, one from her boyfriend and one from father. Now she has presents only from her husband, because she is married. Flowers and gifts for woman are very, very expensive. On this day women do nothing, just eating, talking, playing, and dancing.

Andja is originally from Croatia.

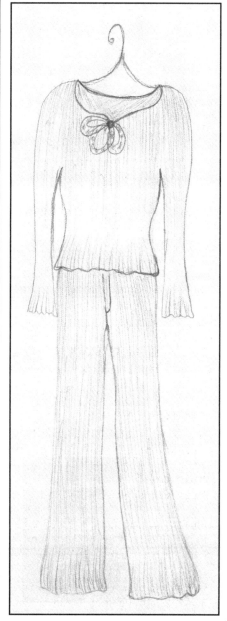

Vue Xiong, Saint Paul

Difference in 20 Years
Eliud Velázquez, Rochester

I am from Mexico. I have two children and I have been living in the United States for 12 years with my family.

When I was a child I remember when the boy liked a girl he sent a letter to the girl first telling her his feelings. Then she answered him yes or no. After that if she said yes, the boy had talked with her parents to get permission. If they had permitted, they can have a relationship. The relationship in that time was the boy came to the girl's house and talked with the girl in front of the parents for 1 or 2 hours. That was all. There was no kiss, no touch the hand, and no go out without somebody.

Those things have been changing through the years. When I was 15 years old, it had changed a little bit. In that time, the girls had more freedom. We only asked our parents if we can have a boyfriend, and they had known him first and maybe they liked him and maybe not. Depends on the parents' decision, but although the parents said no, we said yes, and we had a boyfriend. Anyway, we were more behaved even though at that time we had more restrictions. I like that time more, because it was totally different. Always the boys invited the girls, and the boys paid for everything. Also the boys were more respectful and protective of the ladies.

These customs are still changing until now. Now it is the same between boys and girls, it doesn't matter who starts the dating. Most of the time the girls start the conversation and they don't care about the parent's opinion like before.

Eliud Velázquez is originally from Michoacan, Mexico.

My Culture
Gosa Samu, Columbia Heights

What are some special things that make up my culture? We have special language, clothing, religion, and music. What I think is interesting about my culture is when we have a wedding or holiday, everybody wears special clothes and we make special food. For example: Injera and Doro Wat. We have a lot of things. What I like about my culture is we respect older people and in my country we have a lot of religion. The church ceremonies are on every Sunday and every holiday. What I don't like about my culture is the government of democracy and the lack of women's rights. One thing that would happen to me in my culture is when I got pregnant no one would help me. In this country, everybody got together and they bought a lot of things for my baby and me. In my culture we don't have this tradition. I was very happy.

Gosa Samu is originally from Ethiopia.

Holidays in Somalia
Ahmed Mohamed, Hopkins

There are two national holidays in my country of Somalia. The names of these two holidays are Eid ul-Fitr and Eid al-Adha. These holidays are very well respected in my country. One of them, Eid ul-Fitr, is the day after Ramadan. We give money, food, and clothes to poor people, so we all can be happy on that day. We also decorate our homes. We congratulate each other. The other holiday is Eid al-Adha .We do the same things as for the other holiday. For this holiday, some people go to visit the Holy Land in Saudi Arabia. These holidays are not only important in my country, but they are also very important in many other Muslim countries. These holidays are the only ones on the Muslim calendar.

Ahmed Mohamed is originally from Somalia.

Old-Fashioned Holidays in El Salvador
Miriam Castellanos, Owatonna

Christmas is the time to share, to be together with our families, friends, neighbors, and grandkids. The families start planning what to cook two days before Christmas Eve. Then the families start by buying the ingredients for a dinner and start preparing food. Usually a traditional Christmas meal is tamales, chicken, and turkey. In my family, the tradition is to make tamales for both nights. We prepare all of the ingredients like the flour for tamales, the spices, and the potatoes for the chicken. The banana leaves need to be very soft before you start making tamales.

It is very important to buy a new outfit for Christmas Eve because the tradition is as if we were going to start a new year, so we have to wear something new on both nights.

One of the fun activities is that the children start fireworks at 6:00 p.m., and this goes on until midnight. While the children are watching the fireworks, Santa comes and leaves presents for them under the tree. The children go inside and find their presents and open them after midnight. When it is time, everybody says Merry Christmas, and they give hugs to everyone and wish them the best.

Miriam Castellanos is 45 years old and is originally from El Salvador.

New Year's Eve in America
Belete Gwalu, Saint Paul

On the evening of New Year's Eve I got temporary work plowing snow around University Avenue. The job was difficult for me, because I was not wearing winter clothes. In addition, snow removal requires a lot of force. It seemed that the snow had "signed a love agreement with the land." It was very difficult to separate them from each other. Though it was hard to separate them, I could eventually separate the land and the snow. As a result, on the eve of the New Year, I was earning some money.

Belete Gwalu is originally from Ethiopia.

Marriage in Somalia
Shahira, Blaine

Marriage in Somalia is very important for girls in my country because the family of the man needs to pay the family of the girl. Money or a goat is what the man can pay. The man's family comes to the girl's family. The girl's family needs to make special foods. They mix many foods; meat with vegetables and lamb. After the food, the girl's family welcomes the man's family and the two families eat together. They talk together to get to know each other and then start dancing and singing. The women wear special clothes. Brides wear white colors, everyone wears different colors. After the party the husband and wife go to their own house. Everyone goes home. The marriage ceremony is changing for Somalis in the United States.

Shahira is originally from Somalia.

I'm Proud
Zalina Khan, Brooklyn Park

I'm proud that I decided to come to school 3 days in the week, because in my childhood, I was crying to go to school. My dad used to tell me that one day your prayers will come through, about going to school. Today I'm in school learning more. I'm proud of my great success in school. I'm proud to have my teacher and tutors because of the way they are teaching us. I'm proud to live with my mom at home and the way she is taking care of me with everything in my life. I'm proud to communicate with friends with my device. I'm feeling happy the way my device makes my disabilities improve by being able to communicate with others. I'm proud because I've never missed my weekly masjid prayer in 5 years. I'm proud to be able to go to night prayer during Ramadan's months for the past 4 years every night. I'm proud the way my masjid sisters and brothers are treating me in a very kind way. I will be more proud when my teacher, Rachel, tells me that I passed my test to go over to the reading B class.

Zalina Khan is originally from Guyana.

Sherry Synkiew, Brooklyn Park

Memories of Home

The Citrus Trees
Melissa Urbano, Saint Cloud

What I remember most about my childhood is the time I spent in Mexico at Grandpa's house. There was always something fun to do. I could help feed the chickens and pick the eggs, or just play for fun, but what I really enjoyed the most was the fruit trees.

Grandpa had some land where he planted grapefruit trees, orange trees, guava fruit, peaches, and papaya. So we made sure we were there for every fruit season. I remember the smell of the citrus trees when they were blossoming, especially grapefruit. It is such a strong scent, almost relaxing and mouth watering at the same time. I could hardly wait for the fruit to be ready for me to pick. My cousins and I used to climb up the citrus trees to get to the fruit on top, which was more exposed to the sun. They were the biggest and tastiest, or so we thought. Maybe we were just doing it because it was fun. My grandpa didn't think so. You see, the branches on the citrus trees are not very thick so at times some of the branches would give out and break. Now I understand.

My grandpa and the trees are still there and every year they blossom, only I can't be there anymore. My eyes fill with tears when I get on the phone with him and he tells me, the trees are ready for you to climb on.

Melissa Urbano is a 26 year old Mexican American, but lived most of her life in Mexico. Her and her family moved to the USA in 1997, she moved to the St. Cloud area 3 years ago and is currently attending ABE in St. Cloud. She is working on her GED. In the future she would like to attend college and pursue a career in the medical field. Melissa is currently expecting her first child, and hoping to achieve all of her goals so that she can be a great example for her baby. In her spare time she enjoys going on morning walks and reading.

Seasons
Etalem Lemu, Brooklyn Park

I like four seasons in America and would like to compare with my country, which is Ethiopia. We do have four seasons in Ethiopia, kind of like Minnesota seasons. I want to take one season and compare it to a Minnesota season. That season is winter. Winter in Minnesota and Ethiopia is different because the snow in Minnesota is beautiful, soft, and chilly and everywhere it's bright.

My country is totally different – in the wintertime our "snow" is ice. In the wintertime, ice makes it hard because everybody walks to work and shop because we don't have cars like we drive in Minnesota. God bless America. We have cars to go everywhere we want. In Ethiopia, there is a lot of rain and it is dirty all over the place. That's why I choose to stay in Minnesota.

Untitled
Bilise Ahmed, Minneapolis

My name is Bilise and I am from Ethiopia. The big shopping place in Ethiopia is called Addis Ababa. It is different from the United States as well as school. The last time I visited Ethiopia was 2008. The place I was born is called Wollega. There is shopping around for food, clothes and shoes too.

Bilise Ahmed is originally from Wollega, Ethiopia.

My Background Story
Nadifa, Minnetonka

I am from Somalia and I lived in the capital of Mogadishu. My parent's house was close to the ocean and shipyard. My country has four seasons: two seasons hot, rainy and another two seasons that are normal. My country has two big Muslim holidays and other holidays like Independence Day, Army Day, Labor Day, Mother's Day, Teacher's Day, Teens Day, and other holidays. When I was a child, I learned at school until I finished. After that, I left Somalia. I went to

Saudi Arabia and we lived there ten years. Then we won the visa lottery and we came to the United States in October. After a few weeks, it snowed. When I went outside, I fell into the ground. My kids said, "What happened to my Mom?" Now I am OK. I am driving a car and I am walking. I am studying ESL English and I am looking for job.

Nadifa is originally from Somalia.

Left Behind
Rothana, Elk River

I wrote this story for my three children, so that they would know their mother's story, remember who they are, their history, and to encourage them to be strong and confident in their new land.

In 1975, the Khmer Rouge took over Cambodia. Angka, the chief, separated me away from my family when I was six years old. At first I was happy because I didn't have to feed the chickens and pigs anymore, but after a few days without seeing my parents, I was very sad and homesick. We were made to work very long hours in the rice field, and I was very weak and hungry. One day I became ill with a high fever. I coughed so hard sometimes I would stop breathing. Because of my high fever, I couldn't get up for dinner, so I went to sleep without food. My older brother didn't see me at dinner, so he snuck over to where I was and hid a cooked frog under my pillow, so my roommate wouldn't take it. If the Angka found out that he brought food, he would be punished. I never thanked him enough for what he did for me. Even though he didn't get caught, he later died fighting against the Khmer Rouge.

I received a letter from home that my mom was very sick. After we promised the camp soldier that we would return, he allowed us to go. When we arrived back home, a war broke out between the Khmer Rouge and Vietnam. The sound of guns was all around us. It sounded like popcorn was popping everywhere. The bombs shook the earth beneath us. We heard screams all around us. My mother grabbed me and yelled, "Lay down! Don't get up." I can still feel and smell the bullets passing over my head.

Many bullets whizzed by us, so we jumped into a small pond. I felt something moving behind my back, and was shocked to see I was in a pond full of snakes. My father told us, "Don't move." There I was, frozen in fear. If I jumped up, I would have been hit by bullets, and if I stayed in the pond, I may be bitten by snakes. After awhile the bullets stopped, so we raced out of the pond and kept running.

Rothana is originally from Cambodia.

Childhood
Anonymous, Crystal

I was born in Liberia. My childhood days were the best day in my life. My mom and dad separated when I was a baby. However, my oldest sister took care of me until I was a teen. I went to few school in Liberia but did not graduate from high school because of war that took place in 1998 which cause me to leaved Liberia to Ghana and came to the United States.

National Library
Sviatlana M., Anoka

I am from Belarus. My country is in central Europe, near Russia, next to Poland. A good time to visit my country is in summer: June and July. The weather is nice and everything is green. If you come to Belarus, I think you should visit the National Library. It is located in Minsk, near Independence Avenue, next to the subway "East" and the bus station "Moskovski." It has 17 floors. It is diamond shaped. You can go to the top of the building and see the whole city. You can see many reading rooms, conference rooms, computer rooms, and a café. You can try national food. I think you will have lots of fun if you go to the National Library.

Sviatlana M. is 39 years old and is originally from Belarus.

Life in Laos and the United States
See Vang, Minneapolis

In Laos, I went to school from Monday to Friday. On the weekend, I went to help my parents do the farm work. We raised cows, pigs, chickens and dogs. In my country, there are lots of rainforests and very high mountains. The trees are green all year long. There's no snow in my country. There are only two seasons: winter and summer. In my country, there are no tall buildings and no trains. I miss Laos because it's my birth country and my family still lives there.

In the United States of America, there are many tall buildings, many cars and a lot of snow in the winter. It's too hot in the summer. But I like the United States because there is freedom and peace for everyone and free education for all ages. Now the United States is my home.

See Vang is originally from Laos.

Mae Ra Moe Karen Refugee Camp
P'saw Paw, Saint Paul

I want to tell you about when I lived in the Karen Refugee Camp in Mae Ra Moe, Thailand. I stayed there from March 1997 to February 2004. I liked this camp very much because when I stayed there I was very happy with my husband and a lot of my friends and neighbors who loved and helped me very much. Before when I lived in my native country of Burma, I didn't like vegetables, but at the Karen Refugee Camp I started to like natural vegetables because some people went to find natural vegetables and came back and gave them to everybody. They cooked direct without seasoning and oil. I saw they were strong and healthy all the time, so I ate very well.

This Mae Ra Moe camp stayed between two long mountains. In my home backyard a stream flowed where we bathed and washed clothes. The stream flowed down into the MuYu River. The camp had nine sections and in each section almost two hundred houses. Many homes were built on the hillsides. Section 7-B to Section 7-A was connected only by a string bridge which looked very beautiful from far away. It had a waterfall where many people went to visit. In every section was a primary school. In the camp were two high schools and two hospitals. Many NGO offices were in the camp. We had no electricity and every house used kerosene lamps. All houses were small but for me very nice. They were made of bamboo and were surrounded by banana trees and some vegetables. Some people had cotton plants and made cotton yarn. Then they made cotton clothing and blankets. Sometimes I really miss my Mae Ra Moe Karen Refugee Camp.

P'saw Paw is 40 years old and is originally from Burma

Untitled
Anonymous, Waite Park

In the civil war of Somalia in 1992, I came to Kenya. The resettlement agent helps all the people who come to Kenya. By that time, I was not alone. Me and my family, my mom and my dad, my brothers and sisters, we were all together. In fact, Kenya is a good country because at that time I was an illiterate person who did not know how to read and write, but now I am not. I went to school and I have learned different subjects like Kiswahili, Arabic, and so many others. In Kenya you will get a good education. It is really good to learn something while you are young because education is a vision, while ignorance is darkness. I was living there for many years in Africa. It has good climate. It is warm. All people can adapt with the climate.

How My Life Changed in America
Choe Xiong, Albertville

My life has changed since I came to America. I've had to learn a new language and a new way of life. It has been very difficult for me to learn a new language. English is difficult to learn for the people who grew up in a different country, but I think some day that I will learn to speak good English.

In the United States the biggest change is the way we support our family. Back in Laos, we worked on the farm to support our family but in the United States we work in the factory to support our family. We have many bills to pay in the United States, but in Laos we have only a few bills to pay.

There was a big change in my life when I moved to the United States. I've had a difficult time learning the language, a hard time to support my family and too many bills that make my life difficult.

Choe Xiong is originally from Laos.

Somalia Twenty Years Ago
Deqa Dhagwel Hassan Farah, Minneapolis

My country, Somalia, was beautiful 20 years ago. I liked my country because it is big. It had a government, stereos and theater. I love you, my country.
I like the United States because I feel free. I have a house. I have four children. I am a single mom. In Minnesota there is one problem: snow. But I am happy because I am free.

Deqa Dhagwel Hassan Farah is originally from Somalia.

My Country
Hung Nguyen, Saint Paul

I come from Viet Nam. My country is very wonderful and peaceful. I love the green of my countryside. I like to go walking and look at it. Then I feel very peaceful. I hope everything is all good in the future.

Untitled
Anonymous, Eden Prairie

I am from Somalia. Somalia is a good place to live. My hometown is a beautiful small town called Baydhapo. Many people live there. There are no cars. This city is very busy because the people are all walking on the street. They have nice weather, not too hot or too cold. The weather is very good. The people are friendly. They work together to help. Now I have lived in Eden Prairie for five years. Eden Prairie is a good place to live. I like the school. The people are helpful and friendly.

My Story
Kha Lam, Saint Paul

In Viet Nam, my country has two seasons, summer and rain. People garden rice, vegetables, and fruit. People breed cows, buffalo, pigs and chickens, sew brocades and perhaps go to school. Health services are behind. Pollution is moderate. Roadways are small and traffic jams are regular. There is not food safety. The newspaper and internet are inaccurate. The people have no freedom.

In the United States of America, Minnesota has four seasons: summer, winter, autumn, and spring. I think the winter in Minnesota is very cold and has a lot of snow. People here are tall and fat. The health services are very good and current. The roadways are big and the traffic is good. The air is fresh. In the United States of America the newspaper and Internet is explicit and clear. The religion is free, the people have freedom.

The End

About My Country
Doris Moncada, Somerset, Wisconsin

I am writing about my country. I was born in Honduras. It is beautiful, especially my city, Comayagua. I miss my family and especially my dad. I started a new life in America.

I like American people, because they help me a lot at my schools. They help me find my job and show me how to fill out forms. But my mom, dad, and sisters still live in Honduras. I live here with my husband and my children. I love my family and my puppy, Zuky. In my free time, I like to cook, exercise, and do yoga. Right now, I'm studying English to get a better job for myself. My favorite place in America is my home in Somerset. I love fall in Minnesota, it is very beautiful. I also like to watch the leaves change colors. Christmas in my country has a lot of great festivals. When December begins, all the houses are decorated with multicolored lights, every family has their Christmas tree, and all families get together to cook a lot of food. Tamales and torrejas are special Christmas foods in Honduras.

There are some differences between the Christmas celebration in my country and here in America. Here the people get together in smaller family groups. They don't get together with the whole town, like in Honduras.

I love my old home and my new home.

Doris Moncada is 33 years old and is originally from Honduras.

Somalia
Safiya Mohhamed, Saint Cloud

I'm from Somalia. My family and I are living in the United States. We've been living here for a long time.

My children can speak English fluently, but they don't speak Somali any more. In the future I would like to build a house in my home country. Then I would like to take my children back home and teach them my culture.

Safiya Mohhamed is originally from Somalia.

Autobiography
Hla Tin, Saint Paul

On December 22, 1975, I was born in Burma. I have seven siblings; my family is big. We stayed in a small house. My older sister didn't go to school because she helped my mom take care of my brother. My mom and dad had problems about food for us. When I was three, my older brother and I went to live with my grandparents. When I was five, I went to school near my house every day. I was happy. I had many best friends. Sometimes I went to school early to play skip with them and then I came back home late. My teacher showed me how to play games outside. We were very happy and now I miss them. When I was thirteen, my family moved to the Thailand Refugee Camp and I went to school again. I studied through sixth grade and then stayed home to help take care of my brother and cook. November 21, 1992, I got married. February 10, 1994, my boy Ler Kler Soe was born, and then on June 22, 1999, I got my daughter, Marry Htoo. When she was 3 months, we moved to a new place because Burmese soldiers came and burned my house. They came in 1997 and 1998. Many people died and many people were hurt. The new place was very cold. My daughter and husband got sick. I had big problems because I took care of my daughter at home and my husband was at the hospital for one week. After six months, it got better. The cold was less then. May 15, 2001, I got a job in the camp in reproductive and child health, the first job in my life. Sometimes I was exhausted and confused but I was happy to do that job for seven years. May 14, 2008, I came to the United States. I was amazed because I saw the snow and the trees looked like they had died—I didn't see the leaves. I felt like I was dreaming. I missed my friends and my job but I was happy because my children wanted to go to school to study English. I hope in the future my children will speak English very well. They can help my people. I hear my people cry. I can't do anything. I can't help them. When I think about my people, I feel so sad.

Hla Tin is 36 years old and is originally from Burma.

My Life Before and Now
Kia Vue, Saint Paul

I am from Laos. I am Hmong and I grew up in a small country that has many mountains. As a child, I liked to play with my friends in the park and I liked to go to the farm with my mom and I liked to draw pictures in school. My first job was to help my mom take care of pregnant women and children.

Then I came to the United States in November 2008 and I came by myself. I felt very happy because I got to see a new place. When I was 18 years old, I got married to my husband Hanie in Laos. Then I came to the United States and I had one child, Lucy. She was born in the United States. Now I live in St. Paul, Minnesota. I like this place because it is very beautiful and different from my country. I am seeing new things I never saw before. Now I stay home to take care of my child. I like to visit my friends for fun and I like to go to plays at the park in the summer for fun, too. I like to study English because I need to learn more English and for my future I need a better job and I need to be a good mother for my child.

Kia Vue is originally from Laos.

Farmer Story
Moo Moo Soe, Saint Paul

I was born on June 6, 1972 in Burma. When I was a child, my mom took care of me. When I was 5 years old, I went to school. I learned to read and write in school. My mom and dad were farmers in Burma. Burma is poor. My mom and dad took care of anything the children needed. My mom was busy in the house. We didn't have enough food to eat in Burma. I have five siblings. When I was 18 years old, I moved to the Thailand-Burma border. Here I worked as a nurse at Karen County Hospital for 2 years. In 1990, I got married with my husband. In 1992, I had a baby. In 1997, I moved to a refugee camp. In the camp, many people got sick and many died. The refugee camp was hot. In 2004, I came to America with my family. The first year I had problems in America because I couldn't speak English. In 2005, I started school so I could learn English. In 2009, I moved to the Hmong-American Partnership School so I am happy to learn reading and writing. I thank my teacher for teaching me.

Moo Moo Soe is 40 years old and is originally from Burma.

My Move from the Country
Anonymous, Brooklyn Center

I remember when I was a little girl, my parents planned to move out of the country because we didn't have relatives living near us. We had to move from the country to the city in Laos.

First of all, my father was tearing down the house because the house was made of wood. He needed to build a new house out of wood again. He went to rent a big truck to carry the wood to make a house in a new place. During that time, my brother didn't want to go with my father and my grandmother because he was very carsick when he got in to the car, but my father wanted my brother to go with him. My brother didn't know what to do so he went with my father. They went with the person who owned the truck that my father rented. After that, they went to the city. It took about three days and three nights before they got to the city.

My mother, my sister and I didn't go with my father was because my mother had my younger sister. In Hmong culture, when the woman has a baby,

Armando Gutiérrez Cardenas

she has to stay home for one month or more. That's why we had to wait until my mom got ready to go after my father. I had to stay with her to take care of my little sister. Also, I had to carry a bucket of water every day for my mom. The water was far away from home. Finally, we went to the airport to go to the new house. The first time I got on the airplane was different because I had never seen an airplane before and I was very nervous. It was ok when the airplane went on top of the sky. It's too fast when you travel by airplane. When I got in to the city, it was very different from the country because in the country, we didn't have electronics, TVs, refrigerators, and other things, but I was happy when I saw new different things. These are the reasons why we moved out of country.

It's About My Country
Faisa Abshir Warsame, Minneapolis

I love talking about my country but I don't like the situation that it's in right now. There's a war in Somalia now, and it's been going on for about 20 years. I think if there was peace there, a lot of people would go back. I just hope everything works out for my country. In Somalia a lot of people don't have a place to sleep or food to eat.

Mexico
Rosa, Richfield

Hi, my name is Rosa and I am from Mexico. Back when I was growing up, even though there was more poverty than there is now, people lived in peace. Crime was a problem in the big cities only. Today sadly, crime has extended to small

Owatonna

towns. For example, kidnapping. It used to be an isolated occurrence. Today, it is an everyday crime. It takes so long for individuals to build a better life for their families and kidnappers take that away in a matter of days. Now people in Mexico live in fear. It makes me sad that my family, my friends, and all people in my country have to live in such a violent environment.

However, I am hopeful that Mexico is going to move on. The reason I am optimistic is because I know most people in Mexico is good people, they all want Mexico to be a better place to live.

Rosa is originally from Mexico.

Somalia
Muhubo Kulbi, Eagan

My home country is Somalia. Somalia is part of East Africa. I was born there and lived in Mogadishu for twenty-two years. It is a wonderful place. The weather is great in East Africa. It rains for six months of the year. It is warm and not windy so people still can function as if it isn't raining. Children can still play outside, people still walk most places, and it isn't uncomfortable. The rain makes everything green and beautiful. The other six months of the year the weather is very, very beautiful. It is sunny and about 70 or 80 degrees; not too hot and not too cold. People travel from state to state during this time. People spend most of their time outside. It is very different from the weather in Minnesota.

The most popular business in Somalia is selling livestock, like camels, goats, sheep, and cows. My father was in the camel business. I remember that after he sold some camels he would come home from work with a bag full of money from his sale and a bag full of dates for the family.

It used to be peaceful in Somalia. Before, Somali people worked together and had better lives than they do now. Now it is not a safe place. Before, if people went outside at midnight no one bothered them. Now, people don't go outside much at any time of day or night because they might be shot and killed. Life in Somalia is no longer safe. Children cannot even play outside safely. I feel safe in the United States and feel happy to be here. Life in Somalia is no longer safe but I hope for peace for people there someday.

Muhubo Kulbi is originally from Somalia.

The Differences Between Somalia and the U.S.
Ilyas S. Mohamed, Hopkins

I am from Somalia. I came to the United States one year ago. There are some differences between my homeland and the United States. I have never seen snow in Somalia, but when I came to the United States I saw more than I had ever seen elsewhere. The other difference is the food. When I was in Somalia, I used to eat fresh food that hadn't been refrigerated. Here in the United States it is not normal to eat fresh food.

Ilyas S. Mohamed is originally from Somalia.

The Strange Sound
Der Yang, Saint Paul

When I still lived in Laos, my siblings and I liked to go searching for crabs in a creek far away from my village. We liked to go during the weekend, and also when we had nothing to do. Searching for crabs was one thing that we liked to do to pass the time. It was a fun thing to do. We went many times. There was nothing to be afraid of.

But this time was different. While we were enjoying searching for crabs, suddenly, there was a very loud strange sound coming from the middle of nowhere. When we first heard it, we weren't scared because we thought that it was maybe someone just calling for the pigs to come to eat. Because in my country, people just leave their livestock to run free. When the owners will feed them, they would call the pigs to come to eat. If you have never raised a pig, you will never know that there is a way to call pigs to come to eat.

However, we realized that it was not a human sound, because there were no people living there. It was just a big jungle. When we realized that, we were so scared. We stopped searching right away and ran home. But the way home was very far. We ran as fast as we could. While we were running, we felt like the sound was chasing us. That made us even more scared. We ran without shoes, so we could run faster. At that time, we didn't feel the pain in our feet. But when we got home, our feet were so sore. They even blistered and peeled. The strange sound stopped calling when we got closer to our village. Since then we never went back to the creek.

Der Yang is originally from Laos.

Growing Up on the Farm
Mel Barber, Minneapolis

When I was growing up in Mississippi, there were a lot of things I did not understand. Like one thing, when a person was driving a new car and living in a new home I thought the person was well off.

We worked the farm from sun up to sun down. I will tell you a few things we were raising. We raised soybeans, cotton, and wheat. Also, we raised milo, sunflower seeds, and rice. We raised live stock on the farm, too. The animals were pigs and chickens. We had horses we rode and fed too. The farm was a fun place to be raised up on, but it was hard work.

I just want to tell you a few more things about the farm. They had all kinds of equipment and I used to run the machines. For example, I used to run the combine, cotton picker, and tractor. You must use the equipment right. It is very dangerous. I knew some people who got hurt. I knew some people who got killed.

Mel Barber is originally from Minneapolis, Minnesota.

Childhood in Nicaragua
Eridania John, Elk River

My name is Eridania John. I am from Nicaragua. I have lived in the United States for ten years. I'm married and have two boys, and I am a student of Handke Family Center. Ten years ago I decided to come to this country because I wanted to have a better life.

In Nicaragua, most of the children work at the age of five. I was one of them, so I didn't have an opportunity to study. My mother had to make a choice: buy supplies to go to school or eat. Sometimes we sacrifice ourselves. Some days we ate and some days we didn't, but for my sister and I it was very important to read and write. When I was nine years old, my mother decided not to send us to school at all. For her, making money was more important than school. So I decided when I have my own family not to repeat her mistake.

Growing Up in Mexico
Estefania, Elk River

Hi! I am Estefania. I came from Mexico seventeen years ago. I was born in Guadalajara, Jalisco, one of the most beautiful cities in Mexico. Their food is birria and tortas ahogadas, yummy! Sometimes I want to make the food, but it is too hard to find all the ingredients here in Minnesota. The people who are born in Guadalajara are called Tapatios. Their music is mariachi and their song is "El Jarabe Tapatio." In Mexico it is a tradition to dance to this song in many events, especially on Mother's Day. I remember when I was five years old, I danced to this song on Mother's Day. I was so excited and very nervous because my mom was there to see me and when the song started I forgot the steps. It was so embarrassing, but the boy who was dancing with me said, "It is ok, just pretend nobody is here." So I concentrated on the music and we started to dance. Well, I think it was embarrassing for me, but all the mothers who attended the event were laughing, and that is what we were supposed to do, make their day happy.

Estefania is originally from Mexico.

Coming from Thailand
Moo Ah, Saint Paul

I was born in the year 1980 in Burma village. When I was seven years old, my family moved to Thailand Shoklo refugee camp. We lived there a long time. When I was thirteen years old, my parents didn't have enough money to buy my school uniform. We were very poor. I want to find some money to help my family. I left and worked in Bangkok in barber salon and cut hair, shampoo, and cleaned everything. In 2000, I met my husband in Bangkok. I made best friends for three months and we got married. Since 2009, me and my husband decided to approved interview to UN-HCR office. We have to wait for five months and we passed and came to the United States. I remember the first day my family came to Minnesota. It was on December 28, the first time I saw winter snow falls down white. It was very beautiful.

My Life Story
Htoo Swein, Saint Paul

I was born in Burma, Karen State in 1985. When I was 6 years old, my mother and father left our village because Karen soldiers and Bumese soldiers didn't like Karen people living in the village. We came to Kaw Thoo Lei in 1997. I lived in Thailand in 1997.

I went to the Thailand Tham Him Refugee Camp and lived there for ten years. I started living in the United States in 2009. I came to Minnesota. I had a new life. It's been very hard to learn English in ESL class, but now I can speak English a little.

Htoo Swein is 21 years old and is originally from Burma.

I Love My Country
Pel Moo, Saint Paul

My country is Burma. I love my country very much because I was born and I grew up there. I stayed with my family in my country when I was child. I played and went to school with my friends. My country has many kinds of languages. My country has beautiful places and many kind and helpful people.

Pel Moo is originally from Burma.

My Happiest Moment
Nga Tran, Minneapolis

The happiest moment of my life was when I went to work in the office. When I stood in front of the door of the manager, and opened the door, I saw the manager stand up and shake my hand. Before that I was very nervous. Afterward I was very happy because I had a job. On my birthday my children always celebrate in the house. They said it is important because you don't forget when you are born! What I like best of what I own is my gold ring. I wear it on my hand because I look at it and remember my husband who died eighteen years ago.

Nga Tran is originally from Vietnam.

A Beautiful Memory
Janessa Thao, Saint Paul

My name is Janessa Thao. I'm Hmong, but I was born in a Thailand refugee camp, not in Laos. I became a United States citizen in August 2010. When I lived in Thailand, I remember when I saw many dragonflies in the sky. They were very beautiful and colorful. Some landed on the flowers in a field. The faster dragonflies went over a pond and many landed on the water flowers. For me this will always be a beautiful memory.

Janessa Thao is 27 years old and is originally from Laos.

From My Home in Guyana to My New Home in the United States
Angela Seriram, Fridley

I grew up in Guyana, South America. We lived in a small village. My dad went to work driving and picking up passengers. My mom stayed home cooking, cleaning, and taking care of me and my four sisters. She didn't work outside our home. In my country the weather was very hot. The leaves didn't fall off the trees. We didn't have four seasons. It was never cold. We had lots of rain. We hand-washed our clothes. We bathed outside, and we had toilets outside. We raised goats, chickens, and ducks for our food. We also caught fish in the canals for our mom to cook. We climbed trees and picked coconuts, mangos, papayas, kashu, bananas, five-fingers, and golden apples. We didn't have grocery stores. We bought all of our groceries and toiletries at the outdoor market. For fun we played hopscotch, jump rope, cricket, and swam at the beach and in the canals. Life in my country as I knew it was fun.

When I came to the United States I was very surprised by all the differences from my country. There were many tall buildings, grocery stores, large hospitals, shopping malls, indoor movie theaters, and many other things. Life is much better for me in the United States. I am able to go to school. I can work. I can take a bus and go see many places. I got my license so I can drive wherever I want to. I go see my mom, dad, sisters, and my brother. Our family likes to go to indoor swimming at Grand Rio Water Park. We go putt-putt golfing, ride go-carts, and go to "Disney on Ice." We have done so many fun things here that we didn't experience back home in Guyana.

Angela Seriram is 33 years old and is originally from Guyana.

La Paz, My Home Town
Janneth Aguilar, West Saint Paul

La Paz, B.C.S., Mexico is the city where I was born and grew up. My city is on a bay in the Cortez Sea (Mar de Cortez). It is a beautiful pacific community, so the name La Paz, means peace. It's a tiny city with a blue sea, sandstone desert, and nice weather. In the winter time the temperature goes from 60 to 90 degrees Fahrenheit, but the summer is hot, 100 to 110 degrees. You can spend your time doing different aquatic sports, like scuba, swimming, surfing, fishing, biking, etc. If you travel a few miles to the north, you can watch the gray whales that travel from Alaska to the warmer waters in Mexico where their babies are born.

I miss my city a lot, principally in the winter. I lived 25 years there and I always thought to live all my life in La Paz, but when I got married, I moved to the United States. Now I live in Minnesota with weather totally different than my hometown.

I like so much the summer in Minnesota because is pleasant weather where I can stay outside and enjoy activities with my family.

For me the winter is the worst part because it is difficult to drive on the snowy and slippery roads, and also we need to use layers of clothes to go outside. We can't go out to walk because the sidewalks are under snow and the freezing weather. But I try to enjoy it with my family by making fun activities like snow sliding or simply staying home together to make the winter go faster.

Janneth Aguilar is originally from La Paz, Mexico.

Feelings Toward My Country
Ganga Acharya, Minneapolis

My country Bhutan is small and naturally beautiful and lies between India and China.

About 47,000 square kilometers, Bhutan is surrounded by mountains with big forests. Bhutan was a kingdom country with about 900,000 people. In Bhutan there are 20 states. Thimphu is the capital of Bhutan. My country has different ethnic groups but the government wants people to follow one religion. There was no human rights and democracy in Bhutan.

I was born in a beautiful state called Doban, located on the southeast part of Bhutan.

We had our own house and farm of about 25 acres. We cultivated our rice, biscuits, maize and cardamom. Besides this, we had lots of cattle. We worked in our farm to sell our products. We were spending our life very happy. In our country, the government categorized people in three groups. They are Ngalongs, Sharchops and Lochampas. We belong to Lochampas. The government does not treat our group democratically. We Lochampas ask for our human rights. Instead, we were dust in the eyes of government. The government sent armies to every house of Lochampas and treated us worse. Soldiers stole rice from homes and committed sexual abuse. The king sent soldiers to murder the people living in the country who fought for human rights. This led us to flee our beautiful country. We left in 1991. I miss my motherland. I still remember those mountains near my house and beautiful green forests of my country where I spent half my life.

After we left Bhutan, we came to India. India's government didn't want us staying there. The Indian army took us to Nepal. It was hard because there was nothing to eat and we never got sleep. After we settled comfortably in a refugee camp I started working in HCF as a security guard. The food and shelters were provided by the organization. It was not sufficient for my family, but some things are better than nothing. I started working as a carpenter outside the camp. After seventeen years in refugee camps the UNHCR announced that we could apply to resettle. A big fire burned down 1,228 houses into ashes. My home was included, which made me more interested in resettling. I chose to resettle in the U.S. for a better life.

After six months my process for the U.S. resettlement was completed and I came to U.S. on November 11, 2008.

Comparison About My Life
Hue Her, Minneapolis

I was born in Laos. My family lived in the small town of Laos. My family lived in a wood and bamboo house with a thatched roof made of palm leaves. Every morning my two sisters pounded rice and cooked. After breakfast, my family walked for almost two hours to our mountainside fields and worked all day. Every evening we walked back home. At harvest time, we each carried a backpack basket with rice and corn. I think my family was satisfied with our life so much. However, the peacefulness of our life was disappearing because my country was caught in warfare. The Communist soldiers came to my country and shot many Hmong people.

In 1975 the Communist regime took over my country. My father determined to get us out of my country. My family migrated from Laos to Thailand and we came to the refugee camp of Thailand. Thailand and my country are not different so much. It is a tropical country and the weather is almost the same. We lived in the refugee camp, and we never had any farm. We just had a little garden and waited for the U.N. program to come to help us. They brought rice, meat, fish, and vegetables for the Hmong refugees. Most refugee people did their own jobs. I grew up, studied, and married in the camp. I think Thailand and my country are just a little different.

When I came to the United States, I thought I would have a big change in my life. It was not easy for me to adapt to a new life and new culture, because in the United States most people are working. I can't speak English and I can't work. In the United States they can't walk. They just drive everywhere. The United States has many lures, many bills to pay, and many property taxes. I think it is very hard to adapt to a new life for me.

Childhood Memory
Sokly Chhay, Minneapolis

I am from Cambodia. I lived in Kompong Cham for 30 years. I come from a medium-sized family and have one sister, one brother and I have three kids, two boys and one girl.

My house in Kompong Cham is across from the Mekong River. The weather is sometimes cold and sometimes hot. From January until March it's cold, but not so much, about 50 degrees. From April until October it's very hot. When I was 10 years old, I swam very far in the River because my mom always taught me how to swim and dive. I love swimming. Now my kids love swimming, too.

Sokly Chhay is originally from Cambodia.

Untitled
Issak Mohamed, Minneapolis

On June 16, 1998, I was transferred from Jonvu refugee camp in Mombasa to Kakuma Refugee Camp in Kenya, which is located near Sudan-Kenya border. The Kakuma Refugee Camp is located in semi-arid area and most of the inhabitants are Turkana people. The Turkana tribe is known to be nomadic. Traditionally, Turkana people do not wear clothes, they only wear hides around their private part. They are also armed with weapons and when I was transferred to Kakuma Refugee Camp, our files were handed over to the local UNHCR Office.

At the time, our family moved to Kakuma Refugee Camp and life was very difficult. Kakuma has the harshest climate we have ever seen in our lives. During the daytime the dust storms made it impossible for us to prepare or cook food, therefore, we only cooked our meals at night. Kakuma also had snakes that were found in every corner of the camp. It scared me several nights when I saw a snake in the mat I was sleeping on.

Kakuma also had and still has bandits that attack the camp refugees during the night. They rob any one at the camp and they also rape innocent refugee women. This has caused alarm among the refugee and it made life very difficult and unbearable. Refugees report attacks to the government police, but the police did not take any action, but rather they accused the refugee, who are the victims, of causing the robbery and the rape.

After enduring that difficult life, I received a resettlement program to the United States of America. My whole family and moved to Minnesota. After our arrival of my flight in New York, I was very happy of the law and order of the country and I remembered my early life in Somalia where I lived peacefully among my neighbors and relatives. It reminded me of how beautiful life is and how I missed that beautiful life in Somalia during my refugee years in Kenya.

Childhood Memory
Silvia Martínez, Minneapolis

I remember when I was eight years old. I left my home in the night. I got on a bus and I went to my aunt's home. My mother was worried because she didn't know where I was. My mother looked for me and she didn't find me. When she found me, she was very angry with me. She told my sister, Margaret, that she would hit me and she did it. Then my mother said that I was not good because I was a child and they loved me. Now I understand my mother and I told my daughters my childhood memory. Now I told my daughters that I was a bad child. I fought with my sisters, brothers and neighbors. Every day my teacher called my mother because I fought with my partners.

Silvia Martínez is originally from Mexico.

My Childhood's Scary Story
Zahra Mohammed, Minneapolis

One day some of my friends and I went to the river in my home country. It was an afternoon and our parents were at work. When we came back from school, we ate some lunch and we went swimming. We were in the river a long time. One of us was swimming in a deep place and disappeared in the water. The last time

we saw her, she was in the middle of the river. So we waited a while. The girl didn't come out. When the sun had set we realized that she died. We decided to go back to town. It was so dark. We walked at least two hours from the river to town. Our parents worried about us a lot. When we arrived in town, we went to the missing girl's parents, and we told them what happened. They cried. Most of the people who lived in the town went to the river, and they looked for the girl's body. They didn't find the girl's body. The next morning, the people and the government went together to the river. And they didn't find it, after that time, I decided not go to the river again. I missed my best friend and she was my cousin. Her name was Habiiba. She was thirteen years old. The river was deep and wide and the water moved very strong. All of us didn't have swimming experience. There was lot of alligators in the river, too. Finally, I stopped going to river anymore.

Zahra Mohammed is 38 years old and is originally from Somalia.

My Life
Anonymous, Minneapolis

I came from Somalia but I when grew up, civil war was happening in my country. Then my family and I moved to Kenya. Then we lived there twelve years. Then my father came to the United States. After that, he brought his family to the United States. Then when we came here and my father died. Right now, I live in the United States and I'm studying ESL, because I'm preparing to get my GED diploma!

My Favorite Places
Kazang Xiong, Minneapolis

One of my favorite places in Thailand is Tak. Tak is the place that I want to visit most. I want to go there because it has many places to see such as villages, shops, farms and a beautiful view. If you really want to take a vacation to Thailand, Tak is one of the best places to visit.

Tak is a small village in Thailand. The village is quiet. Most of the houses were built with original bamboo. In the village is a temple where you can go to pray. In Tak, the view is beautiful because everywhere around you is green forest. Also, dramatic mountains surround the village. There is an impressive waterfall near the village. Everything is close to the waterfall. In addition, the forest is a national reserve. In Tak, you don't see a lot of people walking around because they go to the farm every day. Most of them have to walk to the high mountains and farm there. Half of the people in the village have to grow their own food and raise their own animals. During the evening, the exciting night market is fun. You can buy affordable fresh fruit. Also, people there sell a lot of delicious food. There are many good restaurants in Tak. Most of the restaurants have good appetizing food. Around the black market, you will find American food such as KFC and Mc-Donald's. Tak is a small village, but has most of the things you need because of the famous waterfall. All in all, I think Tak is a nice place to visit because of the village, shops, and the view of the waterfall. I think you won't be disappointed if you take a vacation to Tak. Also, I think you will be impressed, too.

Kazang Xiong is originally from Thailand.

When I First Came to the U.S.
Anonymous, Shakopee

When I first came to the U.S. everything was very strange to me because it was a new country. This country is very big and different from my country, Somalia. Somalia always has nice weather. It isn't very cold. It is warm or hot. It doesn't rain so much, but I like my country. But in the U.S. when I compare it to mine it is totally different. Minnesota is very cold in the winter. I never knew this before. Also people in the U.S. come from different countries. They speak many languages. Some people are tall, others short. Some people have black hair and some have blond hair. They also wear short pants. They don't have enough clothes to cover their bodies.

About My Country
Hodan, Eden Prairie

I am from Somaliland. I was born in a beautiful city, Hargeysa. The weather is very nice—not cold, not hot. It is warm. When I was in my country, I lived with my family. I have five brothers and five sisters. We lived in a big house. Then I came to the U.S.A. in 1998. I first moved to Nashville ,Tennessee. Everything was new to me. I lived there ten years. I loved it there because the weather is nice. It is good place to live. Now I live in Eden Prairie, Minnesota. It is beautiful city. The winter weather is too cold and there is a lot of snow, but it is very nice city.

Hodan is originally from Somalia.

Childhood Memory
Sergio Narez, Crystal

When I was a child, I climbed up a tree and the branches broke. I fell down. I passed out. Thank God nothing happened to me. An old man picked me up and carried me to my mom. She was in my house. They didn't know what happened to me. She was scared when she saw me. I couldn't remember what happened. I woke up when I got home. I was ten years old when this happened. I used to live in Mexico.

Sergio Narez is originally from Mexico.

My Favorite Memories from My Childhood
Der Yang, Brooklyn Park

One of my favorite memories from my childhood is when I was 13-14 years old. I had one thing so exciting that happened to me, when I studied at Pun Luang High School.

One day, in March 2002, while my friends and I exercised out of our class, I saw my teacher coming to us. When she got there, she stood in front of us and she told my friends and me that we have to go with the best students to math testing right now. It was so scary because I didn't know this before and I was not ready. She told us again that we had to get ready and go quickly. We still had just one hour. After that, I went back home and brought some books, pens, and other things I needed.

In addition, when we got there, I saw many students who looked like they were very ready. They smiled and talked to each other, but my friends and I were scared. The next minute, I heard someone say "everyone go to your own class right now." I walked slowly to my class and sat on the chair next to the window. Ten minutes after that, I saw a teacher bring some papers to our teacher. When our teacher gave me my test, I felt better. I was feeling excited because the test was not too difficult. During my test, I felt happy and relaxed until I was done.

Finally, after three weeks, my teacher told me I was third in math in our city. I was so happy and my school gave me a beautiful gift. These are my favorite memories.

Der Yang is originally from Laos.

Work for a Better Life
Thitinuntha Ann Osmonson, Saint Louis Park

I am from Thailand where I lived with my parents, my two older brothers Tuk and Tik, a younger sister Jaew, and a younger brother Tom. We lived in a small village in northeast Thailand. My family has a rice farm there. Sharecroppers do the farm work. My parents had a business making and selling noodles. Everyone helped my parents with the noodle business. We all started working in the family business when we were about nine years old. We would hurry home from school, eat quickly, and then work until about 10 PM or later seven days a week.

It is difficult to make a good living in Thailand. Many people go to work in other countries. My oldest brother Tuk went to work in Taiwan and then Japan 19 years ago. Tik moved to Taiwan then South Korea to work 18 years ago. I started working in Taiwan when I was 20. I have also worked in South Korea and New Zealand. My younger sister works in Thai-

land and my younger brother is still in school. My older brothers and I send money home so that the two youngest children can go to college.

Seven years ago when my father died I moved back to Thailand. I met my future husband in Thailand while he was working there. Two years later, I moved to the U.S.A. where we were married.

Like my brothers, I left school after the sixth grade to help with the family business. I studied at home to get my GED. I am happy that I can go to school here to improve my English. The ESL classes are very good. I like my teachers. They are patient and helpful. My English is getting much better. I also enjoy all of the other students. I have friends from all over the world. I am also registered for a class to help me become a U.S. citizen. I expect that I will become a citizen before this summer. When my English gets better, I want to continue my education.

Now I have two jobs. Both of them are at the Southdale mall where I work as a tailor and a therapeutic massage therapist. My husband and I are saving money so I can open my own business. When we retire, we plan to live here during the summer and in Thailand during the winter.

Thitinuntha Ann Osmonson is originally from Thailand.

Untitled
Marie Claire Pambani, Inver Grove Heights

I am from Congo-Kinshasa, Africa. During my ten years in Buta, I met Brigitte. Brigitte was an extreme friend to me, lovely and like a nice sister. The time I met her for the first time it was in the guide group for the girls. We went with two sisters of the Catholic Church to give a gift to the lepers. They lived outside of city.

In this situation, we met and she became the best friend I have ever met, except my husband was my first best friend. She was my second friend and she took to me like my own little sister. If had the trouble I went toward her to get consolation, we rode on the bicycle to an uncle who lived in the farm of coffee, with her wife. To get there was twenty-four kilometers, and farm was off the shore.

Uncle and his wife welcomed us very good. His wife cooked chicken, Liboké and Lituma. Liboké is chicken, pumpkin, onion, tomato, spices—wrapped and boiled. You can make it with fish, meat, cassava, and spinach. To make Lituma, you boil bananas or plantains, and put it in a mortar and mash it. This is a meal preferential for Congolese. We were there for one week, and we came back to the city.

We went every afternoon to the river to swim and Brigitte brought the net to the river to catch the fish. She tied the bag down on my hip. After my family and I moved to the Kinshasa capital of Congo we were separated and met again when we were growing up, I presented Brigitte to my husband like my sister, and we helped each to other until I came to U.S. I can't forget her. I love Brigitte.

Childhood School Memory
Chia, Minneapolis

When I was young, my family lived in a small village on a high hill far from the city. We didn't have many schools and teachers. We had only one school and one teacher. At that time, I was seven years old and I was in second grade. My teacher taught first and second grades in one class, so first grade students sat on the left side and second grade sat on the right side. When I went to third grade, my parents sent me to go to school in the city. I went to live with my uncle and his family. During that time, there were no Hmong people living in that city. Only my uncle lived there because he got a job in the city.

I had never left my parents before, so I missed my parents very much. I felt lonely and cried many times. I didn't like living there because I went to school with only Lao people and I didn't have any friends. When I was in class, I sat with two students at one table, but they didn't like me because I was the only Hmong student. I felt very sad and I wanted to go back home. Two months later, I went back home to my village. I told my parents I didn't want to go back because they didn't like me and I missed them a lot. However, my parents didn't agree with me, they want me to go back to that school. I cried and went back to the school, but I cried all day. A few weeks later, my parents came to take me back home and sent me to a different school.

That school wasn't in the city, but I liked it because all of my friends went to that school. We went to school in the morning and in the afternoon we went back home. It was far from our village about 15 miles and we walked to school. We went to school for about one hour and thirty minutes. Every day, I had to wake up in the morning and prepare my stuff. Even though I walked to school for a long distance, I still liked it better than the school in the city because now I lived with my parents and went to school with my friends.

Chia is originally from Laos.

Maria De Jesus, Stillwater

My School Experience in Korea
Hyekyung Seo, Edina

Most Koreans are obsessed with their children's education. They think that education makes everything possible so that they spend much of their time, money, and effort on it. However, when I look back on my education in Korea, I have mixed emotions. I had three very different educational experiences in my life there.

First, my middle school, a Catholic-based girls' school, was a good window for me to see and know the world. My school's atmosphere was liberal and independent, and it encouraged me to have lots of hands-on experiences: making clothing, cooking, and science experiments. Furthermore, every student was involved in many school activities such as reading contests, choir, art festivals, and informal Olympics.

In contrast, the period of high school was completely the opposite. It was all about studying and tests. A Korean high school was only evaluated by how many students went to a good college. I went to school at seven in the morning with two lunch bags and came home around eleven at night. After school, I headed for a private library for more self-study. Teachers said, "If you sleep for four hours, you can go to the college you want, but if you sleep for five hours, you can't make it." At that time, I only dreamed about passing those three years as quickly as possible.

Finally, my four years of college life was in the middle of political turmoil. Twenty five years ago my whole country was shaken by military dictators. College students were the ones who confronted the government. Many of my friends were arrested, and three of them died because of the security police's torture and tear gas bombs. Even though I was not a radical student, the era called for students to demonstrate. As a result, I realized the power and possibilities we had, and developed confidence about my country's future.

Although I totally agree about the importance of education for this younger generation, I resent Korea placing that same pressure on it as was placed on my generation. I hope that Korea's future education gets focused on preparing the next generation for wholesome living and uncovers possible solutions in a fresh and free way, because it is not healthy to sacrifice their present well being in the name of future progress.

Mgangasima River Story
Nestory S. Harusha, Coon Rapids

When I was 12 years old I went fishing in the Mgangasima River. In this river there were lots of big stones. I slipped on one and I fell down on my back and hit my head. A couple minutes later a woman who was coming from a farm saw the blood in the water. She had a big basket of yucca on her head, so she put down the basket. She asked herself, "Why is there blood in the water?" She decided to follow the river to see where the blood was coming from, until she found me in the river. After she took me out of the water it took about 15 minutes before I was able to know what was going on. She asked me, "Where do you live?" and "Who are your parents?" I told her my parent's names and where our home was. She put me on her back and carried me to our home. There was no hospital, but my mom went to the neighbor to find pills called penicillin. She washed the blood from my head. Then she broke the penicillin and put it on my head where I was injured.

After one month, the woman who had found me in the river came back to our home to visit me. When I saw her, I felt happy. Then I hugged her. She asked me, "Do you know me?" I said, "Yes, I know you. You are the one who saved my life last month." She asked me, "How did I save you?" I answered, "You found me in the Mgangasima River." After that I caught a rooster, and I gave it to her as a gift.

Nestory S. Harusha is 27 years old and is originally from Tanzania.

How Somalia Is Different from the United States
Hibo, Blaine

In Somalia we live all together in one house: mother and father, brothers and sisters, aunts and uncles, children and grandparents. Each family in the United States lives separately, husband and wife, and kids only.

The weather in Somalia is different from the United States. In Somalia it's very hot. Sometimes it's rainy, sometimes it's windy. We only have two seasons. Here in Minnesota we have four seasons: winter, spring, summer, and fall. In Minnesota the weather is very cold and snowy in winter. Spring can be both sunny and rainy. Summer is often warm and sunny. In fall, it's cold and the leaves fall off trees.

Another difference between Somalia and the United States of America is level of education. In Somalia all people can go to school, from first grade to high school. You have to pay and it's expensive. If you have money you can pay for a good school, but some people can't pay and so they can't go to school. In the United States of America all people can go to school. The school is also free for people to learn to read, write, and speak English. They have nice teachers here and if you have questions, they help you. In the United States of America when you finish high school you can go to college.

Hibo is originally from Somalia.

Welcome to Mexico
Adriana García, Blaine

I am from Mexico. My country is beautiful and a neighbor of the United States. There are five million people. People in my country are friendly and hospitable. The opinions that tourists have of people in Mexico are good. When we have free time we like to know about other countries, and having parties is common in my country. The weather in my country depends on the four seasons of the year. The best time to visit my country is December. It is a month of traditional party. It is common for the family to get together. Typical food in my country is tacos; Mexican Food is recognized all over the world.

In my country it's difficult to find a job. Many people in my country are not working. There is a lot of crime and violence. One thing that is better in the United States than in my country is the food; everything is more natural. One thing that is better in the United States than in my country is lifestyle. It's possible to find a better job, the house, and the school for children. What I miss most about my native county is my family; it is very important to me. One interesting thing about my native country is culture. My country has rich history and culture. I love my country.

Adriana García is 37 years old and is originally from Mexico.

Story About My Life
Anab Jibril, Saint Cloud

When I look at my eyes, I am amazed! I love them so much because I can't see without them. I can see everything I want to. I can't do anything without them. I can say that my eyes are my remote.

Before 1991 when the Civil War waged in my country, I was with my family. I was so happy but after that I lost my family. And my dear mother died during that war. I grew up with my aunt and her children. We came to Uganda. After three years she left me in Uganda. At that time I was so sad, but I tried to forget everything about the past and I tried to solve all my problems. Now I enjoy life one day at a time. And my eyes give me reason to be happy!

That is my true story of my life.

Untitled
Fali Prosper, Saint Paul

I'm from Congo in Africa (DRC). My country is the third biggest country in Africa; found in the center of Africa's map.

My country has many riches, such as valuable minerals, ex. Diamonds, etc. about it. Today my country has a problem of war between two tribes and the neighbor country came in my country to take some wealth.

Today my country is the first country for violence in the world.

Everybody help us pray to God to help us reach peace.

I like Africa and I like my country.

Fali Prosper is originally from Congo.

For Those I Love

Friendship
Sartu Ahmed, Minneapolis

I remember when I left my friends back home in Ethiopia. It was my last night before I had to leave the country. I remember when we all sat outside and were looking at the sky. The weather was so beautiful that you could see the clear sky. I remember that we all were sitting outside of my house and watching the stars and a beautiful moon. We also told stories to each other, made each other laugh and supported one another. That was the best and last time of my life in Ethiopia.

Friendship is like a breeze. You can't hold it, taste it, smell it or feel it. A friend is a person to laugh and cry with. An inspiration is someone who lends you a helping hand, though friends may not be forever. A friend is neither a shadow nor a servant but someone who holds a piece of a person in his or her heart. A friend is someone who shares a smile. A friend is someone who brightens up your day. What makes a person a friend? It is by saying your love will stay in my heart forever.

Sartu Ahmed is 27 years old and a student at Northside ABE. She came to the United States almost 11 years ago from Ethiopia and now lives in Minneapolis. She has two kids. Abdunasir is 4 years old, and Amir is 2 years old. Her third baby is due soon. She enjoys reading any kind of story and teaching her kids in her free time. In her future, her dream is to get her diploma, and (Insha Allah) if God is willing, go to college and get her nursing degree.

My Grandfather
Mary Lay, Saint Paul

I'm a Karen refugee from Burma, but I grew up in Thailand. I came to the United States in 2010. I remember my grandfather. His name is Saw Bee. He is 76 years old. He has a wife, two sons, and two daughters. He is from Burma, but lives in a refugee camp in Thailand. My grandfather is a pastor who loves our Karen people and they love him. He is very kind. My grandfather is also good for his children. When he talks to them they listen to him. I love my grandfather. I think in the future I'll come back to see him.

Mary Lay is originally from Burma.

My Best Friend
Til Gurung, Saint Paul

My best friend is Ram. He is a strong guy. He always shares his difficult problems to me. He is a very helpful person. He always helped the poor people by giving them rice, food, firewood, money, clothes, and positive education. He is a responsible person. He always thinks good of people. In fact, he is a humble and soft guy. He is living in a small village in Nepal. He is a really brilliant and healthy person. He is my devoted friend. I love him very much. I miss him every day. May God bless my best friend.

Til Gurung is originally from Nepal.

Love Song
Zoua Her Vang, Minneapolis

How can I let go from the one that I always love, but today have let go the love we have from now will have no more. All the promises we have in heart, your precious smell I kept. How should I let it go cause I kept it in my lung, how should I let go should let go let go of you. Everything that I had because of you... How should I forget you in my life if don't have you I couldn't live. There's only one way that, can move

you that is when I no longer live. Then I will forget you. Even though today you will go away from me I will still remember you in my entire life. How should I forget you, forget you in my life. If I don't have you I couldn't live there's only one way that can move you from me. That when I no longer live. Then I will forget you, even though today you will go away from me. I will still remember you in my entire life. I will still remember you because you was my loved.

Zoua Her Vang is originally from Thailand.

Family
Akech Majok, Coon Rapids

My grandma is from Bor village in South Sudan. She moved to Malakal then back to Bor. She had eleven children and my mother was the second youngest. She is important to me because she helped my mother when my mother was pregnant with me and my dad died. Grandma is also important to me because she told me about my life in the future. She taught me how to cook and sew and many other things. My grandma was close to my mother because my mother loved her a lot. Momma always worried about her mother. Momma wanted Grandma to feel special. She helped my grandma with the rest of her life. Grandma died in 1988 at 65 years old.

Akech Majok is originally from South Sudan.

Spotless
Shelia M., Minneapolis

When I got my kitten I was very happy because she was a prayer answered. I wanted a kitten that was all white, with green eyes and with a very gentle spirit that I could name Spotless. Most white cats that I've seen have blue eyes. She was found on the lady's lawn like she dropped out of heaven. I know she was an answer to my prayers. She would walk up to me and put her paw on my lap and say a sweet hello with a purr that was totally different than anything I've heard. I would have a vase of fresh flowers on my dining table and she always had to stick her paw into the vase to touch the water and knock it over. It would make me so mad.

As she grew into a full-grown cat her tail was beautiful. When she walked in the room, she walked with a prance like a horse in a show. Spotless was a sweet cat. I had to give her away. So my nephew took her and treated her like a little princess. She brought lots of joy in to my life when I needed it, and I am very thankful.

My Friend and My Family

Seyfu Berhane, Eagan

I was born in the big city Addis Ababa, Ethiopia in 1980. When I was a child I had a best friend named Dawit. We played together all the time. We were the same age, started school on the same day, and we ate together often. We were actually more than best friends, we were like brothers.

One afternoon Dawit surprised me. He won the Diversity Visa Lottery to come to the United States! He arrived here in 1999. In 2003 my good friend sponsored his family and me to come to the United States. When I moved here life was hard and I had many problems. It was difficult to learn English so I started school in Minneapolis. I could not find a job and it was hard to adapt to the cold weather.

I miss my country a lot but I give thanks to God for all the good things in my life. I have lived in this country for seven years. I have a good job and I work hard every day. I have wonderful children that I enjoy spending time with. I feel very happy.

Seyfu Berhane is originally from Ethiopia.

A Horrible Day at the Park

Juliana, Minneapolis

One day in the summer, I went to the park with my boyfriend. It looked like it was going to be a beautiful and perfect day. I was a little bit afraid about insects, but I thought that nothing was going to happen because I was protected by my boyfriend.

We sat on the ground under a tree, and we started talking and laughing. We were really enjoying our first day at the park. Then I felt something walking on my feet. It was an ugly and big, black worm. I was terrified looking at the worm, but my boyfriend took it and said, "Are you afraid of this? This is nothing; it is just a worm." After that, I was nervous and scared and I wanted to go home, but I didn't say anything.

We continued talking for a few minutes. I looked at the ground around us, and when I looked at my boyfriend, there were many worms on his shirt and jeans. I got up quickly, and I started screaming, jumping, and running. I wanted to stay away from him, but he got up and followed me. He was laughing a lot because it was so funny, but for me it was a horrible day.

My Most Supportive Person

Mrs. Rizvi, Elk River

Every man in his life has someone who lends support to him or her. The support may be physical, emotional, or financial. My life is no exception. I have been very lucky in this regard. God has been very kind to me and gave me a special and loving mother.

Unfortunately, my father expired leaving behind me and my three brothers. There was nobody to look after us. At this critical stage my mother came forward. She gave us love and affection, and above all, food and other needs of life. She was very particular about character building. She made us useful and ordinary members of the society. To achieve her aim she had to work very hard. She fought this battle single-handedly to accomplish the dual role of father and mother. My mother fought the tough battle of life. She passed away leaving behind unforgettable memories of love, affection, and sacrifice for her family. She left the world with consolation that she had done justice to her duty. I pray to Almighty God, may He shower His choicest blessings on her soul and rest her in heaven. Amen.

A Healing Experience
Mari Naw, Saint Paul

My name is Mari Naw. I come from Burma. Yesterday I went to my friend's home. Her daughter was very sick and had a very high fever. The pastor came to my friend's home and also some Karen people. All together we prayed and read the Bible. In a few minutes her daughter was very good, but she could not speak. The Pastor took her head and prayed and she began to talk. Her family and all people were very happy. God was very powerful. Then I came back home with my family at 9:00 p.m. I hope her daughter will be very good, happy, and strong.

Mari Naw is originally from Burma.

My Grandpa
Heather Farris, Mapleton

You taught me a lot. You taught me to drive both the cars and the tractors. You taught me politics before I understood. Showed me the world! If there was one more day I would tell you, I miss you and love you. That I am grateful for you helping raise me. That no matter what, I want to be a lawyer someday. Even if it takes me 'till I am a hundred. Because that is the one thing we always talked about.

My Story
Chai Kao Lor, Minneapolis

My country, Thailand, has very hot summers. It has no snow. When I drive the car it's better for me. My country is small. There are no lost people in Thailand. It has lost many trees. My country has many farmers.

My country has no freedom. I don't like my country. It's dirty. It's not good for me. I move to America. I think America is beautiful. I like American freedom. America has work for me and helps my family. My family is happy in America.

The Gift
Nadia Saleem, Minneapolis

The best gift is a plastic rose. It is from my husband. He gave it to me on Valentine's Day five years ago. It is special for me because when he bought it from the shop some TV channel interviewed him and asked him, "What are you doing?" He told them, "I want to buy a flower for my wife," and talked about me in lovely words and respectfully. All our friends saw him and called me to tell me that they saw him on TV and that he bought a flower for me.

Nadia Saleem is originally from Jordan.

Anthony Chapple

Aurora

Health Check-up
Sara, Minneapolis

One way to have good health is to make a check up one time a year, because it is very important. In the actual life, we suffer too much sickness. Most of women are dead from the cancer of breast and cervical cancer. These types of cancer are very strongest when you don't receive a treatment on time. It's easier to overcome if you discover the sickness before it advances. Many people have this cancer, and know the chemotherapy and biopsy are very difficult, because the people suffer vomit, the hair falls down, and the people feel dizzy and feel weak. After that, if the person is strong and has fortress they can overcome that, but if they can't, they die.

I ask for all women who never made the pap-smear test or mammogram test, please make one every year. It is very important to save our life, and discover the sickness on time.

This information is dedicated to my grandmother who died of the cancer.

Sara is originally from Mexico.

Love Is Important in Our Lives
Paw Gay, Saint Paul

Love is important from everybody.
There are many kinds of love. Love is just a feeling. If you think it is true, love can confuse you if you don't know about it. Love is special for everyone. Love may make you cry and make you smile at the same time. When you love somebody your life seems to be for the long-term. If you don't know how to use it, love can be very dangerous.

There are different kinds of love. Love between family members, love for your parents, love for your kids, and love for your friends. The love between a boy and a girl is a special love. People who love each other always like to be happy. If you have love in your home, your home is a home sweet home.

Paw Gay is originally from Burma.

Being a Mother
Makoya, Coon Rapids

It's fun being a mother. I have three beautiful children, two girls and a boy. Their ages are 11, 9, and 7 years old. My 11-year-old is very fun to be around. She helps to cheer me up. When I am sad she tells me jokes. She also helps me with my school work. I am thankful to have her. My 9-year-old is the cleaner of the family. She loves to clean the kitchen and cook breakfast. Drawing is her passion. She draws people and animals.

A Gift from Joe
Chuol Juay, Coon Rapids

The nicest gift I have ever had was a winter coat. A missionary man who became my friend gave me this winter coat because he thought that it would be very helpful to me. I received this coat when I was a new arrival to this country. I still have it to this day, and I will keep it as long as I am living in Minnesota. The missionary man told me that he was very much aware of the weather of my country. That was why he gave me that wonderful and heavy winter coat. I didn't like it at first, but as soon as it started snowing, it made me love this coat forever and ever. Thanks, my friend, Joe.

Chuol Juay is originally from Sudan.

My Memory
Ka Chang, Mounds View

The second day I was in America, I met Keng, my husband. He was my brother-in-law's older sister's son, but I had never met him before. That day he invited me to go on a date with him. At that time it was very difficult for me because day time in America was night time in Thailand, so I was very tired and funny. It was only my second day in America, too. We went to the Mall of America. I was very shy with him, and I didn't talk much. I saw a lot of people walking in the mall. There were many things that I had never seen or heard before like a new language, black people and white people. They were big and tall. I had never seen this in my life. I saw many things and smelled a lot of things like foods, perfumes, and other things. It made me sick. I felt a little dizzy, so I walked side by side, and I held Keng's hand without asking him. He took good care of me all day long. After that we went home, and then one month later, we feel in love with each other. We always walked in the park near my house after work and school. One year later on June 9, 2006, we were married.

Right now we have a good life. My husband goes to work every day, and I go to school every day, too. I also have a part-time job. One more thing that we still want in our lives is a baby. We hold God will give this destiny to us and to our life.

The Classmate Interview
Tatiana Biles, Byron

When I interviewed Helina last week in writing class, it gave me the chance not only to know her better but also to appreciate some facts make this classmate unique.

Helina is from Ethiopia. She has lived in the United States about one and a half years with her husband and brother. She works as a cell phone manager. Helina got a visa to the United States recently as the member of the "green card lottery" and it changed her life very strongly. She likes to spend time with the close people—to cook some special food for them, to read books. She is very attached to her family. She knows her husband from childhood.

Helina has a clear understanding about her professional long-term goals. She is an IT person who can talk about computers very extensively. Her technical English is more advanced than regular. Her work in the telecoms branch makes her satisfied because it's close to her original specialization.

Helina impressed me by her strong social position to help motherhood, especially for the education system. She looks sad when she talks about conditions of children's education institutions and the level of life for many children in Africa. She wants to help this system and adopt a child from Africa in the future.

Helina is a young beautiful woman with smiling eyes and friendly, kind manners. She is optimistic and inquisitive— a brave and active person. I believe that she will realize her wishes because they are clear, inspiring and cordial. I felt myself more bold and energized after my talk with Helina. She showed me an example of courage and kindness.

God Is Always with Me
Isabel Suazo, Shakopee

When I was 14 years old, I went from my little town, Los Terrones, Guerrero, Mexico, to Guadalajara, Jalisco, Mexico. I went there because I was very bored in my town and I'm a very curious person. I like to experiment with different things. But I am very careful when I do something different. While I was in Guadalajara, Jalisco, I lived with my Aunt Rosita. She helped me to get a fake ID with another name that stated I was 18. I needed this because I was only 14 and I needed a job. I went to work at a large company doing quality control. It was fun and I made new friends. My life was definitely different.

One day, one of my friends invited me to a bonfire at a cabin far away from the company. I was very excited. We planned to go on Friday on the company bus when we finished our work. I thought I was just going with my friends. When we got on the bus I was scared because I didn't know what to do when we arrived. The men started the bonfire, music, drinking, and dancing. When all of this began I wanted to leave. However, my friend said we had to stay until 6 am! But the bus driver agreed to take me right away. On the way back the bus became stuck in a hole on the road. So I got off the bus and started walking. It was very cold. I was scared because I didn't know where I was at. I started to cry because the road was very dark and I was all alone. I was praying to God. I said, "Please, send to me an angel to take care of me because you are the only one I can trust." Suddenly, I saw a big rock beside the freeway. Painted on it was a picture of the Virgin of Guadalupe! I thought that this was the angel that God sent me to guide me to safety. I saw a bridge and then I saw the company. I was very happy because I felt safe. I had been walking for 4 hours.

Today, I still believe that God will take care of me. Thank you, God. I love you.

Isabel Suazo is 27 years old and is originally from Mexico.

My Sweet Shandel
Uniek Styles, Saint Cloud

Just the thought of her gives me butterflies. Feeling like a six-year-old who has a crush on his teacher is the feeling that takes form. Like a cut getting deeper and deeper. In a way that changes the definition of beauty itself. Her eyes are bright wide sparkling reflecting only me. Her smile wide, ear to ear, dimples showing slight fear. Yet she moves forward, faces toward a future of us. Leaving the hurt behind she and I have intertwined. I am in her eyes and she is in mine forever. Together, there is no such place as time. We are still. Traffic stops. No wind blows. The sun shines perfectly and reflects the freckles on her nose. That hair of an angel, no, that of a goddess. With all my love, I promise, as witnessed from above, to be completely honest. I will be here, never leave, in sickness. Can't fall, won't fail. Will count sheep as they jump bails. She completes me, no other woman can come close to competing. Asked her for her hand in marriage, she was completely stunned. An exciting yes, spoken in soft breaths, so excited she barely speaks. One of our strongest moments left my sweet Shandel weak in the knees. Tears of joy streamline her face, sweet embrace my sweet Shandel. I love you, you love me, we equal eternity. Soul mates, face to face, I speak my vows. Promise to love you here on out. As these words surround us a lovely storm of bliss, electric charge felt on my lips, when we kiss. My sweet Shandel. My wife, I will make it home to you soon. My sweet Shandel. I will be home, complete, I love you. My sweet Shandel.

Great Love Knows No Bounds
Lily Ding, Plymouth

Great love knows no bounds. I was fortunate to witness this in person on my way to America. While waiting at the airport gate, I saw a thin Asian boy without a leg in a wheelchair. He was about 12 years old. There were two white children playing with him. Two adults were standing behind them. They were all waiting at the priority boarding line. I thought they might have just adopted the Asian boy and now were taking him home to America. I watched them happily board the plane, and I followed them onto the same flight.

I have read many articles about American families adopting Asian children, and I admire these families greatly. But this was the first time that I actually saw a disabled child being adopted and so well loved and cared for. I was deeply touched. I know adoption demands many sacrifices and adopting a disabled child would be that much more challenging. All through the long and boring flight I wondered what great love motivated their devotion to their cause.

After the plane landed and the passengers disembarked, I was again moved by what I saw. The young father was holding the Asian boy in his arms and walking slowly ahead of the crowd. The two children were pulling their small carry-on bags and walking briskly, and their mother was walking behind them pulling a suitcase. At the corner, the man stopped to wait for his family to catch up. Everyone hurried by, but I slowed down to watch them with great interest. As I walked past them I saw them talking, smiling, and having so much fun. The Asian boy even poked at the man's face, and the father seemed to enjoy his touch and his tease. Although we never exchanged a single word, and did not even make direct eye contact, I could feel the love, joy, and happiness freely flowing among them. This is indeed the greatest love: no colors, no races, and no boundaries.

I have a dream to someday meet this family who unknowingly brought so much joy and love to my heart on the first day I arrived in this country. I want to talk to them, to understand them, and to learn from them the great love of the American people. I want to be like them and spread this great unselfish love all around the world.

Lily Ding is originally from China.

Ukrainian Village Volunteers
Oksana, Andover

It would be very, very good if we had more humanitarian persons or organizations than we have now. In my small village, Podvirne, we still have an organization to help old people who don't have any relatives in our village. There are six volunteers who help them. They come to their houses and bring food or clothes. They help do household chores – cleaning, cooking, washing, and fixing the house. They also help people prepare for winter by chopping wood and bringing it into the house. The volunteers help Grandma or Grandpa to get to doctors' appointments or to visit friends. All old people still have a piece of land around the house.

It is very important for people to have their own property. Thank you for all these people who still have big hearts. God bless them.

Oksana is originally from Ukraine.

A Special Birthday
Silvia C., Blaine

One of the nicest gifts that I received was on one of my birthdays. That was one of the best things in my life because it was a hard time due to past difficulties with my health. I didn't think to make something to celebrate, but my kids gave me the surprises. They knew what kind of flowers I liked and bought them. That for me was a bountiful gift. Why? Their gifts were given at the moment when I needed support, and the memories are ones that I'll never forget in my life. I loved the plants because they made me happy and feel like I had life again. Thanks to my kids and my love to them.

Silvia C. is originally from Mexico.

Jodi Sperandio   Buffalo

Good Friends
Ka Khang, Minneapolis

In 1980, I was about 8 years old. I lived in the Ban Vinai Camp. I had many friends. We played together and went to school together. After two years, I stopped school. My parents moved to different place. I didn't see my friends for a long time. I missed them so much. Now some still live in Thailand and some came to the U.S.

When I moved to different place, I met another girl. Her name is Ploua. We are very good friends too. We learned how to sew together and we went to shopping together. Five years after, I got married and I missed her so much. And after three years, I came to the U.S. She stayed with her parents. And after that she got married and she came to the U.S. Now she lives in California. We talk on the phone every night. She came to visit me and I went to visit her last year. Now we so happy because we are still very good friends.

Thank you for reading my story.

Ka Khang is originally from Laos.

My First Dog
Miguel López, Minneapolis

When I was born, my parents decided to buy a dog. His name was Gyro. My mom and dad thought that it would be the best gift for their first child. He was about 3 weeks old when I was born. I don't remember him until I was 5 years old. But my parents always reminded me how my relationship with Gyro was, and they said that I didn't want to leave him alone at home.

There were more dogs in the house but no one like Gyro. He was unique. I used to come home late at night from school, and I remember my house was five blocks from the bus stop. Gyro always was waiting for me at the bus stop or half way. Even though my arrival times were different, he knew when I was coming home.

Time passed and he was getting old but that didn't stop him for meeting me at the bus stop. It used to make me feel so bad that he walked five blocks to meet me see him tired, so I carried him in my arms on the way back home.

Then one time he was 20 years old, and he disappeared forever. My mom told me that dogs run away when they are very close to die. We couldn't find him anywhere. My whole family and I were sad for years because Gyro meant a lot for all of us. He changed our lives.

Miguel López is originally from Ecuador.

Missing My Parents
Fernando Arzimendi, Coon Rapids

My name is Fernando and I was named for my dad. My dad was a really nice person. I don't remember much about my mom. Her name was Obdulia and she died when I was only six years old. I was raised by one of my sisters. My dad lived in Mexico City which was three hours from Morelos, the state where I lived. He used to come to Morelos every weekend to give money to my sister and visit us. My whole family would go out every Sunday and do a barbecue and play games like soccer, baseball, and volleyball. When I turned sixteen I decided to come to the United States. It was really hard to leave them. My dad left early that Sunday. He didn't want to cry when I left.

We used to talk on the phone at least once a week. He was proud of me, and I was proud of him, of course. A year and a half later, I was on my way to work, and I got the worst call of my life. One of my sisters called and said that my dad had been killed.

It is really hard to live without parents. You never get used to it. But you can learn a lot from life. You learn how to appreciate things and understand people. I miss them a lot, but I keep going on to do my best in life, just like they are both still alive and I am still trying to make them proud of me.

Fernando Arzimendi is originally from Mexico.

My Life
Anonymous, Saint Louis Park

A person I share with my life is my husband. His name is Abdulahi. He is from Somalia and he came to U.S.A. in 1999. I came to U.S.A. in August of 2005. We both met in the U.S.A. and got married. At that moment I was attending high school. After one year, I got pregnant and was attending school. Life was not easy at that time. When I had my first baby, I stayed home for one month. After that, I went back to school. I attended school for eight months and I got pregnant with my next baby. When my next baby was born I dropped out of high school, but no matter what, I have two beautiful kids and a nice husband. I still have time to go learn.

Friend
Maria P, Saint Louis Park

What is a friend? To me a friend is helpful when she needs somebody to speak, and to share what I know. I have a friend. I met her when I was in preschool but now we can't see each other because she is in a different country.

We still talk by telephone. When I came here I met a new friend. She is my best friend, too. She teaches me how to make different recipes of food from her country. She is Mexican and she learns to prepare my recipes from Ecuador, too. She helps me to take care of my kids when I have to go some place. She is a really good friend.

My Life in the U.S.
Anonymous, Saint Louis Park

My name is Rany. I come from Cambodia. I came to Minnesota in 2008. I came here to live with my husband. I like Minnesota but I don't like the winter in Minnesota. It is so cold.

My life is hard right now because I keep looking for a GED, a job, and a driver's license. I think when I get everything I need, I will have a good life.

I have a wonderful family-in-law; they always help me and teach me well. I want to say thanks to my husband and his family. They are so sweet, lovely and friendly.

Story
María Tigre, Saint Louis Park

My name is Maria and I'm from Ecuador, one of the most beautiful countries. I came to this country in 2002 and it was very different for me, even the people. There were many things to learn, especially about being away from my family and my friends. I miss them a lot.

In 2003 I had my son, the best and most beautiful person in my life. Every day he makes everything more easier for me. I feel very blessed to have him with me now. Soon he will be 8 years old and I'm very proud all of what we have done together.

My Short Stories
Bounthanh Saengtarahn, Saint Cloud

My name is Bounthanh Saengtarahn. I have one baby boy. My baby is very energetic and he is very active. When he is at home he is running around, opening the refrigerator, opening bathroom doors, shutting doors, and turning on the T.V. He likes the free life. He doesn't like to be interrupted.

I love all of my children. I have four children. Their names are Ouy, Ann, Joe, and Amy. Ouy is very beautiful. She is working now. She helps me a lot. Ann is in high school. She is very nice. She helps me with clothes. Joe is very good, too. He helps me with cooking. Amy is very nice. She goes to school every day.

I came to the United States in December, 1990. It was something new for me, the Milwaukee snow and cold. My first winter surprised me. I had never seen snow in my life. When I looked through the window it was very beautiful but the weather was not good! Now I live in Saint Cloud, Minnesota and the weather is the same!

When God Was with Me
Yuniba Montoya, Shakopee

When I was 21 years old, I was pregnant for the first time. My husband and I were very happy while we were waiting for the baby to be born. When I was 3 months pregnant, I was diagnosed with preeclampsia. My body changed but it was not like other pregnant women. My body had too much liquid. Some liquid passed through my skin on my legs and my stomach and was visible outside. I was scared because I wanted my baby to live. The doctor told me, "When you have a headache you need to go to the hospital." One day, I had a severe headache that was impossible to tolerate.

I went to the hospital quickly because I could have convulsions. The doctor took me into to a dark room because I could not tolerate light or sound. When I was in this room, I started to sing and to pray to God. I saw a white light and I felt peace in my heart. I felt God was with me. When the doctor came to check me, he looked at me and said that I was fine. I would

need to stay there for a few hours to be observed. I had a cesarean at eight months of pregnancy. When I was in surgery, my blood pressure was high and I couldn't breathe.

I felt the doctor cutting my stomach. I didn't know if it was the pain or the anesthesia but I couldn't sleep. I didn't want to sleep because I wanted to see my baby. When my baby was born I couldn't hear his cry because my head was very confused from the anesthesia. When the doctor showed me my baby, I heard the doctor's voice from very far away. When I saw my baby I fainted. The nurses checked on me when I woke up and I felt better. I asked where my baby was. They answered that my baby was a boy and he was good. He needed to stay in the incubator because he was born at eight months. When I went to my room, the nurse came with my son.

I couldn't explain my rejoicing when I saw my son. He was too little, but for me he was the most beautiful baby.

Yuniba Montoya is 33 years old and is originally from Mexico.

My Everyday Hero
Anita Kimball, Minneapolis

My every day hero is God. I say God because He is the one who wakes me up. He gives me air, light, food, money, kids, family, and a teacher who can help me understand what I need to know.

Another reason He is my hero is when I call on Him, He's there. When I'm down and out He picks me up when I cry. He says something to me. He also gives me a feeling I can't explain.

I'm blessed to say that He is my father and my brother. He will always be there for me. I have to do right by Him and keep going to church praising His name. God laid down for me and that's not all. I look at what He went through for all our sins.

My Father has always been good to me. I love him for everything. I'm blessed to still be here with my family and friends. Also, I'm able to get up and go wherever I want. When the car is down He gets it back running. He took me back when I was sinning.

He gave me my baby girl back and He gave me a son that I always wanted. I say thank you for that.

This is the reason why I say God is my hero. He is always on time no matter what. He will never let you down no matter what. Call His name and mean what you say and my Father will bless you in His name. Take time out and say thank you, thank you, thank you God.

Angelica's Story
Angelica, Otsego

My name is Angelica. I was born in Soledad de Doblado. It's a small city of Veracruz. I lived there for 8 years. My family and I moved to Veracruz Port, that was the better for my education. I have three sisters and one brother. They're wonderful people, but I didn't see them for six years. I came to Minnesota with my friend and it was very difficult because Veracruz is coast and means it is very hot. Minnesota is beautiful. I never appreciated well the seasons. Despite the weather so different, that I have to pick up the leaves in the fall and remove the snow in the winter, and I don't speak English. I'm happy because my daughter was born here. She is three years old, is a bit difficult to understand because she speaks English better than Spanish, but it does not matter because she tells me every day in Spanish, Yo te quiero mucho a tu. When she says a tu she means a ti, and at least I can answer, I love you so much in English to her.

Angelica is 36 years old and is originally from Mexico.

Coming to My Life
Yanet Escalante, Austin

I love my life and I think everything is working well. If I work hard I will get what I want. I love to dream about a lot of different things and follow them looking for the right way to be successful. I have two wonderful children and an understanding husband who takes care of me. They are my life. They are the motor that moves me to be a better person every day. I also like to help people no matter what kind of people they are; I like to share some stuff that they really need like clothes, shoes, etc. That why every day I thank God for giving me health and peace. He is the best friend and never fails even you don't remember him. He is there next you giving you a hand and his shoulder to cry on. When you have problems or happiness He is always waiting for you to share with him. Don't be afraid to talk with Him because He is happy when everybody is happy.

The Birth of My Second Daughter
Anonymous, Golden Valley

That time was a difficult pregnancy because I had a small birthing problem. My doctor said, "This is a very dangerous pregnancy." I didn't wait 9 months for birth. I waited 7 or 8 months. One day suddenly I had high blood pressure and I went to Park Nicollet Emergency Room. My doctor checked my blood pressure. It was high. He referred me to Abbot Hospital. That time I was 5 and ½ months pregnant. The Abbott Hospital Emergency Doctor checked my pressure. It was still high. Finally the doctor decided to do a C-section and take my baby. That time my baby girl weighed 1 pound 2 oz. She stayed in Abbott Hospital 3 months. After that she came home. She is now 5 years old. I say every day thank you God for my daughter.

Poetry and Prose

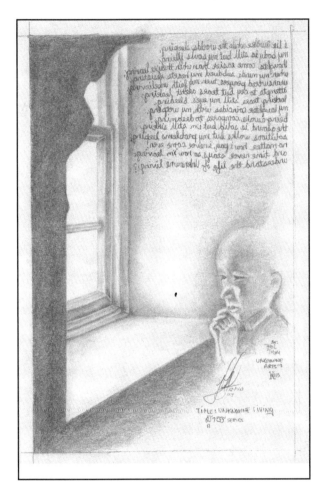

Unknowne Living
Thol Thim, Rochester

I lie awake while the world's sleeping,
My body is still but my soul's fleeing.
Thoughts come easier than when they're leaving,
When my mind's subdued my heart's resisting,
Unanswered prayers turn my faith unbelieving.
Attempts to cry but tears aren't leaking,
Lacking tears, still my eye's bleeding,
My laughter coincides with my weeping.
Being awake compares to dreaming,
The ground is solid though I'm still sinking.
Solution walks but my problems leaping,
Now matter how I pay I never come even.
And time never stays so now I'm leaving,
Understand the life of unknown living.

Thol Thim is 26 years old and is originally from Cambodia.

There It Went
Keshaun P. Guy, Annandale

I'm alone in this world without anywhere to go,
Without a shoulder to lean on
And with no one to know.

Alone in this world where forgiveness is a sin,
Where success is only based
On the color of your skin.

Alone in this world where my ancestors never made it,
With so many kids
Of my color who are uneducated.

Alone in this world where my parents disowned me,
And then turned their back on me
As if they don't know me!

Alone in this world where I'm digging my own hole,
Preparing my own grave
As my body gets cold.

Alone in this world where brothers kill brothers,
There's no love in the air,
Not even for their own mothers.

Alone in this world where racism is cool,
Where if your skin is black
You'll be treated like a fool.

Alone in this world where no one understands my pain,
Even if I let it go
The hurt still remains.

Alone in this world where I was scared to have kids
I never wanted my son
To experience the life that I live.

And even though, in my heart, I really want to change,
The only thing my homies tell me
Is to charge it to the Game.

Alone in this world where I'm concerned about my family,

All I wanna do is teach them
A little thing called reality.

Alone in this world where I think about my son,
How much he really needs me
And the hard times to come.

I'm alone in this world where I've been through so much.
I'm just showing you my experiences
Because it's never enough.

I'm alone in this world where many hate each other.
Maybe in the Afterlife
We can have love for one another!

Knot
Lydia Perkins, Minneapolis

Here I stand with my
Life tied in knots.
Knots that I made
Tied with time.
One rope is self-righteous

Self-critical and many more
Now I sit down to
Undo what I did.
Ask, I heard the
Teacher say,
Time to get started.
And one knot
Gets untied.

Lydia Perkins is 57 years old and is originally from Minneapolis, Minnesota.

I Like Work

Mohamed A Dawe, Saint Paul

My country is Ethiopia.
My language is Oromo.
When I was a child, my first job was farming.
I moved to this country for freedom.
I feel summer because more flowers, more colored
leaves on the trees.
Winter, rain and snow, the bitter cold.
I came to the U.S. with my family.
I am married. My wife's name is Maco Falam.
I have more children born in Ethiopia.
I live now in the United States, Minnesota, Saint Paul.
I like the Hmong-American Partnership School.
I am working. I want to become an American citizen.

Mohamed A Dawe is 54 years old and is originally from Ethiopia.

Peace Peace

Zaman Albdeer, Coon Rapids

I wish for peace in my country.
I wish for peace everywhere.
Peace to the world.

I pray to my God
Please give us peace in our lives.
I don't cry anymore.

I like the color white.
White is the symbol of peace.
I wish to change my clothes
From black to white.

White is the color of peace

Let us live in peace.
When you open the ways for peace
We will welcome you into our
Lives.

Zaman Albdeer is originally from Iraq.

Haiku

John Strle, Virginia

Eyes are now opened
Free from restrain of closed pain
When end is begin

John Strle is 33 years old and is originally from Subic Bay, Philippines.

Love

Tommy D. Holloway, Jr., Duluth

Love is a magic show
You never know what may happen

Tommy D Holloway, Jr. is 23 years old and is originally from the United States.

Patricia

Patricia Reyes Hernández, Austin

Playing with my children
Always ready to help others
Thankful for life
Raising two children
Improving in my studies
Christmas is a good holiday
Invitation to be happy
Accomplishing a lot during the day is important for me

Doomed, Damned, and Outcast
Rochelle, Cloquet

It seems I live in a make-believe world,
Inside a cage I created with words,
A place where sinew is the fabric of time, and the sky
is drawn by skeleton birds.
I live in a place that doesn't seem to exist. Where peo-
ple never relent with my screams,
A bomb of negative energy I have built,
From twisted visions in my dreams.
Trapped in a cage of anger and fury,
The bars buckle under sympathy and distress.
Guarded by the blood red hounds of hell,
Which melt to and from the darkness.
My eyes alone hold the story of a pain,
I cannot even begin to voice,
Disguised in a human skin,
In this world devoid of free choice.
I have locked myself deep inside,
A solitary component surrounded by empty space.
Nothing can reach me now.
I am hidden behind a glass face.
Even my thoughts are not my own.
I cannot seem to sleep at night,
In fear of dangers that lurk within me,
Obscured from my sight.
But from within my warped prison,
I see the truths of days gone by,
I can experience the pains of life,
And then long eternally to die.
No one can understand for I never let them in.
I block out all emotion,
And blank them from my mind.
Nothing will ever stop me now,
I will move forward and leave everyone behind.
There are people who try to get in
They ask questions which I cannot comprehend,
They make my cage of words tighten,
And make me hunger for the end.
Eventually they back off and I am left alone
No one bothers me anymore.
I have peace at last.
I have finally realized I am not alone,
We are doomed, damned, and outcast.

True Love
Mark Lewis, Duluth

When you find true love
You know it from the first second it passes by
From every kiss from her lips
Every smile on her face
And each look into her eyes
When you find true love
It's like a song that doesn't sing
There's no need for words to communicate
You just know what each other means
When you find true love
You protect it letting no one cause her harm
And when you fall asleep at night
On her neck you lay your arm
When you find true love
You close your heart
Allowing no other love inside
And you love her out in the open
Because there is no need to hide

Strangers
Ben Briggs, Cloquet

Warning watching a world at war in dreams
Terrible trouble touch our children in tears
The pompous politics are profound
In a lazy lust, greed lingers
Over a vast ocean omnipresent forces obliterate
Mimicking a miserable past
Destruction daring many culture's deity
Ignorance wearing armor indecently
Here, harmoniously helping ones who hinder
Fortitude without feign, life in balance forever
Perplexed, pleading against the pious preposterous
Acts that are about to proliferate

Ben Briggs is originally from USA.

My Mind Is Blank
Princeton Witherspoon, Duluth

My mind is blank
It's like I'm wandering in space
It's hard to think
When all I can think about are the days
The days I'm counting down
To leave from this place (NERCC)
The day I leave
I'm going to look back to see how far I've come
For the better or the worst, I'm looking for a change
But I am who I am; I still have the same name
Don't know how I made it this far
But whatever it was kept me going like blood in my veins
I'm in a tight spot as if the biggest animal trapped in a small cage
Physically, they might lock me down, but mentally not my brain

Princeton Witherspoon is 22 years old and is originally from Saint Louis.

My Life in the U.S.
J. Cesar, Austin

June is the month of my father's birthday.
Use the dictionary to find the meaning of any new word
Like playing sports on the weekends
I would like, someday, to go back to my country, Mexico.
Occupied in the afternoon because of my job.

Again It Rains Down
Richard Vickerman, Cokato

When I bow my head and close my eyes
I pray for the rain to end, but for some reason I can't stop getting soaked.
The lightning bolts twisting around me while the thunder rattles my bones.

I scream out inside, "Stop, please just stop! I cannot take it anymore!"
Wiping the tears that form in the nooks of my eyes on my soaked sleeve,
I wish this monstrosity would just pack up and leave me to pick up the pieces
Of my wreckage that have been tossed about the land.
For it is I that is weak compared to the blowing storm
That has its forsaken grip on me, crippling my soul.
So I stand here with a bowed head and a broken heart,
Asking why I must ride this wave of destruction and pain.
Standing at the beckoning Gates of Hell, waiting for the hasp to open,
Unlocking bolts so that I can take my place with the other desolate
And condemned souls anticipating defeat.
The Rain continues to fall down on me.
Finding nothing but emptiness inside of me
I scream aloud this time, my piercing shriek landing only on deaf ears
And witnessed by blind eyes unfulfilling in their purpose.
I can only bow my head and close my eyes and pray to God above for relief
From the Storm Clouds that Again Rain Down…

I Don't Believe!
Azar Sharafshahi, Woodbury

I don't believe winter will end.
I don't believe the lake's ice will melt.
I don't believe the geese will return.
I don't believe the trees will grow leaves again.
I don't believe the buds will open.
I don't believe the sun will shine.
I don't believe everything will change.
I don't believe anything, but one day it will happen.

Blake's Helper
Helene M. Trebesch, New Ulm

It was ten thirty at night. The cool fall drizzle added to Blake's misery. He pulled his coat tightly around him as he stared through the music store window. He wished the dark night would swallow him whole.

At the young age of twelve, he had a police file against him. He had joined the Blade Runners at the tender age of nine. He was looking for friends, thrills and the support from other kids, which he didn't receive from his own dad. He had started feeling uncomfortable with the gang, but had heard of other kids leaving gangs. The consequence would not be a pretty picture!

In half an hour, he and his gang would bomb the store. He didn't know why. He didn't want to be here, but he didn't want to be beat up either. Blake jumped as Rafael spoke to him. "I would leave here if I was you. Your gang is going to try bombing the store soon!"

"Why? Are you going to stop them yourself?"

"Not by myself."

Blake looked the cop. "I don't want to be here, but I don't want to be beat up or killed, either."

"I can understand that. I was beat up, too."

Blake looked at Rafael more closely. "You were a gang member? But, you are so hefty!"

"I was skinny then. Don't worry about dying so young. God has other plans for you. He won't let them kill you."

"How did you know I was scared of being killed? What plan does God have for me?"

"I just know. God wants you to talk to groups of young boys about the life as a gang member. He also wants them to know that just like you, God loves them and He hurts when they get hurt."

Blake in wonderment asked, "God still love me?"

Rafael exclaimed, "Yes. Now GO! I have to stop the bombing. I will contact you about when and where to talk with the kids."

"Thanks for showing me the wonderful love of the Transformer of Lives!"

As Blake ran for safety, he was awestruck by how God had just used Rafael in saving his life. When he had reached cover, he bowed his head and said, "Thank you, God, for still loving me and saving me from the dreadful life of a gang."

Baha'i House of Worship in India
Kamal Moosavi, Maple Grove

The Baha'i House of Worship in India looks like the lotus flower. The lotus flower symbolizes purity for the Indian people. It has nine entrances and it's open to everybody from any religion. The building only has curved lines and it has three levels: the first level symbolizes unity of mankind, second level symbolizes unity of all religions, and the third level symbolizes unity of God. In the Baha'i House of Worship in India there are Holy books of all religions, and there is no clergy. The nine entrances symbolize the grand religions in the world, including Judaism (Moses), Hinduism (Krishna), Zoroastrianism (Zoroaster), Buddhism (Buda), Christianity (Jesus Christ), Islam (Mohammad), Babi (The Bab) and Baha'i (Baha'u'llah). The Baha'i House of Worship in India is the most visited building in the world. You can see the pictures at http://www.bahaihouseofworship.in

Kamal Moosavi is originally from Iran.

Honest for All
Youa Thao, Saint Paul

Once upon a time in a small village, there was a widow. She was very poor with no one to care about her. She lived in a small house that was set away from the other houses.

One day, the youngest son of the dragon had shape shifted like a white deer and came to the village. The people in the village kept chasing the white deer and killed it. Then they shared the meat with every house in the village, but not the widow. One week later, the dragon family found out that their son was killed in that village. Then the village had big trouble with a heavy rain for seven days. The village was flooded all over everywhere, except the widow, because she didn't eat any meat from the white deer. So, all the people in the village died because of the flood.

Your Smile
Verónica Nieto, Saint Louis Park

I always knew I wanted you.
I dreamed of your smile.
The day that you came into this world I was scared.
I was alone giving birth to you; your father had to watch over your older brother. After five hours of labor there you were, big and healthy.
I was excited but worried, you didn't make a sound, and all you did was look around.
They put you into my arms and you wouldn't keep your eyes off of me.
And with a few words I said, "Hi baby, I'm your mama." You smiled so big.
That beautiful smile that I would always dream of.

Verónica Nieto is 26 years old and is originally from San Salvador, El Salvador.

My Life
Davin M.S. Jenkins, Duluth

I lived my life too fast
I know this time now has to be my first
I lived my life in anger
I walked the path of fear and danger
I lived my life being lost
Committed crimes getting money at any cost
I lived my life to the least
Waiting on the day I must face the beast
Now I'm living my life with love
I'm waiting on the chance to rise above

The Love in Me...The Lover in You
Ramon Smith, Saint Peter

Open your eyes can't you see
That it's just the lover in me
How I notice the little things
Accessories like little toe rings
Full of life my gift of speech to you
My favorite way to hold out my hand and reach to you
Preach to you maybe but only for a minute
The lover reminds me it's time to get in it
Even when it's steamy hot I want you close
The lover in me raises my glass for a toast
I'm all this and that can't you see
My favorite attribute is the lover in me

Time after time you see me through
It is for the lover in you
The lover in you allows you to see
My big heart and the lover in me
No more lies I'll be so true
When it's so good the lover in you
The lover in you brings me joy all the time
Thinking of you all the time
Say what I say but what it is, is what I do
And it is for the lover in you

The Halls of Justice
Amanda Dunning, Buffalo

Sit and watch
As you strain the minds
Of the Strong and Weak;

Euphoric in time…Crime
Will survive you as you
Paint the walls with ink

Water
Muktar Ganno, Minneapolis

Water is very important
We drink for thirst
Water for cooking
Water for cleaning
Water for living
Water for dying
Water for swimming
Life without water is very dangerous
We use it to wash our clothes
Water is important for all of us
The animals drink it and the plants

The water resource comes from
Oceans, seas, lakes
Rivers, streams
From ground
Wells, springs
From clouds in the sky
Snow comes from west
The rain raining from east to west
All green comes by water
Summer is nice
Winter is snow
All is ice
We like four seasons
Spring, autumn, winter, and summer
The flowers grow up with the water

A Father's Love
Kwon Lapreed Gullie, Beaver Bay

Welcome to the world, my boy, my girl
Pretty little faces, head full of curls
Time won't be wasted, that will be true
Cover her in pink, cover him in blue
Hold my little finger, squeeze with your might
A kiss on the cheek, that's what you like
When it comes to trouble, I'll be there to save ya
You will be Knecrid, you will be Nevaeh

Snow and Sun
Phan, Minneapolis

Everyone thinks that they are so different
But not really, they are living together.
Right now, Snow covers land and sky
And Sun covers Snow, land and sky.

Sun is hot and Snow is cold
How can they live with each other?
But they can and make a nice couple
And I feel that they are magic.

Sun likes Fire and Snow likes Water
Fire and Water cannot live together
But Sun and Snow can, even complete
Sun keeps warm Snow, Snow makes less Sun.

If someday no Sun in Snow's life
Snow would be sad and Sky is dark
This could be happen in our life
Just Snow and Sun always together.

Phan is originally from Vietnam.

Mr. Patikulapa (Spider)
Jeff Kulah, Minneapolis

Once upon a time, there lived a spider named Patikulapa. He lived between two villages in Liberia. He usually performed many tricks during Hunger Season. In that part of the world we have two major seasons that are impossible to change. It began from generations back. So Mr. Patikulapa was invited to two villages for Christmas parties. These parties were scheduled at the same time. He told both of the hosts to tie a rope on his waist in order to get to the party on time when the food is ready. He made the appointments with both of the towns at the same time.

When the hour came for the parties, both of these villagers began to pull the rope at the same time and same speed. When Patikulapa began to feel the pains on his waist, he started crying. His wife heard his voice and came out; she asked him whether he was O.K. He replied, "Does this look O.K to you, when my waist is getting smaller? I want you to go right now and tell the people in the nearby village and let them know that I am dying from my own greediness. Let them know that no man can do two things at the same time because one will always overcome the other."

In real life, as a human, you need to be content with what you have, rather than having a daydream of someone else's expectations.

Jeff Kulah is originally from Liberia.

Cultural Marriage
Deka, Woodbury

Here is a story about a well-documented cultural marriage.

There was a well-mannered, obedient lady who had reached the age to get married. She was the youngest daughter in the family. One sunny day she informed her parents about an upcoming get together with the man she wanted for her future husband. She took her mother into a different room to break the news about the man who was coming to the house requesting their blessing to marry the girl. Her mother replied, yes daughter he must first come to the house where you grew up and meet the family.

After a long wait, he came and met the family and asked for their blessing to marry their daughter. Her father said yes we agree to let you marry our...oldest daughter.

The young man was very surprised, this was not the daughter he planned to marry. He wanted to marry the one he loved, the youngest daughter.

The one he loved came out and said if you love me, you need to marry my older sister. It is our culture, the oldest daughter gets married before the youngest daughter.

The man left the house with pain in his heart and said in a very loud voice "Culture of love!"
In the end, the man did not marry either daughter. If he could not have one he loved, he didn't want to marry.

There It Went
Jason Olson, Buffalo

Today can't see Tomorrow
And Tomorrow forgot Yesterday
Before it even happened.
Yesterday knows the Present
Ain't no present.
When it comes to living in the Future
Because the Future means nothing
When you describe it to the Past.
The Past never wanted Right Now
To finally show up.
And when it did,
The Clock refused to stop long enough
To let you recognize this very space in time.

Dreamers
Silviano, Minneapolis

My little one
Telling me aloud
I still have a dream.

What does dream mean, papa?

The trees can dream?
With a long spring.
The flowers can dream?
With shiny bees.
The wind can dream?
With new mountains and valleys to see
The sun can dream?
With souls to warm up.
The rain can dream?
With being a majestic lake.

Papa what else can dream?

The color dream,
With being only colors not people
The weapons dream
With being musical instruments

The wars dream,
With being colorful parades
The earth dreams,
With main fullness.
What about your dream, papa?
My dream is to continue dreaming
Because dreams are hope of our reality.

I Wonder Why I Feel Sad
April F. Romero, Cloquet

I wonder why I feel sad,
Is it because I feel bad,
Or is it because I feel glad,
I wonder why I feel sad,
Is it because of my meds,
Something I've read,
That made me confused,
I wonder why I feel sad,
Is it because of something I've watched,
Or how much it cost,
I wonder why I feel sad,
Is it because of my family,
No, not really,
I wonder why I feel sad,
Is it the clothes I wear,
That's not fair,
Well, does anyone care?

I Love My Name
Flor, Austin

Friendly with people
Loving my family
Optimist about life
Relationships with people

Flor is originally from Mexico.

Not Again—Not Again...
Mr. Grbich, Waite Park

Have you ever awoke from a dream and thought, man that was one real and vivid dream!? Then you think, maybe I am still dreaming and I just dreamt I woke up or am dreaming about dreaming you woke from a dream. However it works, it is weird.

This dream started out with me sitting on a park bench like Forrest Gump, but I did not have a box of chocolates or the dorky clothing. I am sitting there and I look across the road and see this guy leaning up against a sweet bike with baskets on it. He is smoking a cigarette and has some tattoos, a black bracelet on one wrist, and a watch on the other wrist. He looks pretty normal. He has a black t-shirt on that has some writing on it that I cannot read, a pair of blue jeans, and cowboy boots.

At first, I thought he was flipping me the bird, but it turned out to be a peace sign. As I get closer to him I can read the writing on his t-shirt. I get up to him and I notice he has the strangest eyes I have ever seen. They are all black and shiny. Real crazy. I was going to ask if they were contacts but he first says, "Hey pal, have you ever been abducted?" I tell him, "No, I do not think so, at least." He says, "Dude, I have. Let me tell you about it."

He was about to say something when he just stops and looks at me. He jumps on his sweet pedal ride with the baskets and bikes down the street. Out of the corner of my eye I see police cars coming. They remind me of catfish for some weird reason. Maybe it is just because they are roundish and slither up on you. Anyways, I see them roll up on the guy with crazy eyes like he was bait. They corner him, men jump out of the vehicle in their para-military uniforms and point weapons at him. They are yelling and pointing. They grab him and place him in the back of one of the catfishes. I can see him look over his shoulder back at me, this time those crazy eyes say without saying, "Not again." And there goes an abductee...

It Serves You Right
Houa B. Vang, Minneapolis

A child named Chalie had to go to help his father do farming. On one summer morning, when Chalie and his father reached the field, he saw many of his father's pumpkins bearing and hanging down from each small vine. They looked weak and cheerless. Then he glanced at a big tree beside the field that had some small fruit on the high place of it, which looked very strong and cheerful. He observed and compared those two kinds of plants over and over about the justice.

So Chalie went to ask his father a question. "Dad," he called his father curiously. "Take a look! The pumpkin trees are just a short and crawl on the ground to carry the big pumpkins and they look so hard and tired. But the big and high branches of that tree only get the small-small fruit, which looks unsatisfying for it to carry. If I meet with God, I could ask him to switch bearing for them. Do you agree with me?"

Chalie's father smiled and was quiet for a moment. "You might be thinking too much, man!" His father said. "That is their fate, and you don't worry. If you do, you will understand, okay!"

After his father gave him a suggestion, they were going to continue their jobs until noon. The sun was very shiny and they got hot and tired. Chalie's father let him take a rest and sit under the tree that they were talking about that morning. Suddenly, the wind was blowing at Chalie and he was oblivious to the whole thing. So the small fruit over his head fell down to hit him bluntly on his head, but he was not so hurt and it was okay to put up with. Then he looked up to those fruit again and again. "Oh, my gosh!" he shouted softly and said. "Now I'm understanding the solution very clearly about these two kinds of fruit. If just the small fruit can make me hurt; if that big pumpkin over there and fell on me, I may get knocked out on the ground or hurt more seriously." He continued to suggest to himself. "So, they should stay in each place as before. I agree with God right now." After that, Chalie and his father got back home in the evening, he shared this funny event with me.

Influence of Technology
Mouna Driouch, Rochester

There is no doubt that technology has affected all of our lives whether it is positive or negative. Personally, I am very interested about any new phone, laptop, TV, software etc. I find technology is very wild world where you can image anything you want to. First, the reason why I found technology useful and essential in my daily life is the way I can call my family overseas and see them live. I will spend more than 10 dollars for just a half hour, on other hand I could use Skype and speak with them for hours. I just need a computer, webcam, and internet access.

Technology makes our lives easy and enjoyable. There are very high technology televisions with a 3-D option. There are ATMs everywhere which help you withdraw your money within seconds. Phones with their touch screens have many applications and options like GPS, music, internet, games, etc.

The most important thing that technology brought is the internet. It is a great and powerful way to access to information. Personally, I learn so many new things through the internet like English grammar, computer skills and vocabulary. Today most of the universities offer classes online to facilitate education for students.

As we can see, technology has great advantages. Unfortunately, it has very serious consequences for people that misunderstand the appropriate usage of technology.

Using computer for many hours can develop mental and physical issues like addiction to games, vision problems, and headaches. Recently, it was a show on TV discussing how technology is affecting new generation. For example, in South Korea thousands of teenagers are staying over nights to play violent computer games. Some Korean hospitals are now providing treatments for teenagers to control their addiction to the computer games and internet. Schools are teaching children how to balance the way of using the internet and games so it will not impact their education.

The worst effect is that technology can cause death. Studies show that more than 28 percent of car accidents are caused by using the phone or texting while driving. Finally, it is very important to know how to take advantages of technology. It is a great way to communicate, facilitate your life, and educate yourself. On the other hand, you have to make sure to protect your children from being addicted to computer and the internet.

Mouna Driouch is originally from Morocco.

Origin of the Name 'Mexico' and Why We Speak Spanish
Christian B., Saint Paul

I want to tell you about why my country of origin is called Mexico and why we speak Spanish. Everything began when Christopher Columbus discovered the Americas (The New World). During that time, many Spanish explorers made expeditions in that new world. Many of the expeditions were in the central and south parts of Mexico. They encountered people from different cultures like the Azteca, Maya, Tolteca, Olmeca.

One of the more important cultures was the Azteca. Their language was Nahuatl and they governed by king Montezuma II. The Aztecs built a great capital city with big pyramids, on a large lake and called it Tenochtitlan (in Nahuatl it means the place of prickly pear cactus). That territory was called Mexico (from the Nahuatl Metztli=Moon and Xictli=Navel). This means "place in the center of the moon" The Aztecs believed in different Gods, like Tezcatlipoca (God of the sky and earth), Huitzilopochtli (God of war), and Tlaloc (God of rain). They offered human sacrifices to their Gods.

The Aztecs were good at astrology, agriculture, art, and architecture. They also knew about medical plants, (we still use this knowledge today in Mexico). But in 1519, Hernán Cortes, a Spanish man, caused the fall of the Aztec Empire. The Aztecs were forced by the Spanish to adopt the Spanish language and religion. Then a new culture was born. I was born into this Mestizo culture. It is part of me even though I am now a part of the culture of the United States.

New Horizons
Álvaro Barrios Sarmiento, Minneapolis

I am an emigrant with luggage,
Full of dreams, aspirations, and hopes.

Dreams are the way of encouraging myself,
To achieve my goals day, by day.

Aspirations are the wings that make me,
Fly in a world full of opportunities.

Hopes are the auroras, the lights that allow me to see,
Throughout this short pathway called life.

Soaring farther from my own horizons makes my world bigger,
And always full of dreams, aspirations, and hopes.

Álvaro Barrios Sarmiento is originally from Colombia.

My Love
R. Lawrence Smith, LeSueur

I've been in love over the years
With the great sound of hip hop music to my ears,
Ready go – to the steady flow
Rather I'm just listening or watching the live show,
Hip hop sometimes gets people's lips locked
It takes time to learn so burn your wrist watch,
Put the clock around your neck like Flavor Flav
The ones who are Public Enemies act all brave,
From the cradle to the grave I've been in
The Fresh Prince at 5 and too short at 10,
Those were my cassettes,
Sometimes I burst out and yell a few bars like I got Tourette's,
This is the effect and it just don't stop
30 years and I still love you, hip hop.

Red Roses
Lontavia M. Powell, Minneapolis

I define myself as a rose
I'm very subtle and closed in
Then eventually I begin to blossom
Show the beautiful and elegant
Person that I really am
Roses are red and
Tulips are different colors
I adore my sisters and love my brothers
Roses are used for
Weddings, funerals,
Compliments in clubs
Roses have thorns
So does life
I know this because
I pricked myself at least twice
Roses have a way of saying
What can't be said
And the color of speechless
Comes in Red,
Roses

Lontavia M. Powell is 18 years old and is originally from Minneapolis, Minnesota.

The Love of God
Martín Torres Balderas, Saint Paul

God likes peace with us.
Doesn't want fights.
Doesn't want deaths.
And doesn't want wars.
God likes when we are brothers and
Forever make peace.

Martin Torres Balderas is originally from Ciudad Valles, San Luis Potosi, Mexico.

The Beauty of a Black Woman

Shannon Knight, Minneapolis

She's made of unique black chocolate, white chocolate, caramel makes her complete.
From her head to her feet, the beauty of a black woman who dares to compete.
Formed from a man's rib, not from dirt or sticks, the potter molds to be mother of men.
Eve, girl, you were so blessed, the first woman called before the rest.
Body soft as a peach, the beauty of a black woman.
She was made to be sweet, helper of her soul mate, waiting to be reached.
She is a Queen that is worth more than riches.
A virtuous woman to be respected by many.
She bore the king child, rejected by many.
It's blessed to be a woman and not follow behind riches, to lie on your back to be called witches.
She's no man's mistress, so he shouldn't dare to complain
Or treat her like she came out of the garbage can.
Man, you are blessed to find a woman like this, while you are out working she's also making ends meet. The beauty of a black woman who dares to compete.

Shannon Knight is 40 years old and is originally from New Orleans, Louisiana.

Black Outs

Bradley Smith, Aurora

Waking up days later
Waking up in a different town
Waking up in an unfamiliar room
Waking up wondering what happened
Waking up to doctors and nurses
Waking up not knowing I almost died
Waking up, actually, now I think I'll stay up

Bradley Smith is 19 years old and is originally from Virginia, Minnesota.

Morning Sunshine

Muzamil Yahya, Minneapolis

Morning sunshine
If you're like the moon
I'm able to see you every morning

Morning sunshine
I should be peaceful
If I see you every day
My lover we have an addiction for each other
We live in different places but we have great love for each other

Morning sunshine
You are a wonderful, graceful, lovely girl
Like a rose, there are no words to describe you
I love you a lot
My sunny place
If you do not live, there is no bright

Morning sunshine
So how can I live where you are not living?
But if you live far away from me, I should not stop giving my love to you
My chocolate, when we will see each other?
Is that day coming?
I love you, my sweet
And you love your Casanova

Morning sunshine
This love has to go on forever
I love you
I always think about you

Morning sunshine
When you call from that distant location
I feel good and all my stress is gone

Hey! My sunshine comes and releases that bright sun onto my face
Hopefully I will see you if God says
Hopefully I will see you if God says

Oh Flower Wonderful Flower
Anonymous, Minneapolis

Oh flowers, flowers
So beautiful, beautiful
Flowers your color is so good flowers
You have a good fragrance flowers, flowers
You make Love

Flower your aroma is so wonderful
I love too much your color flowers
Flower, flower you make all families around the world
so happy
Flower, flower you are so pretty
OH wonderful flower
Flowers, flowers I look at your color and it makes me
happy
All the time you have a beautiful color for different
occasions

When I cut the flower, it smells so good
Flowers, flowers you make me so happy
Your garden is so beautiful
I like to be a gardener

Untitled
Gail Simpson, Buffalo

I'm so alone in this cell every day,
So many emotions and feelings making me gray.
As I sit here and start to think,
I wish all of this pain could be flushed down the sink.

I see that sad look on my daughter's face.
I cry and am sad cuz I'm still in this place.
I admit I've done something I knew wasn't right.
Here I still sit in this jail trying to put up a good fight.

I have this addiction that I know is no good.
If I could go back and change things, I certainly would.
So here is my plea to get the help that I need
And, that I, in turn, may plant that sobering seed.

I need treatment to help me get rid of this
So that I can be there for the things I already miss.
At the end of the day when I pass this test
Will you be there saying that I sure did my best?

I'm here to thank you for all of the support;
Yes, especially when my temper has been short.
I can tell you that I remain steadfast all day long.
I do this so you know that I, too, can be strong.

My Major Love and Queen
214018, Rush City

You're outstanding and most dominate.
You make it you're priority to be the best lady and
mother
To our family that we love.
I'm only half the spark of your glowing soul.
You're my better half and you're greater and superior
to be
Most high to any queen's throne.
You're most important to my world more than any
other
Woman or thing.
You are my lady, the love of my life.

You're the most magnificent and closest noble woman
in
My heart and sight.
You're love is all I can feel all through the night.
You're heart is loyal and faithful, my love,
I deeply understand you and grasp your every word
And thought.
I truly accept every bit of you in this world.
My Queen and major love.

To Rachel, my major love and Queen

She Don't Believe in Love
Darrin Buckhalton, Minneapolis

She don't believe in Love, that's something she won't do.
The Love in her has died, from all that she's been through.
She lies awake at night, in her bed all alone.
She said she don't believe in Love; that's a sad, sad song.

She don't Love him anymore, she wonders why she's still tryin'.
She stares at herself in the mirror till she starts cryin.'
She's got X's and O's, sweet kisses and hugs,
But what she needs in life she can't get enough of.

She has kids and a dog, a cute little kitten, too.
But she won't believe in Love. That's something she refuses to do.
No, she won't believe in Love. She says it's just out of season.
She's been hurt too many times, so I guess she has good reason.

There is no romance in her life in the winter or summer time.
She said the excitement has died; she's already got the papers signed.
She used to soar from Love high above the clouds flyin'.
Now she has no faith in Love; she said, "What's the use in tryin?"

She don't believe in Love, that's something she won't do.
The Love in her has died, from all that she's been through.
She lies awake at night, in her bed all alone.
She said she don't believe in Love; that's a sad, sad song.

She has a beautiful smile. It could light up the night.
She's a gorgeous woman, and a boring man's wife.
Just how lovely she is, I don't think she has a clue.
I long to tell her, "If Love doesn't exist, then how could I Love you?"

Angel
Raleon Moore, Saginaw

An angel is what you can turn into when your time under the sun is done
Being an angel can make you a guardian and that responsibility
Can make you not want to become one
I could describe you as an angel, though it's something I've never seen
Tell you about their white robes, their halos and prettiest of wings
If you have questions about angels, I've heard there're answers in the church
If you open up your eyes, you might see an angel on earth
That single mother with three kids who sends all of them to college
The sponsor who saved another's life just by being a recovered alcoholic
The woman who gets a child out of the street just seconds before being hit
The coach who believes in you and won't let you quit
The teenage girl who kept her baby even after the father split
The dad who, to support his family, works 12-hour shifts
Though an angel is a spiritual figure most seem to say
I bet you've seen an angel almost every day.

Story Behind Glory!
Jane Agnatodji, Crystal

Behind every glory,
There is a story!
Your present trials are
Your tomorrow's testimonies!
Never dispute your little beginnings,
And never forget that your trials are your testimonies!

Life and Death (Into the Pit of Hell)
Michael Harris, Hibbing

Another night in hell
Locked inside a bloody cell
My head wants to explode
And I don't feel too well

I'm always freezing cold
The sight, the sound, the smell
Life was so good
Then into the pit I fell

Death and brutality
Borderlines of insanity
Falling over the edge
The worst of humanity

The things I've seen
Every damned day
Make me want to spread wings
Makes me want to fly away

The devil is inside of us all
I am here to say
I can't take any more
I want to crawl away

Life will always suck
Waking up hurts in the worst way
Burning for all of eternity
I can't hide anyplace

Another night in hell
And I don't feel too well
The sight, the sound, the smell
Locked inside a bloody cell

I hate the world
Psychotic schizo brain
Want to leave this earth
All I ever feel is pain

Another night in hell
I don't feel too well
The sight, the sound, the smell
Into the pit I fell

Michael Harris is 41 years old and is originally from USA.

Prison and Life
Bozel Rulford, Le Sueur

The game liked me
But I liked it back
I was fighting with a gun
And the gun was black
Down the barrel of that black hole
In it took a lot of souls
And the prison bars weren't too far
With my body in a cage
And my mind in a jar
The casket in a graveyard wasn't far
So the night I sleep
I will fight with bad dreams
And my heart will weep
The game I played wasn't fair
The life out of prison
My body wasn't there
The people I fight with
A gun and a knife
High off of drugs
And my mind wasn't right
I got out and learned my lesson
Now my daughter and son are now who I'm protecting
I leave with this quote
"Listen to what I wrote – you will always
Have a future
But live your life with HOPE"

Jail Cell
Clifford Owen, Faribault

Sun's shining brightly in my cell.
Everyday I think I'm in hell.
I've got a pencil and some paper.
The Chaplain tells me to thank my maker.
But I don't want to give up, see.
This life I'm living, to me I'm free.
Running with the boys downtown,
Everyday one of us was a clown,
and we didn't care how many people we drown.
In our hate, anger, pain, and sorrow,
We just want to live to see tomorrow.
We run, we cheat, we steal, we fight.
We are the ones who have never seen the light.
Someday we'll throw in the towel and stop the fight.
I quit. I'm done. I don't want to live a life on the run.
Now, I'm back in a cell and there's no way out.
I'm changing my life beyond a reasonable doubt.
Making choices that are beneficial to my health, now
my cell's locked and I'm not on the inside.
Now I'm free, free.

Life is so much easier for me!

My Mom
Anonymous, Saint Louis Park

Mom years too many years have passed without that
I can't finally admit that you are my reason to live
without you I could not survive sometimes life is not
gifts, and I often in the dumps the only person on I
count it's you mom you have all I need very often I
feel like everything is surrendering but thanks to you
I get there to persevere. I wanted you to know that I
miss you and I need you to be there all the time like
my sister, my best friend, because you know me better
than anyone.
Out of sight near the heart love you.

A Vision of Home
Chad Erickson, Duluth

At peace now riding on my time machine,
I see the oceans and vast lands,
My time has come to an end served on earth,
Never more am I able to set foot on.
Endlessly comfortable on this fluffy cloud,
As I admire the beautiful sights below,
The peace and quiet is enlightening on my journey,
Never again to possess the loves of a social life.
I venture around the world through the atmosphere,
Seeing places I've never been to before,
As the new sights bring a smile to my thoughts,
A better sensation than being lost in a fog on earth.
Not knowing when this would end I kept thinking,
Were there any positive moments in the physical life,
That I once adored and fully cherished?
A while later I realize I'm getting farther away.
This is when it sets in I'm on my way,
Away to a place where all is kind and gentle,
A place where I can feel free again,
Real and true, I'm on my way to Heaven.

Trouble and Pain
Jawane Chatman, Duluth

Living the night life is full of trouble and pain
Trying to fit in just so I won't lose instead of gain
It's just nothing but trouble and pain
Fight after fight, night after night
Happiness is still out of range
It's just my life...full of trouble and pain.

Love
Shaun Tanzy, Saginaw

Love is sweet and kind
And what I wish could be mine
Love can also lead you blindly
Hoping one day it finds me.

Struggles and Decisions

The Other Side of the Wall
Sabrina Kolleck, Champlin

I was born in Germany in 1982. The woman who gave birth to me is not my mom but she will always be the person who helped me find my real parents!

I got adopted when I was two. The woman in whose belly I had grown was a kid herself! Her boyfriend was gone; her mom let her choose, either her or me. Still in school and no perspective, but still she had the strength to admit that she would not be the lovely caretaker I needed her to be.

In tears, she ran to social services. With shivering hands, she signed the contract that placed my life in the hands of strangers. That took away all her rights to know about my life in the future, all her rights to hug me and tell me that she loves me.

It wasn't the first time they told her she could still be a good mother, but she knew better. She was sick of all the daycare programs she made me go to, sick of all the sleepless nights when she woke me up because of her crying and sobbing, sick of her life the way it was.

She handed over my little ducky called *gaggchen*. "Well, give her chocolate. She will be quiet and follow you around." Then she set me on the ground. No good-bye, no turn around. She just left.

There I was. Me and my new mom, my new dad, and my new older brother. Me with my infected earrings, my too-small worn-out shoes, my matted, tangly long hair, and my gaggchen. The first day I was fine. It was exciting to make new friends. The second day it dawned on me that I was on my own now. No one was coming back to pick me up. But there was this family who cared about me, who loved me without even knowing me. Who wanted me to become a part of them. With arms wide open they were trying to comfort me. But it was still me. Just me! I stopped eating, stopped talking, stopped listening. I didn't want to have these feelings anymore. Didn't want to feel anything at all. I just wanted to be happy. That was the first time I leaned against the wall and wished I could disappear behind it.

Sabrina Kolleck was born in Kiel, Germany. She was adopted at the age of two and grew up in a small town in West Germany. She has a degree as a Preschool teacher and ECE (Early Childhood Education). Sabrina moved to Minnesota with her husband in 2008 and is now a proud mother of a 3 year old. In her free time, Sabrina enjoys dancing with the Minnesota Dance Ensemble. She has always loved to write but has never shared these with anyone, she is happy and thrilled to be published.

I Was Scared of Phone Calls
Maymun Mohamed, Minneapolis

I was scared of phone calls because I could not speak English well. If I tried to call many companies because they sent bills but I did not agree with that, it was difficult when I tried to call them. I felt shy and I felt disappointed. When they said, "What did you say, Ma'am?" or, "I did not understand what you said." I hung up the phone. But right now I can call them if I have any questions about my bills. I said, "Guys, the bill you sent to me isn't right." I feel comfortable to call anywhere now. I am not worried about calls.

Maymun Mohamed is originally from Somalia.

How Illiteracy Impacted My Life
Lukman Abdile, Saint Cloud

I will never forget how illiteracy and ignorance affected me. When I was a very young boy, I used to look after cows. One day the cows were grazing and eating grass in a field on a pastureland in the evening. I was bringing them home. As I was walking after the cows, a branch of a tree hit my left eye. I felt pain and there was no hospital, clinic, or any health facility close to the area. But there were a few eye drops in a small open bottle or container which had been previously used by somebody else a long time ago. So my elder brother picked it up and put it in my eye. Immediately, I lost my left eye's vision permanently. Maybe the medicine was expired or maybe it was bad. Nobody could read the instructions on the medicine. This experience made me feel that I wanted to get an education. After this happened, my family decided to send me to school. I got my high school diploma last year, and my goal is to continue my education. It is very important in my life.

My Worst Experience
Mohamed, Minneapolis

When I first came to the United States it was difficult to ride the bus. One day I went to take the bus and I asked the bus driver where to put the money. He said, "Do you know how to ride the bus?" I said I don't know and after that I got confused. I put in five dollars and it worked. Then I got off the bus. The bus driver asked me if I wanted a ticket. It was hard to learn and get used to the system. This is why I decided to learn how to drive. That's my worst time in the U.S.A.

Mohamed is 27 years old and is originally from Somalia.

How I Made Friends with the Snow
Ablavi Adjagoudou, Minneapolis

When I first came to the United States, it was difficult for me to walk in the snow. I couldn't go out. I was very cold. I remember every morning, when I brought my son to the bus stop for school, I came home and I took a nap immediately.

My worst problem was falling down in the snow sometimes. One day the bus came late by a few minutes because there was snow on the ground. When I went back home, I was very sick for one week. I'm afraid of snow, so I started school late in the last year.

Now, I'm walking carefully. I'm thinking it's a little better. I can go out when the weather is very cold.

Ablavi Adjagoudou is 40 years old and is originally from Togo.

A Confusing Experience
Ana Santos, Saint Cloud

When I first came to this country, it was very difficult for me to understand English. I remember when I came back home the first time after living in the United States for four years. My very worst experience was the time when I decided to go back home. The first bad thing that happened to me was I missed the flight because I did not understand where the gate was. Then, when I finally found the gate, it was too late because the flight was gone. Then, I waited until the next day to get the correct flight to my country. But when I came back to the United States, I had a different confusing problem again. From my country to Minnesota, we do not have direct flights. At the time, I did my transfer in Miami. Then I was looking around and I decided to ask a question of one woman who was near to me. I said, "Where are you going?" She said, "I'm going to Sao Paulo." I said, "thanks." But I decided to follow her. Then she went to the gate she was looking for. Then I decided to ask a question to the correct person who was working for the airport. "Where is this flight going?" She answered, "This flight is going to Sao Paulo, Brazil." Then I was so scared to miss the flight again. I was confused because I was looking for the flight to Saint Paul, Minnesota, and I did not understand much English. But fortunately, the woman who was working for the airport helped. She sent me to the correct place. Then I was so happy because I was on the correct flight to get home.

You Are Royalty
Roslyn Plummer, Golden Valley

Ruiz and I have so much in common. I returned to school after having children and overcoming a crack addiction. Some friends and family members felt that I wouldn't make it; it would take me too many years to complete my education and that I'd be too old. They were concerned that no one would hire me once I was done. My parents wanted a better life for me and now, at this age, I want it for myself.

While using drugs and alcohol for a number of years I finally got tired of being sick and tired. I had already wasted more than 25 years of my life in total darkness. So, about two years ago I returned to school. Frightened, not knowing what to expect, constantly asking myself, "Can I do this? Am I too old?" Well, I graduated with honors. But something was missing. I realized that I wanted more. I want to be an RN. So here I am back in school again preparing myself for college, still afraid and even doubting myself.

Contrary to what others think or believe, I will become a nurse one day. I refuse to be deterred from my goals. Yes, it's difficult trying to balance school, home, and work. However, to live a more conservative, traditional, and fulfilling lifestyle, I must sustain my education. I chose the nursing field because I want to help others. I would like to heal people if I can, because I care for people.

Like Ruiz, who is a person that I read about in my College Prep class at Northside ABE, my spiritual father delivers messages to me through spiritual music. The Lord says, "You are royalty." The message says that I'm born for greatness. God sees my failures. He wants me to see myself in the future. He says do not judge myself from my failures. He wants to see me as an entrepreneur, the head not the tail. I am royalty.

Roslyn Plummer is 59 years old and is originally from the United States.

My First Driving in the Snow
Pascal Kabamba, Brooklyn Park

Driving in the snow was one of the experiences I had never had. I still remember that morning I got up at 3:00 a.m. and it was snowing. That was my first snow. I had to drive twenty miles to work. I was a new driver, but I started to drive a car one month before. Many things happened in my head. Can I call my supervisor and tell him that I can't drive in the snow? Can I call one of my friends to pick me up? In the driveway, my car was whiter than I had ever seen before and the sky was so light we could think that it was already ten in the morning. Finally, I decided to drive. After removing snow from my car's hood, windows and lights, I ran the car and heater for 20 minutes until the car was warm.

On the road, it was an occasion for me to remember what I learned about winter driving: no stopping suddenly, avoid accelerating abruptly, adjust speed to road conditions. I was scared alone in my car, especially when I thought that I didn't have some items for the first aid kit, like a shovel, blanket, jumper cables, lighter and so on. I still remember that day the snow accumulation was around 6 to 8 inches, the road surface was slippery and I drove 20 to 25 miles per hour. I think God protected me and I reached my destination without problems. That was my first experience driving in the snow.

My Long Journey
Kebbeh Murray, Hinckley

My name is Kebbeh Murray. I was born in Liberia, Africa. I have four children, two boys and two girls. They are still in Monrovia in Liberia, Africa. My husband was killed in the Liberian War in 2002.

My Uncle Jimmy was in Minneapolis working in a meat shop and met Dennis Murray. They were selling goat meat. Jimmy went to Monrovia and brought back some pictures of the family to show Marie, my cousin who lives in Minnesota. Dennis saw the pictures and picked me out. He told Jimmy he wanted me to be his wife. He had not talked to me at all! Dennis sent me some money and the next day I bought a phone. We talked on the phone many times for six months. I could not read or write at all! Dennis e-mailed me and my Uncle Joe read them to me. Then I told my Uncle Joe and he e-mailed Dennis back for me. Dennis tried to petition me as his fiancé and immigration refused. They said he had to meet me in person. So, Dennis flew to Monrovia and stayed for ten days. We got married June 5, 2008.

Dennis petitioned again to bring me to Minnesota but it was refused. He got a lawyer. We had to get two people to sign an affidavit. Dennis and Marie signed it. After two and a half years it was approved. I came to the United States by myself in September of 2010.

We now live in Hinckley, Minnesota on a hobby farm. I am happy to be here! I am going to GED classes to learn to read and write. I want to get my diploma. I also want to get my United States Citizenship. My biggest wish is to get my children here with me.

My Life in the United States
Manuel Barbosa, Gaylord

When I came from Mexico to the United States, I arrived at Atlanta, GA. When I came, I lived with my friends. I begin to work with them at a carpet factory. I worked for two years and after that I got another job. I started to work in construction building. I worked for one year and five months and then I decided to come to Minnesota. I talked to my cousin because he was here in Minnesota. When I arrived, I began to work in maintenance at the Golden Egg Farms. I have worked for four years in Minnesota, because it is nice and quiet here and the people are very friendly and interesting. I like Minnesota

Helping Others
Pedro Ramírez, Brooklyn Park

I moved from Chicago in 1998 and came to Minneapolis, Minnesota. When got here, I found a lot of Hispanic people who did not know much English, and they had to pay people who knew only a little English to translate for them. I felt so bad for a lot of them. My cousin Carmelo told them that I speak English and they can come to me to ask for help with translation. Sometimes I went with them to the hospital, clinic, or a job application and sometimes I helped them over the phone. Most of them tried to pay me but I refused to accept any money from them. I just am so happy when I can help others.

How Autism Changed My Life
Anonymous, Shakopee

I'm the mother of two children who are autistic. When I first came to this country, I had many dreams for my family: to have a better life, work, and my children could have better opportunities to study.

When my first boy was born, I thought everything was perfect, but soon I noticed something was different. I became very nervous and worried about him. The doctor said he has signs of autism. This was then confirmed by a specialist and I felt very bad. Then I became pregnant and was very happy. I thought my new baby would be healthy and together we could help my big boy.

When my new baby boy was born, I asked the pediatrician if it was possible that my new baby could be autistic, too. He told me, it was possible but we had to wait two months for the results. After two months, the doctor told me, "I'm sorry but your little boy has autism, too."

It was very hard for me to know that both of our children have Autism. Some people criticize me and my children, because my children act differently. They don't understand anything about me and my wonderful boys. While this used to bother me, I have learned to ignore it. All the criticism has helped me do better and be happier.

What is Autism? Autism is a brain disorder that affects the development of children starting at a young age. Some signs of Autism:
1. - Little or no eye contact
2. - Language delay
3. - Turning around in circles
4. - Using repetitive action or words
5. - Playing alone and apart from other children, etc.

I hope my story can help other people to learn about Autism and what the signs are. If you suspect your child has these symptoms, talk with the child's doctor and they will help you. Always remember all children are beautiful.

My First Time to the U.S.A.
Mohamed Awal Traore, Minneapolis

My first journey by airplane was from Africa to the United States. I arrived at MSP airport on May 12, 2010. After filling the immigration form that was given to me, my friend Leon welcomed me with a big hug. When we got out of the airport, Leon had forgotten where he parked his car. We were struggling to find the car by going from one parking lot to another. At that time, I couldn't walk very well because my ankle was painful due to an accident I had a few days before I left my country. Although the winter ended, I was feeling cold. I couldn't stand the weather. The situation made me sad and all I could say in my heart was, "What is

this? Is it the United States people talked about?"

At the end of the day, we found the car and now Leon could see a smile on my face. We went home safely. I will never forget that day, it was memorable.

Mohamed Awal Traore is originally from Togo.

My First Winter in the U.S.
Edgar Lema, Minneapolis

When I arrived on November 4th, 2000 in Burlington, North Carolina, a long frigid winter was approaching. I have never endured the cold climate before, so coping to this new climate was challenging for me.

Doug Atkinson   Duluth

During the first day of my arrival, I saw snow everywhere. I ventured around the neighborhood to explore the new environment. I found out that trees had no leaves, and all of them look liked dead trees except for some evergreens. Also I ran across with some squirrels which were playing—chasing one another up and down the tree. For me these rodents meant a delicacy meat, but later I found out that these critters can carry some diseases because they scavenge their food from the garbage dumpsters. On the way home, I grabbed a handful of snow, but it melted away before I reached home.

As the days went by, my excitement about snow diminished. I felt cold whenever I was outdoors. I got some frostbite in my ears and nose. I spent many gloomy days indoors, but I didn't want to be defeated. Soon I learned to cope to the cold climate by observing what my neighbors did.

A drastic change in place and climate was not easy for me. I was determined to overcome this new environment, so I did it. As the years have passed, I have learned to respect nature. Winter is a wonderful thing that God has created.

Edgar Lema is originally from Republic of Ecuador.

My Worst Phone Experience
Blanca Ochoa, Minneapolis.

When I first came to the United States, it was difficult for me to use the phone. I couldn't understand. I was looking for job. I called a temporary job to ask if they had any position open, but he couldn't understand me. He said can you repeat that one more time. I repeated it three times and he didn't understand. He asked me if I had someone with me who spoke English. I didn't have anybody. He told me you need to speak English clearly, when you are ready you call me again or come here. Then he hung up the phone hard and mad. I felt sad at the time. I didn't want to call any place because I thought no one understood me. Now I feel better when I call some places to pay the bills or ask any question. Sometimes they understand me or I try different ways.

Untitled
Fadumo Farah, Minneapolis

When I first came to the U.S., it was difficult for me. I couldn't understand English on the phone. One day my case manager for welfare called my home phone. I picked up my phone and I said, "Hello." She said, "Can I speak to Fadumo?" I said, "Yes, I am Fadumo." Well, she told me something about my benefits and she wouldn't explain that for welfare I had eight months. After that, I felt happy because I thought she called me for a job. Then I answered. I said, "I got a job!" She laughed so much. I heard her laugh really hard. I felt shy then. She said, "Fadumo, I will call you again," She hung up the phone. Finally, she sent me a paper and she explained what benefits I got.

Fadumo Farah is originally from Galkacyo, Somalia.

Reality
Damen Washington Jr., Minneapolis

Abandonment. Growing up in the hood was hard on me, I had to strive and survive the best I could. But my having the willingness to want to get out the hood, I knew I had to do what I had to do to get out. I overcame and jumped over obstacles and hurdles to get where I wanted to be. I want to be prosperous in life. I don't want to be another statistic in life. I want to be able to show and prove that all black men are not drug dealers or in the penitentiary, or a thug. There's more to life than that. I am one who is here to set an example for the rest of my brothers. We can make it no matter what the strife or struggle is. We can overcome it. And for those who cannot relate to this, then you're on your own. God bless you.

My First Year in the U.S.
Ansar Gedi, Saint Louis Park

I came from Hargeisa, Somaliland. I am 23 years old. I came to Minneapolis in 2007. When I got off the plane my brother was there to pick me up. It was in the middle of winter. Everything was white and the road was slippery. I saw some homeless people and I was scared for them.

Ansar Gedi is 23 years old and is originally from Hargeisa, Somaliland.

Stuck in Transition
Raymond Waddell, Oak Park Heights

I am currently incarcerated in Oak Park Heights Prison in Minnesota. Though I've been in prison since the age of 18, I've been in and out of the judicial system since I was 11 years old. Growing up, school wasn't a priority in my family. We were more worried about our next meal or where we would sleep that night.

Earning my GED was one of my biggest accomplishments. I am now enrolled in the prison's Transition to Post-Secondary program. The goal of this program is to get adult GED graduates ready for college. I believe I have excelled in this class and now know that I want a college education majoring in psychology.

By focusing on my education, I've realized that I can still make a difference while in prison. I have a 15 year old daughter and knowing what I do now, I refuse to let her slack in school. I let her know that education is her number one priority and I also know that I need to lead by example. This is one reason why I intend to graduate from college. I want to show her that nothing is unobtainable if you put your mind to it.

Right now, I'm working on two goals. The first is my freedom. I have a life sentence which means I'm eligible for parole in 30 years, but I'm continuing to fight for my freedom. I'm waiting on a decision from the courts right now. Hopefully, I will not have to do 30 years. The second goal is trying to obtain the funds to pay for my correspondence courses while still in prison. Unfortunately, I cannot apply for financial aid or Pell Grants because I am incarcerated. With a psychology degree, I want to mentor at-risk kids and become a motivational speaker. Without tuition funding, however, I'm stuck in limbo. My teacher and I have come up with a plan for the time being. She has prepared college course material as if I were in college majoring in psychology already. I must say, it's hard work but I can't wait for the real thing.

The funding barrier won't stop me from reaching my goals. I know that both my daughter and I will receive a college education and that this transition time is temporary.

We Cannot Turn Back
Denise Reyes, Saint Cloud

When I first read the *I Have a Dream* speech, I had many mixed feelings. Mostly, I was mad at the nation we live in. To realize that we still live in a racist place, being judged by not only the color of our skin, but the stereotypes: where we live, what we wear, and the kind of car we drive. Sad, but so very true.

I couldn't help but think of my children and the things they will face in this world. How cruel will it choose to be towards them? I remember a time when

I had to explain to my 8-year-old son, 7 at the time, why this lady stopped us as we were walking out of her store. She thought I had stolen something, and later told the police that she had just caught two Native American girls, days early, stealing. I sat in my car crying. My son asked me why she did that. When I told him what she said about the other Native American girls, he said to me, "But what does that have to do with you, mom?" I was lost at words to say to him. My sons are half-black, and I now know that the world will see them as a black men.

There is a lot of injustice in this world, and a lot of hurt. I could've chosen to stay mad at what happen to me that day, but for what? That would only teach my children to hate. Martin Luther King Jr. says not to distrust white people, for some of them stand with us for freedom. He also said "We cannot walk alone... we shall march ahead. We cannot turn back." I won't look back at what happened to me and have hatred in my heart because I want my children to know love and forgiveness.

My Worst Driving Experience
Norberta P. Olmedo, Minneapolis

When I first came to the U.S., it was difficult for me. I didn't understand all the road signs because I didn't know English.

My first day of driving class, I went to drive and my friend said, "Stap." I asked, "What does 'stap' mean?" He responded, "Stap means wait." "When you see the red sign," I asked. "Yes." But the red sign said "Stop" not "Stap." English is written and read differently than Spanish. Now, English is much easier for me. I'm proud of myself because I understand more English.

Norberta P. Olmedo is originally from Oaxaca, Mexico.

My Hard Experience
Rizki Handarumsari, Minneapolis

It was a bad story.

It happened to me when I wanted to reach the bus which drove down my street. I went to the bus stop. I saw an old lady who was standing at the bus stop. When she saw me, she looked at me from my head to my feet. She immediately grabbed her handbag, and didn't stop looking at me. She looked so worried, like I would take her handbag from her. I thought fast, I walked little bit away from her. I was angry. It was a big problem. I took a deep breath to make me feel better. I tried to calm down and it helped me so much to handle my emotions.

Should I make a problem with that old lady? No I didn't. She reminded me of my mother. I could not fight with the woman of that age. I remembered what my mother told me when I would leave my country. She asked me to be more patient and think positive. That old lady made me think. Maybe she had a problem with strangers.

From this experience, it made me think deeply. I have to be more careful. And from then on, I always keep space from a woman who brings the hand bag.

Rizki Handarumsari is 40 years old and is originally from Indonesia.

My First Month in America
Anonymous, Mankato

I came to America in March, 2001 and the first place I came was Pittsburgh, Pennsylvania. At first things were very hard for me. There were no Somali people there and my caseworker did not speak Somali. I did not speak English that much so the communication was hard. He found me someone from Somalia on the phone to interpret.

That is the way we communicated. After one month, my caseworker found me a job. It was from 7:00 am to 3:00 pm. I did not have a car and the weather was cold. My caseworker told me, "You have to ride the bus." The bus was difficult to ride because it always arrived at a different time. Sometimes I had to stand outside for 30 minutes. Sometimes I missed the bus so I would have to wait for another 30 minutes. My caseworker told me, "If you don't arrive on time to work, you will be fired and no one else will hire you." So I was scared to be late and always worried about the bus.

A Difficult Part of My Life
M. Alonso, Shakopee

I had one brother two years older than me. We were very close siblings and friends. We were always together. We protected and defended each other and we had a happy childhood. But everything changed when I fell in love with one person who my brother didn't like. I knew what my brother thought and I told him that I was not with him anymore. I continued seeing this person in secret and then I was pregnant. I felt afraid because my family didn't like him either. I made a decision to abandon my family and leave my house in secret. I didn't have enough courage to tell the truth.

I came to this country and then my daughter Litzy, was born. I decided to call my family and tell them I was so sorry. That was a very, very difficult thing to do. I was the most remorseful when I spoke with my inseparable brother because he told me, "You were my favorite sister, I was always proud of you. I thought you were an intelligent and strong woman, able to do and say anything, but now I feel let down." When he told me that, I felt very bad and sad. This was one more sad moment in my life.

I didn't see my brother for many years, but two years ago he came here. I knew I would see him face to face. I thought he wouldn't speak to me. When we saw each other he hugged me and I started to cry. He told me not to worry. Everything was fine. We will always be brother and sister.

The relationship between my brother and I is not the same as when we were children. It is much better. We speak on the phone and he loves my children. That is most important to me. Now I know that young people do not think things through and sometimes make hasty decisions. People need to mature. When

I matured, I understood the position of my family. I learned that the family is the most important thing that anybody can have.

M. Alonso is originally from Puebla, Mexico.

Something I Did on My Own and It Was a Big Mistake
Sandra E. Paredes, Minneapolis

The weekend ended, and Monday I come back to work even happier because on Saturday I just got married. But I never expected what was going to happen that day. All my co-workers were giving congratulations to me.

I used to work for a restaurant and I was working as a cashier that day. I was at the back of the house and one of my co-workers called my name. I had customer to charge for my co-worker. My co-worker had a food order with a beer in a tray. I only had to charge. I saw my co-worker with the ID, so I asked, "did you check the ID?" She said yes. I charged and gave the receipt. While I was handling the receipt, two guys came closer to the register. They were undercover police officers. They did these in order to see if the restaurant was following the alcohol standard. So that meant that I just sold alcohol to someone under 21 years old.

I felt so bad and I couldn't say a word. My face turned red and I felt like my blood stopped circulating. I felt annoyed and I looked at my co-worker's face and I didn't say a word because ultimately to check the ID was my responsibility. I always use to check ID even to older persons with gray hair. But that day I didn't check it by myself. That was a biggest mistake I ever made. It changed my life forever. The undercover police officers wrote a report and I had to go to court. The day of the court I was arrested by the ICE. This lesson I will never forget and it doesn't make me proud of myself, but I learned that following the law is my own responsibility.

I didn't know serving alcohol to someone under 21 years old would make me a criminal. If you are new in this country try to learn about the laws.

The Unexpected
Gloria M., Shakopee

When I came to this country it was very difficult because I didn't understand any English. I was very insecure. But when I started to work and take the bus, my life changed because I gained self-confidence. When my first baby was born, that moment was a very happy time in my life, but after twenty days, he was very sick. We were also feeding him the wrong formula. This made him worse so we took him to the doctor. He told us my son needed surgery! This made me very sad, but it was needed. Today he is very strong and it is fun to hear him talking. He is my big boy.

One year later, I was pregnant again and my second boy was born with a tumor in one eye. When he was six months old he had surgery and he is fine now. My first thought afterwards was, "Maybe there is something wrong with me?" and I decided to not have any more children.

Seven years later, I was pregnant again. This was different from the others. Our baby boy was very big, strong and a perfect little boy. However, we were once again faced with another illness. This time it was very serious. I took him to the hospital because he had pain in his legs, but the doctor advised us it was just growing pains and not to worry. When he was three, my doctor detected Leukemia and my first feelings were anger, sadness, and other emotions. I wondered if God was punishing me and I didn't know why.

When I look at my children, I ask myself, "What's wrong with me?" Maybe I did something bad, wrong, or maybe I am to blame. I really am not sure why all of this has happened to me. But I cannot let it affect my life. I can only thank God for my wonderful family. I love my children with all of their faults. They are warm and loving children and I would not change anything today.

Gloria M. is 33 years old and is originally from Mexico City, Mexico.

How Lottery Visa Change My Life
Anonymous, Minneapolis

It was in the Summer of 2007 when I got a visa to come to America. That was the greatest news I've heard in a long time. I was so happy that I am going to be the first one in my family to visit the country of Uncle Sam (America).

My life in Togo wasn't an easy one. My mother was poor, so I did everything I could to help my family. I used to work for so many hours, but I got little money at the end of the month. In Togo, we get paid per month, not per hour like in America, so I had to be very careful in my spending.

One day, my cousin advised me to play the lottery visa, which is a program the U.S.A created to help immigrants come to work in the U.S.A. Surprisingly, I won. I was awarded a free visa to come to America. I knew from then that my life will be better because I am going to have the opportunity to have a decent job and save more money. Even though the government is taking a lot of money from my paycheck, I am happy. My life is better than it used to be. I put my sisters and brother in one of the best school in Kpalimé, Togo for a good education. My mom has her own business, and she is living in a beautiful apartment.

One day, I will finish building my house, so we can all live together again. Thanks to America for changing my life.

A Story of My Life
Anonymous, Brooklyn Park

I was born at Mercy Hospital, in Anoka, Minnesota. My mom was a single parent. We moved from place to place a lot. I stayed with my mom up till I was about five years old. My mom brought me to my grandma and grandpa's house. It was fun because my big sister lived with them.

When Sunday came along I was waiting for my mom to pick me up. I was waiting all day for someone who wasn't coming. I got use to living with my grandparents and sister. I got into school and met some new friends. Everything was perfect for me after I knew my mom wasn't coming back to get me.

A couple of months went by and everything went downhill for me. My grandma beat me with all types of random things she could find. I never did nothing wrong—well I didn't think so anyways. My grandma never put her hands on my sister. So I got it in my head that I had to be doing something wrong for her to do that.

I tried my best to stay on my grandma's good side but then again she was still hitting me. I went through this for two and a half years. I get this phone call from my mom saying that she was in treatment and she will be out soon and wanted to know if I wanted to come back to live with her and I said yes.

My mom got out and I was so happy to move back with her because I missed her with all my heart and I didn't want to be hit no more. That's when my mom and I moved to North Minneapolis. That's where I started my life as a new person.

My Way to Cope with Hard of Hearing Stress
Angela A. A., Austin

I am a hard of hearing, but this doesn't affect my life anymore. As a hard of hearing woman, I want to share with other people the skills I use to cope with hard of hearing stress.

First, I want to explain what hard of hearing stress looks like. When it is difficult for you to hear what people are saying, you feel frustrated. Then talking to people stresses you out, because you think that you will not be able to answer correctly or you feel uncomfortable to ask them to repeat what they said to you. Hard of hearing people may find themselves useless.

I have encountered all these stresses, but I have developed some manners to help me cope with them. When people talked to me, I used to watch their mouths, and tried to read on their lips. Sometimes, I asked them to speak louder and more slowly. I also tried, every morning, when I wake up, to stay in good mood all day long.

All these things help me to hear more and be able to communicate with people. I don't feel frustrated anymore, because I think, I'm worth something. By this writing, I want to talk to other hard of hearing people. I want to tell them that they are worth something, that life is great, that God is there to help them, to help us. So never give up.

Deaf Child Girl
Chrissy Moore, Bloomington

Hi, my name is Chrissy. I was born in Minnesota and my whole family lives in Minneapolis. I was born totally deaf because my mom was sick from chicken pox while pregnant. I grew up with my family who are hearing so I felt left out with no communication with my family. I felt sad that no one would talk with me. I felt mad wishing I was hearing like my family. I didn't understand why I couldn't hear and couldn't talk. I went to school and I learned lots of sign language and my family learned sign, too. I am so happy; I can talk with my family forever!

Chrissy Moore is 36 years old and is originally from Minneapolis, Minnesota.

Difficult Time in My Life
C. Ruiz, Saint James

Something that happened to me that affected and changed my life was when, after a week, that I gave birth to my son Jamin. I felt sick and I couldn't breathe so I had to be taken to the emergency room. When the doctor checked me and did some tests he told me that I had gallstones and that I was passing a gallstone into my pancreas. They decided to transfer me to the hospital in Mankato. When I arrived there they gave me some pain medicine and told me that they were going to do everything they could to make me feel better. After a week, I was just getting worse, so again I had to be transferred, this time to Saint Mary's Hospital in Rochester. And even though I was really sick I could only think of my newborn baby and my husband. Both needed me, and the fact that I was away from my baby that I so longed for

and had waited for, made me sad. When I was transferred to Rochester, I stayed in that hospital for two months, and one week in the intensive care unit. I thought I wasn't going to live, because everything was getting complicated. I almost died because of a blood clot.

What kept me going and fighting for my life was my baby boy and my husband who never left my side during those difficult times. What I learned from this experience was that I need to cherish every moment in life and spend as much time as I can with my family. I always let them know that I love them and how important they are to me.

Moving from Mexico to United States
Alejandro Galicia, Minneapolis

Four years ago, I was moving from Mexico my country to United States. So I was sad because I left my mom, sisters and friends. Then when I was here, I felt happy because here is my father, so he taught everything about United States. So my life was start. The first year I was in focus to learn English and work. It was very difficult to do both, but never impossible. So right now, my life is very good and I know almost everything about this city. Also I know English.

Every day I learn something about the United States of America. Minneapolis is good place to live, is beautiful because have many lakes, park, river, stores, etc.

Alejandro Galicia is 21 years old and is originally from Mexico.

Decision
Miguel Angel Bautista, Saint Paul

I have had many decisions in my life, but most important was to decide to move to the United States. It has been the hardest one. I was 18 years old when I did it. I still remember when I didn't know what to do, when I had to decide between school and my family. I don't know but when this comes to my mind I almost cry. I think it is because I miss back home. Now I have been living here for 6 years. I can't believe it, but it is true.

Living in United States is difficult especially for immigrants. Everything is new and so different from my country. My experience has been exciting and strange. It has been exciting because I have made many things that I never thought. I never imagined speaking English. I never thought to be in the United States and see its beautiful places. I never thought to meet people from different countries. Also it has been strange because I didn't want to be here. I remember when I was a younger and I said that I would never emigrate to the United States. That was because I had an uncle here and he most the time he neglected his family. So now I can say, never split up because it comes to fall to your face (I am here) or in other words never say no.

This decision has had advantages and disadvantages. Everything around my family changed since I came here. Now my younger brother is in the university. That's what he wanted when he was at the high school, so I made him a promise to help him. But on the other hand, I am still dreaming of going to college. Although advantages or disadvantages I feel happy to be here, and to help my family. Maybe the next decision is to go back home and try to reach my goals because it is never late to make dreams come true.

Miguel Angel Bautista is 24 years old and is originally from Hidalgo, Mexico.

My Life in the U.S.A.
Anonymous, Minneapolis

First, when I was coming to the U.S.A., I was thinking that life is easy. I will be able to find a job in a month, but it was not how I thought. I was a guest for my cousin and her husband. She and her husband both were working, and they used to leave home early in the morning. I was by myself at home every day. I did not know where to go or who to call, so I kept sleeping.

After one week of being on and off the bed, I was tired of sleeping. I did not know where to start to look for a job or school because I did not know how to take the bus. After one month, one of my neighbors asked me if I am interested in learning how to take the city bus. I said, "Yes, I would be so glad if you can show me." When I learned how to take the bus, I registered for school and looked for a job. I started school and found a job.

Finally, my life is very different than before. I am so excited by overcoming all the difficulties. Now I am married to an honest husband that I love, and I have a happy life. I am rejoiced with my life in the United States of America and my husband.

Change Is Always Good
Angela M., Minneapolis

I remember when I came to Minnesota when I was 7 years old. I was sad when I left Oregon and left friends and family behind. When I came to Minnesota I was nervous and excited to meet my other family and nervous of going to a new school and meet new people. I remember meeting my family and noticed I had a lot of cousins, aunts, and uncles in Minnesota. Entering a new school was scary. I was scared I wouldn't make any friends or meet new people. In about a month I had made friends who I had things in common. Being in a new state, a new home, a new school and meeting new people can be hard especially since I grew up in a different state. But change has made a big difference in my life since I moved here to Minnesota from Oregon because I've met more people, have more friends and have a lot more family I can spend time with them.

Angela M. is 20 years old and is originally from Los Angeles, California.

My Life Experiences
Anonymous, Minneapolis

In 1987, I was born in Laos. When I was three days old, my brother and I got sick! My mom and dad took us to the doctor. I was sick for 1 month and for a week, I couldn't eat anything. They didn't let me come home until I could eat, because when I was sick I couldn't move my mouth so I couldn't drink milk. Then an old man came to our house. He felt bad for us. The old man taught my dad about medication. They gave it to me. I got better and they let me go home. There was a bald spot on my head because that is how they put water in my head. My dad's brother helped pay and the Thailand government helped pay a little and my mom and dad paid too. They paid for injections. I could hear, but then I became sick and lost my hearing. I was almost dead.

The area I lived in was damaged because of the war. We tried to escape from the war. We walked from Laos to Thailand. We came to the United States around 1990. My dad's brother helped us find a home. At first, we were living with them then the United States government helped find a new house for us.

When I was a little kid in kindergarten, I used a hearing aid box. I could hear voices. I was 6 or 10 old years. Now they have new hearing aid technology. During high school, I didn't have a hearing aid. Some students were deaf and some were hearing in my class. My left ear can hear a little and my right ear can't hear at all. I was mainstreamed for my art, cooking, and pottery class. I needed an interpreter for my mainstream classes. In 12th grade, I helped my friend clean up little sticks on the ground. My friend tried to lift a big log. The big log hit my head. I lost my memory. For a few days, I couldn't remember anything. My mom found out about me and took me to the hospital. But I didn't know it. The nurse tried to check me. The nurse found out my head is the problem. The nurse told me, "Your brain had a concussion." One and a half years later I was a bit better. Sometimes I forget for things.

The Earthquake Broke the Capital of Haiti
Michelle Lieske, Owatonna

On January 12, 2010, an earthquake happened in my country of Haiti. During this period I was in bed talking to my husband. He had just flown into Haiti at about ten o'clock that morning, and the earthquake happened later that day about 3:53 p.m. My family was on the roof and I was lying in my bed at the same time. I was surprised by what happened, because earthquakes rarely happen in Haiti. It had never happened before. I was lying still in my bed when I saw the ceiling shake and things were falling down at the same time. My husband and I ran out and went on the roof. Finally, my family left our home and went into the street. We were so lucky only one house fell down in my neighborhood. However, a child was killed. We slept in a big yard for ten days. After, my husband and I moved to the United States on January 22, 2010.

Michelle Lieske is 28 years old and is originally from Haiti.

Why I Left My Homeland
Hser Hser Eh, Saint Paul

A long time ago when I was a child, I lived in a big village in Burma. We had a lot of villages. Every Sunday I went to Sunday school and I had a lot of friends and was very happy. We had a small house in a large garden area. It was beautiful for me because around our small bamboo house my dad and mom planted many kinds of flowers like a fence. We also had many kinds of fruit trees and a lot of vegetables. I'll never forget my poor life in my homeland and I'll miss it forever.

My parents didn't want to leave Burma, but because of the war we had to go or our family would be killed by the Burmese soldiers. Our village was near the Burmese army camp and there were so many problems. One night when everyone was gone to sleep I heard the gun sounds a lot around my village. It was serious and dangerous, and we had to be safe in a hole under the ground. After three days we had to leave, and in 1988 I became a refugee at the Burma and Thailand border. I was very happy in the refugee camp because I had the opportunity to go to school and study when I was young. Then in 2007 I got the chance to come to the United States with my family. Now we all live in Roseville where we are safe and happy.

Hser Hser Eh is originally from Burma.

Coming to America
Anonymous, Minneapolis

I departed from Ecuador on December 3, 1999. I came with my friend. I came to the United States because I tried to improve my life. Ecuador is a country which is very hard to live because there are not many opportunities to get a job.

My destination city was Minneapolis. I flew from Quito to Costa Rica and stayed few days right there. After that, I flew to Guadalajara, Mexico. After that, I got a bus to go to Ciudad Juarez. I walked to the border and got a flight to Chicago, and then from Chicago to here. I came here with my cousin in his car. The time approximately was 29 days. I don't have a real idea about how far the distance was.

I despaired about my family, because I knew I wouldn't see them for long time. I had a little idea about this country, but when I was here it was very different to listen than you feel. I have nostalgia sometimes when I talk with my friends and family and remember some events what I had there. I am trying to finish school and then I am going back to my country.

A Terrifying Winter Day
Alejandro Olivo Arenas, Richfield

It was many winters ago, about the first day of January. It was a really bad snowing day. It was very cold. My friend and I were driving back from work. Well, I was driving and my friend was a passenger. The road was very slippery. It was frozen. Suddenly, I lost control of my car. I stepped on my brake pedal, but that action didn't help very much. Then we turned around many times. I remember I could hear my friend screaming because he was too scared while I was fighting to keep the car under control. Then, when the car finally stopped we were very happy that nothing happened to us. Since that day, I am always cautious and I try to drive more slowly then I usually drive. In conclusion, now I think that it's better to be a few minutes late, than to be involved in a terrible accident.

Alejandro Olivo Arenas is 37 years old and is originally from Mexico.

My Life as a Kid Growing Up
Omar Cross, Minneapolis

I was born in Chicago, IL into a family with three brothers, which meant that we did not have a lot of money. My mother didn't have a job at the time so our life wasn't that good. We didn't have good things like other families did, but we had each other as a family. When I was growing up, I didn't have good clothes or shoes that other kids have. That made me mad, but as a little kid I didn't have no control of life, I had to deal with what I had. I used to play games with my friends but they didn't want to play with me because the way I used to smell or the way I used to dress. The kids I used to play with had that good stuff that I always wanted. But like I said, my mother didn't have a job, and my dad couldn't take care of me like he wanted to, so my life was hard growing up. But I made a promise to myself that when I got older I was going to take better care of myself and have all the clothes and shoes that I didn't have when I was a kid. God is great, thank you for all the understanding that you gave to me.

Now that I'm older, I can eat, so can my kids. Thank you, Lord, for blessing me. Ha Ha, it's funny when you go through life with nothing as a kid, and as you get older God gives you a gift, and that's me staying on top.

How I Grew Up
Symone Walton, Minneapolis

I am from Vallejo, California. I grew up learning nothing but the street life. I lost my childhood at the age of twelve. I was a rebellious teen, smoking marijuana, fighting and sleeping with grown men. I was thirteen when I had my first official boyfriend or man because he wasn't a boy. One night I ran away from home to be with him. We went down to Chicago where he was from and possibly still stays.

He sold drugs. He was what many females thought was cute. He was a dope boy and my life with him was hell. Yeah, money was good, but all money isn't good money. At thirteen years old I let a twenty-four-year-old man abuse me mentally and emotionally. It was never physical, but it felt that way. I was two months pregnant when the girl he was cheating with jumped me with a group of her friends, and I lost my baby.

After that I ran back home and got locked up in a juvenile facility in my hometown. Three months after I was released, we moved to Minnesota and I got in even more trouble than I did back home in and out of county home school, Elmore Academy, Eau Claire Academy and Saint Joseph's. I am very intelligent, have good grades, but I dropped out of high school.

Out of everything that I did and everything that happened in my life, the only thing I regret is not going to school when I was so close to graduating. Now I haven't given up on myself. I am going to get my GED and go to college at eighteen.

I'm glad I caught myself before I hit twenty-one or older. I'm still young and still have a chance. And in the future, when I do have kids, I am going to make sure their life is not like mine. I love all my flaws and myself. You want to know how I got this far and have all my radiance. LIVING WITHOUT REGRETS.

Symone Walton is 18 years old and is originally from California.

Joining the Army
Fredy Antonio Ramírez, Andover

When I joined the Army, it was a big decision. Although it was hard being in the Army, it was something that I wanted to do in my life.

For the first time, it took a lot of nerves because I know it is hard to be in the Army. But, I didn't know exactly what was going on there. I still remember the day the lieutenant sent a member of the army with me to cut my hair. After they cut my hair, I looked very unusual because they shaved my head.

When I got there, I realized it was not going to be easy for me in the first month. I was confused and nervous because everything was really hard. But, after a couple of months, I was feeling good. In the Army, you have to wake up at 3:00 a.m. every day to run three miles and come back, take a shower and be ready in five minutes. Then we had to train. We would practice combat fighting and shooting as though nothing had happened.

Leaving Laos
Sython Louangsyharaj, Saint Cloud

It was about 7 p.m., my brother and I were playing with our cousin outside of my Grandma's house. My mom was inside cooking supper.

My dad came home from work. He worked for the fire department. We sat down for supper and my dad said we were leaving, I didn't understand what he was talking about so my brother and I asked him. He said we were leaving for America and I said, "Why?" He told us for a better life.

We waited for midnight to leave because there was a party and all the police would be there so they wouldn't be guarding the Mekong River. We said goodbye Grandma. It was hard because we loved her very much. We didn't say goodbye to any of my cousins because dad didn't want it to get out to the police.

We left for the river front. We had to be very quiet so no one would hear us. If we got caught we would not see my dad again. The police would harm him.

We waited for my dad and his friend by the shore while they looked for the canoe that they had tipped in the river earlier that day. When they found it my dad came back to get us. We had to be careful, because across the river there was a spotlight.

We made it to the river and got in the canoe. My dad and his friend stayed in the water with garbage bags tied to their arms and floated with the canoe across the river. Until this day I don't know how we didn't get caught. We made it across the river to Thailand. We waited in the woods until morning. A van came and picked us up to bring us to a refugee camp.

I was scared. I didn't know what was going to happen to us. We made it to the camp. That's where we stayed, studied English, learned American culture, for a year. We moved to the Philippines for nine months then we came to America it was 1981. We lived with a friend of my parents. They were our sponsor. They lived in Anoka, Minnesota. That's where I went to school and saw my first snowfall. I had never seen snow before.

The Life in My Country
Pah Er, Saint Paul

I was born in Burma in 1986. I started school in my village when I was 7 years old. I went to school about 3 years in my village. I had 1 sister and 2 brothers. I'm the older son, and I helped my parents in the farm. My parents taught me how to know about the farm, and we planted the rice and vegetables. We made a barn near the farm. When the Burmese soldiers came to my village they broke our house, barn, and rice. They put the fire in the house and killed many people in my village. We couldn't live in our village, and we moved to a refugee camp. We lived in a Thailand refugee camp for about 14 years. When I arrived to the Thailand refugee camp I went to school again. I moved to the Thailand refugee camp with my parents, brothers, and sister. I got married when I was 20 years old. I had worked in Thailand refugee camp for about 3 years.

Pah Er is originally from Burma.

Journey
Samiya Abubakar, Minneapolis

When I came to America in 2006 I didn't speak English and I didn't know how to drive a car. I didn't know anyone. I only know my sister's home and I wanted to work but I didn't know how to find a job and didn't know to go to schools. Everybody was busy and I cried. After six months I got a friend. I took the license test and started a job too and learned to speak English.

My First Winter in Minnesota
Mauro Castro G., Richfield

The first time when I saw the snow it was incredible. It was so nice. But days after when the snow started melting, I was kind of scared. The temperature went lower and lower. The cold was terrible. I never had felt the cold in Mexico. It is a different temperature between Mexico and U.S.A. Now I enjoy the snow. I like when we have snowstorms. It's fun. Driving on the snow is a good experience. Otherwise, it could be dangerous. I don't know, but I will miss snow when I have to move back to Mexico.

Jason Hegg, Duluth

How I Made Friends with the Bus
Jeanne Kisongo, Minneapolis

When I first came to the United States, it was very difficult for me to use buses. I couldn't understand people in person when they talked to me at the bus stop. I remembered one time I was lost because I didn't know which bus I could take. My worst problem was the bus schedule. I couldn't understand people when they asked me in the bus. I couldn't understand what they said. I was very nervous. Now, using the bus is much easier for me. I enjoy taking the bus and like to talk to the people.

Jeanne Kisongo is originally from Congo.

First Time in an Airplane
Anonymous, Eden Prairie

My first time I flew in an airplane was when I came to America. That was a long trip. It took about two days, but after 30 minutes I started to smell food. I felt nauseous and vomited constantly the whole time in the airplane, so my stomach was empty. I didn't eat or drink. Even after I made my final destination and slept about five hours and I felt better and ate and drank, I still didn't like airplanes. Six years later I decided to go back home, so I needed to take an airplane again, even though I remembered my illness. My second time I flew I didn't feel sick. I enjoyed the airplane flight.

A Memory Date
Marie Therese, Minneapolis

On January 12, between 4:20 p.m. and 4:45, an earthquake struck Haiti. Two-thirds of the country was affected. People were not prepared for this terrible moment. I was home with my daughter, she was five months old, and I was studying on the balcony. My daughter was sitting next to me. When I first felt the shaking, I thought it was cars on the street outside my house, but the shaking continued and I knew it was not the cars. I braced my daughter's chair against the wall. I hung on to the balcony railing, and looked up at the trees to make sure they were not falling. I saw the hill around my house collapse and fall into the street. Meanwhile, the communication stopped. The street was crowded with people injured. They were asking for help and it was getting dark, each intersection had a group of people. Also, some of them laid down on the sidewalk. They were singing and praying with hope. I slept for five days on the sidewalk, and after that, I flew to Orlando, where I stayed for two days before I came to Minnesota. God saved me, and I thank his looking after me everywhere I go.

Marie Therese is originally from Haiti.

My Language Experience
Fartun Nuh, Minneapolis

When I came to the United States I didn't speak English so when I went to the hospital I needed someone to speak two languages. If I didn't get that person, the doctors told me to stay at the hospital until they got someone who speaks my language. One thing happened to me. I was working at a hotel in downtown Minneapolis in 1998. It was Ramadan time. I didn't eat all day because I fasted and our group leader told us to come downstairs when our hours ended. When I came downstairs the big boss came and said, "You have to go back and finish your work," but I couldn't because that day we had a lot of work. We didn't eat any food all day and had no energy. Also our hours ended and I didn't speak English. He told me, "If you don't finish your work you can't go home," but I didn't know how to say I couldn't finish my work because I didn't have time left.

I Am Proud of Myself
Nasra Omer, Minneapolis

The first day that I felt proud of myself was when I succeeded in saving the life of my friend. It was in 1992 in the refugee camp in Nairobi, Kenya. The situation was when the friend of mine had developed a very serious mental illness that could have killed her life if she didn't get medical treatment. Her mental problem was too complicated to be treated with local clinics.

The local clinics refused to admit her to Agakhan Hospital, the most expensive hospital in the horn of Africa. I decided to do something before my friend died. First, I went to local communities to report her situation but the response was not as good as I wanted. Then I changed course by organizing a group of refugee members and contacted churches and mosques. My group and I went to local businessmen too.

The first response from church was very great. The church contacted the Agakhan Hospital and signed that the churches would cover 100% of the bills for her treatment. My group and I took the patient, my friend, to Agakhan Hospital. My friend recovered from her illness and went back to her normal life.

To me that was the day that I realized that anything is possible if there is perseverance, dedication, and determination.

Nasra Omer is originally from Ethiopia.

My First Month in Minnesota
Lydie Ngoy, Minneapolis

I came to U.S.A. in October 30, 2010. I found this country so bad. I complain the weather in Minnesota. It is too cold, snow. I sometimes have a headache. The days are shorter than the night. I must stay at home every day because outside it is cold. I must wear boots, a sweater, a jacket, and gloves every day.

I found Minnesota too cold because in my country it is hot now. I must learn English because I want to find a good job in Minnesota. It is very difficult to find a job. I want to move in California next month. I hope in California, the weather is more comfortable for me and I might find job after little time.

Doing Something Difficult
Blia Vue, Minneapolis

A difficult thing was when my dad didn't want to come to the United States. It was very difficult to make him understand, but at the last minute, he agreed to take my family to the United States. When we first came here, it was difficult for me because I didn't understand English. I was not used to the food and fruit in America. I felt like I was born a second time.

One day, my brother and sister-in-law, who came to the United States before my family, came and asked me to go to school. She took me to school. I was shy and afraid because I never saw tall people with blue and green eyes. But, I decided to learn English because it would be the one way to support my family in the future.

Three years later, I graduated. I had three kids without a husband. I had no chance to go back to school, so I decided to go to work. When I got my first job, I was really happy because my job was a machine operator. At that time, my English was not very good. It was difficult for me to learn my job but I think I tried my best because I needed money to support my family.

Three years later, I got laid off because the company went out of business. I also got married in that time, so my three kids and I moved to another city with my husband. When we got there, I also found a job over there too. The job was sewing machine operator. It was my favorite job.

During that time, I had two things to worry about, my husband running away and my dad being sick. I didn't know what to do, so I decided to quit my job and leave my husband. I came back to Green Bay to take care of my dad. Two months after that, he passed away. I was so sad and felt sorry about my life.

Two months later, I went back to visit my sister in my country. I also met my husband over there and we got married right away. Nine months later, I brought him to the U.S. to Appleton, Wisconsin. Two months after that, we moved to Minneapolis. Now we have lived in North Minneapolis for almost five years.

Blia Vue is 33 years old and is originally from Laos.

Coming to the United States
Mai, Coon Rapids

I came to the United States in July 2007 from Laos. The reason I came here is my husband lives in the United States and I married him. I came here with nobody. My trip was 24 hours because I went from China to New York. I brought pictures of my family and clothes with me because I didn't have any clothes in America, so I thought the first day here I could wear my clothes. I was too tired to go shopping for clothes. I brought my family pictures because sometimes when I miss my family, I look at their pictures often. I saw McDonald's and a nice house on the first day in the United States. On my first in the United States, I felt nervous and tired because I didn't know what to do in the United States, and I felt different from other people. On my first day in the United States I slept for 8 hours. When I woke up my mother-in-law and my husband took me shopping for clothes, shoes, and shampoo at Kohl's. The best thing about living here is when I met my husband and he helped me come to the United States. The worst thing about living here is snow because I feel cold. The thing I don't miss is farming a lot in my native country. I wouldn't like to go back to my country and live there. I like my new life in the United States.

Mai is originally from Laos.

The Law of Life
D. Barrios, Austin

When I came for the first time to the United States, I was eighteen years old and I had just finished my high school. I decided to come to work for one year, save money and then go back to Mexico and go to college. I got here in August of 2006 and in September I started working. After four years, I still live in Minnesota, and like many other people that immigrate to United States, I am prolonging my stay because it would be hard to come back again if I decide to move to Mexico at this time.

Many of the people I know miss their countries and their families, but since some of them are not legal in this country, they must take advantage of being here and work to save money and give to their families a better life. Crossing the border it's becoming harder and harder and each time it's more secure, at the point that many people die in the attempt of crossing. Many people have been here for a long time and don't even know their relatives in Mexico and their relatives in Mexico don't know their children that were born here. Until somebody decides to do something about it, things will remain the same.

Coming to U.S.A is Very Stressful
Marwa Abubaker, Austin

We moved from Africa to the U.S. in 2005 because we were looking for a better living condition, and we wanted to go to school.

When we arrived we faced some obstacles. The first obstacle was language, I could read English but I couldn't understand people when they speak. Another obstacle I was pregnant with my first daughter when we moved here, and my husband had no job. Back in Africa it was hot and dry, and we arrived here during winter so it was very cold for me. I missed my friend and relatives and it was not easy for me to call them at that time. Because of all of the above, I felt stressed at that time. Sometime I used to cry. Now I can better cope with my stress in different ways. I like playing games and laughing with my daughter. Also I used to watch movies especially dramatic ones. Sometime I used to write stories about what I felt and this helped me a lot. Also I used to post some of those stories on the internet and that was fun.

What I Like Most About the United States
Aisha Sheikh, Columbia Heights

What I like most about the United States is if I don't have money I can go to school. If I don't have food I can get food. My biggest surprise was seeing people wearing short clothes and kissing outside. It is different because in my country, the houses are very strong. When I came to this country, the difficult things were speaking English and taking the bus.

Aisha Sheikh is originally from Somalia.

Learning and Lessons

The First Afro-American President
David M Looney, Minneapolis

The thought of having an African-American running our country is overwhelming. The reality is that Barack Obama is not totally black. His mother was white which tells us he is mixed racially. A person of color leading our country is something I thought I would never see in my time.

As a child, any images we would read or see about a black person would either be as a slave, or pictures of black people being lynched. After seeing so much negative stuff about our people, you really begin to think that you will never amount to anything. I remember in my history class all we were taught about was white people, their achievements, and how much they succeeded in everything.

I look back and think how sad it is to hate another person because the color of their skin, or worse yet, to be looked upon as not even a people. I think about all of the achievements that black people have accomplished, things we've invented, and the sacrifices we have made to get to where we are now. I don't remember what triggered the movement that led to the recognition or the making public of our achievements, but I was so proud to learn that there were many things that blacks have invented. People like George Washington Carver, Eli Whitney, Rosa Parks, Maya Angelou, Harriet Tubman, and all the others who felt they could make a difference and not just for themselves, but for the better of society. These pioneers paved the way for this historical event to happen now. Barack studied every morning, and his mother would wake him up as a child to make sure he knew his lesson for school each day. Most of all, it was the determination that Barack had within himself to succeed in life. There is this old saying of black people, "If you wanted to hide something from a black person, put it in a book." It makes me proud to see other people open those books and take advantage of whatever they read in order to better themselves and society.

One of the greatest achievements a person of color could ever accomplish is to take this country in the shape it's in and slowly but surely turn it around. I really hope Barack Obama is the person who initiates this process and that the president who follows him continues it.

David, born in Saint Paul, Minnesota, dropped out of high school in the 11th grade. He did not have the interest, motivation and support to stay and graduate. After he left high school, he went to work and has always had a job, retiring after 31 years at Honeywell as a punch press operator. Presently he is on the ministerial staff at St. Alban's COGIC in Saint Paul. David has six children, all high school graduates, and two with college degrees. His interests include playing jazz and gospel music on the guitar and working with his hands especially in auto mechanics.

How I Made Friends with Getting a Ride
Abdi Hassan Kulmiye (Ayare), Saint Louis Park

When I first came to this country it was difficult to get a ride. I couldn't understand the character of the people, but I got rides with people who had a different opinion. I remember the first time I called my friend I said, "Please give me a ride." He said, "Please wait for me." I said, "Wait what?" I thought that wait meant, "I will give you ride."

My worst ride problem was calling my friend. When I called someone else, he didn't answer the phone. I couldn't understand the people who lived in my village. I used to try to get information I needed.

One night I called another friend when the weather was 13 degrees. He shut off the phone. I responded to an automated massage for English that said, "Please leave a message."

Now getting places is much easier for me. I enjoy driving a car, and I don't like to refuse someone a ride because I understand the problem about someone who doesn't have a ride.

Abdi Hassan Kulmiye (Ayare) is originally from Somalia.

My Worst Bus Ride
Sahro B., Minneapolis

First, when I came to the United States, it was difficult to ride a bus. I didn't know what time the bus was coming. Sometimes when I was near a bus, he drove off and he didn't stop. Sometimes the weather was cold and snowing, and it was difficult to stand at the bus stop.

Second, the bus driver needed change so I was looking for change at night. It was difficult to use a bus card. The card needed to be put in the right place and I was putting it in the wrong place. The bus driver said, "What are you doing?" And I said, "I don't know how to use a card."

Finally I understood everything about riding a bus and I am so happy.

Sahro B. is originally from Somalia.

My First Trip to Honduras
Cenovia Lagunas, Marshall

My name is Cenovia. I'm from Mexico. For 10 years I have been a United States citizen. It is wonderful! For a long time, I had a wish to make a trip to Honduras but I was scared and full of emotion. Then on November 15, 2010, I had the opportunity to visit Honduras but I was scared because I heard bad news about people being killed.

Then my ticket was ready and my departure was November 15, 2010, from Minneapolis to Chicago. Something was wrong with the airplane in Chicago. I was waiting 4 hours. Then I took the airplane to Miami. When I arrived in Miami, the airplane was gone and the next airplane wouldn't depart until the next day at 12 p.m. The good thing was that the company gave me some coupons for dinner, a night in a hotel, and a breakfast— free!

Then I flew to Honduras and finally I arrived in Honduras. It was wonderful! The people and costumes were different. The things I liked were banana fries and the people were friendly. I made friends and I am ready to go again. They'll wait for me too.

Cenovia Lagunas is 49 years old and is originally from Mexico.

How I Got Back
Deonna Link, Minneapolis

How I got back in school is that I was looking for a job and all the jobs were taken by high school kids. I am a grown woman and I have two high school kids. I need a career and will let the high school kids get that $6.75-$7.00 dollar an hour job. So I have to go back to school to get my G.E.D. At first, I didn't want to do it. I thought to myself, my little sister did it, I can do it too! So I got up the next morning and took the pre-test to see what I needed help on. From that day I am on my way to getting my G.E.D. so that I can have a career. The career that I want is to be a RN, because I like to help people. So, that is how I got back in school.

Deonna Link is originally from Chicago.

Sewing Mittens
Mei Schilling, Esko

This is very exciting to hear the information that my teacher wants to teach my class on sewing mittens. I first saw the material and it was just unbelievable. How can I make the mittens like my teacher? This seems to be very difficult for me. Then my teacher says, "If you study diligently it will be simple." Then she helped me cut the material and pin it together. She taught me how to sew. I had never used a sewing machine before in my country so I will be very careful with my hands, and I have to work my feet to match my hands. I think this is not easy for me. With the help of the teacher, I spent two hours to sew one mitten. I was very happy. I know that I am sewing very slowly, but I know that as I learn more I can sew faster. Now I can sew mittens very good and very fast too.

I am very happy to have this class. I learn a lot from my teacher. I learn the English language from this class. I also have the opportunity to learn other things as well, like sewing, cooking, and gardening. I am very thankful my teacher is my English teacher and also my life coach. I also like this class as it lets me improve a little each day.

Bucks
Kyunghee Yoon, Minneapolis.

When I first came to this country, it was very difficult for me to buy something at market. I couldn't understand "BUCKS." I guessed that it was "BOXES." But it's dollars. At the first time, it was very funny for me. Now I'm getting better slowly.

Kyunghee Yoon is originally from Korea.

How to Communicate with People
Suleiman, Minneapolis

I remember when I first came to the United States, it was difficult for me to communicate with people. I couldn't understand American people when they spoke English. It was extremely difficult for me when Americans spoke English. I remember the first time I took the bus. An African American guy said to me, "What's up?" and I said, "What?" I didn't know "What's up?" can mean "How are you doing?" My worst communication problem was asking directions. When I asked for directions for example, I couldn't understand and I couldn't get the directions I needed. Now I speak English well and I understand American people. So I'm very proud to learn English and to communicate with American people.

Suleiman is originally from Hargeisa, Somaliland.

Education
Fadumo Ali, Minneapolis

Education is very important for every human being on earth, especially if you are an immigrant and you come to the United States. Some of us, when we come here to the United States, don't know any English. Wherever you go you will need an interpreter, even for something that you want to be private. I can understand what it means going through that situation, and I have seen many of my relatives go through it. It is very stressful and disappointing.

There are many opportunities in this country; there are schools everywhere. Adult education is free because the government pays for it. You can learn English from basic to GED. After you graduate you can go to college. If you are eligible you can get free college, get your degree, and have a good career of your dream. Don't say I can't learn because I am an immigrant and don't know any English. Yes you can, if you work hard. There are many immigrants who came here to the United States and they didn't speak English. They learned basic English then went to college and went to university, and now they have a good career.

Fadumo Ali is 28 years old and is originally from Somalia.

Getting My Driver's License
Chao Vang, Saint Paul

My name is Chao. I was born in Laos. I grew up in a Thailand refugee camp. I came to the United States in 2004. After three months I got my driver's permit. Six months later I went to test for the driver's license. My first time to take it, I felt nervous because the man who tested me was a white person. He was tall and big. He talked very loud and fast. That made me scared. So my sister told him to speak slowly to me because she knew that I was nervous with him. After that he talked slowly but I didn't pass. Four weeks later I went back to take it the second time so I passed and got my driver's license.

Chao Vang is originally from Laos.

Untitled
Alvaro Ortega, Minneapolis

My name is Alvaro Ortega. I am from Mexico. I want to tell people how important education is, because you can understand when you talk to someone if they have good education. When you don't understand, the people look down on you and then ignore you. So, I want to tell people how important it is to me to learn English, because when I want to say something it is really hard for me, so I'm in the school to learn English. I hope one day I can talk very well.

The Big Truck
Humberto Miranda, New Brighton

The first time that I drove the truck, I was working for a construction company. My coworker and I went to another state and we were coming back to Minnesota. We usually used this truck for all the equipment, obviously. Seriously, that took me a lot of nerve when I thought about how driving the truck was going to be like? I think that's what everyone thinks when they do something that they never have done before.

This truck made me feel so weird. The seat is bigger than the seat of a regular car that I have been driving for my whole life. Although I didn't care about how big the steering wheel or the pedals were. Everything is all almost the same, but in large sizes! And most of them are manual. But it was automatic and that helped me a lot.

The view is totally different from the biggest truck. You can see many things better than when you drive just a regular car on four wheels. I think when you're driving a truck nobody will trouble you because you are driving the truck. Which means, that you're more powerful on the road.

Finally I'll say a big truck is a big truck. It looks different from outside and inside and also feels different when you're driving it. And finally when I got off of the truck I realized that driving was almost the same as driving my car but just a little more difficult.

Humberto Miranda is originally from Mexico.

Where You Want Your Life to Lead You
Tiffany Meggers, Alexandria

When I was a little girl, I dreamed that my life would have lots of money and I'd have everything in my life. After finishing high school, I entered a nursing program; the program was for three years which helped my dream to come true. When I was in the hospital, suddenly I heard a gentle voice, "Hi there." In front of me, there was a young man; he was an ophthalmology doctor, who looked at me with his adoring eyes. In a minute, my heart was beating too fast. I was thrilled, and we were falling in love. After passing the examination for graduation, I had my nursing license. Then we had a big wedding.

My life from high level was dropped down to low level because the Communist took over South Vietnam. They wanted to impoverish everybody. All of bourgeois intellectuals must be brainwashed. They said, "You guys will take a course for ten days." But in their political prisons, it took from three to eighteen years. At that time, I had two kids and was 4 months pregnant. I had a hard time taking care of my three young children. I was a twenty-four year old who was being very loyal to my husband. I traveled many miles looking for any prisons where my husband might be incarcerated! After leaving his prison, my husband worked in a hospital as an ophthalmology doctor. Next, he cheated on me. To stop my crying, I got a divorce. I was thirty-six years old.

When I was fifty-nine years old, my youngest daughter (she is thirty-six years old) told me, "Mom, stop thinking of us, you need to think of yourself for the rest of your life." She loves me so much and wants to warm my heart so I can enjoy the rest of my life. Then, I got married with Bill Meggers, that why I am living in Alexandria, Minnesota where I can see snow everywhere. We just celebrated one year wedding anniversary. I wonder that how many years do God gives me for the rest of my life? I want to say, "Thanks, God! Thank you, America! Thanks to my husband, Bill, and Thanks, Mom! (Bill's mother), and all of the members of the Meggers family. You guys received me in your family and truly love me." Thank you.

Tiffany Meggers is 60 years old and is originally from Vietnam.

My First Travel to the United States
Ismail Mohamed, Saint Paul

This is the first time in my life in America. I have a very long distance prayer for my home country.
I am really proud to live in another country. My great problem was that I didn't know anyone and I had no father, mother, brother, sister or family here and much worse was that I couldn't speak English. Lord, what to do?

I arrived at the Minneapolis-Saint Paul airport, Terminal 1.

Then I had the choice. A man came directly to me and asked me if I was Somali and I said yes and replied with pride, "I'm your responsibility."

And finally I left him with joy and I can start to learn. I can stay in Minneapolis-Saint Paul and get a school education for persons over 20 years at the Hubbs Center. I am learning reading and writing there. Before, I could not do anything, not even the computer. Thank you, Hubbs Center!

New Americans
Shoua Xiong, Columbia Heights

I would like to stay in the United States because it doesn't have war. Also we have good government to make laws for everybody and help the students go to school. The government pays for the buses and for some students' lunches. Every student has the equal right to learn good things they want. Also, I am happy about the safety in my life. I have lived in the United States for twenty-one years. I think I will live here because we have good government and rules for everybody to use. I think some Americans are not polite to some people because they don't know where the new people come from or why they came to the United States. All the new people have different hair, languages, and skin, and some Americans think they are bad. But some Americans understand the new people and they are polite.

Shoua Xiong is originally from Laos.

Learning to Be a Helpful Mother
Lucero Rodríguez, Shakopee

My name is Lucero. I am 22 years old. I have two children and I am pregnant with my third. I'm a student at Family Literacy because I hope to learn English to help my children to be successful in school and their lives.

I like to attend school, especially the parenting class. I learn something new every day that can help my children. This subject is very important for parents because sometimes we do not know how to do fun activities with our children. I learn many good things in parenting. For example, I know how to read fun books with my sons. I learned to have patience and how I can talk with them and they understand me very well. Another thing I learned is to listen to their wishes and feelings. My goal is to be the best mother I can for my children.

Lucero Rodríguez is 22 years old, and is originally from Puebla, Mexico.

What a Surprise!
Hau Cin, Saint Paul

Oh, I remember my first snow experience in the United States on a Friday morning, November 12, 2010. I got up early in the morning at 5:00. Then I prayed for my family and my native country. After that, I looked outside from the window. I saw the white field. Everything was white. Everything had a white hat. I called my wife. "Honey, come and look outside. Everything is white same as a cotton field," I said, "Oh, my God! This is great and very beautiful," she replied.

Hau Cin is originally from Burma.

My Dream
Juan Carlos, Bloomington

I was born in Mexico and I grew up in the town. When I was ten years old, I told my parents I wanted to be a teacher. They told me I will go to a university, but six years later, I was annoyed and depressed because they didn't have money to pay the semesters at the university. We talked about the situation and I decided to quit college and go to the United States.

I lived in New Jersey for five years. I was drinking too much alcohol every weekend at the nightclubs. I always thought about when I was sixteen years old and in college. After that, I moved to Minnesota. I will never understand why God called me because He changed my life forever. I follow Him and trust in the Lord Jesus. I believe in the Holy Trinity, I want God to be my number one.

Juan Carlos is originally from Mexico.

Look Around Closely!
Yassamin Mehdi, Coon Rapids

Coon Rapids Dam is my favorite place. When I feel stress, I go there. The Mississippi River divides the park in two. Each side has weeping willows and pine trees, and between them you can see vines, yarrow, Angelonia, daisies, and lady slipper flowers.

The dam on the Mississippi River makes a nice view. There is a path on the dam. You can walk over it and hear the sound of the waterfall. This park is almost two miles long. There are also three ponds and many rest areas with places to barbecue. You can see Canadian geese, seagulls, and Mergansers swimming around.

I like the four seasons in this park. It is very special in the fall. Every fall I wish to be an artist, so I can draw pictures of how it looks. In winter, all the trees and the ground look like they are wearing a white blanket. The river and pond are frozen, and you can see small tents on the pond where people are fishing in the winter. In spring, the weather is just perfect for walking and smelling the fresh air. This is the only place I can enjoy and not feel stressed out.

Yassamin Mehdi is originally from Iraq.

Body Snatchers
Dee Livingston, Brooklyn Center

I attend school in North Minneapolis. One morning, as I pulled into the parking lot for class I noticed two buses parked aside North High School. One bus dropped off two students, the other bus dropped off only one student. She was pregnant. As I got out of my car, I looked around me and wondered where in the world have the kids gone. North High School looks like a ghost town. Kids drop out of school for all sorts of reasons, but how do you explain it? Was the whole school grabbed by the body snatchers? One has to wonder what the future of North Minneapolis will be like. What will the world be like for kids who can't see what's happening? What will the future hold for them? And, where are the kids who will help create the future? What will happen when so many kids will be dropping out of school? There will be no potential doctors, lawyers, engineers, or business owners to set up shop on this side of town. I don't know the answers to everything, but I do know, as I walk through these doors, I can feel good because I am shaping my own destiny one day at a time.

Dee Livingston is originally from Kansas City, Missouri

Learning English
Jasmine Cao, Saint Louis Park

I am from China. I came to the United States about four months ago. Now I go to school to learn English from Monday to Friday. I have been going to school since October of last year. I like it here because the teacher is very good and is patient. My listening skills and pronunciation have improved. I was sad recently. I was in the customer service class, and I liked it, but my English is not good enough. I don't always understand when someone speaks English fast in the class. So yesterday I told my teacher, "I want to give up, I'm so sorry. When my English improves, I'll return to class. Thanks, Todd." This morning I am studying ESL in my former class. Now I am glad.

Jasmine Cao is originally from China.

Making Decisions
Marie Bounds, Minneapolis

In my life, I've made lots of decisions. Some of them have been too fast without thinking them all the way through and often not thinking of the consequences that follow them. One of the good decisions I have made is achieving my GED and diploma. I want to experience the feeling that I finally completed a task and that one day my life will be better. Getting my GED will help me get that good job and enhance my skills and someday I plan to further my education. My dream is someday I will be able to provide a better home and place for my kids in a better neighborhood and someday even have my own transportation. With all of those achievements, I hope one day to look up and watch my daughter and my adult children smile in laughter being proud of their mom doing something positive in this stage of her life. I'm seeing them make better choices in their lives. One day when we're all having Sunday dinner I will be able to tell them how now I understand what they were going through in school and actually mean it. It will be nice sharing with them my experiences and the frustrations and hard work as well.

A Story About My Life
Samuel Rubio, Minneapolis

I began to travel when I was 13 years old. First, I went to Mexico City. I worked there for about two or three months. It was my first experience in the city. After that, I started traveling by bus everywhere around different countries. It was difficult but I was very happy. It was what I wanted to do when I was only ten years old. I came to the U.S.A. in 1989. After less than a year in the U.S.A., I went back to Mexico. My family was very happy, especially my mom and my father. My next step was Guatemala. I went to a small town. I met an old man and his wife. They were very poor, but they were very nice people. They saw me like their son. I traveled to Guatemala many times but it was in Mexico where I started to see the differences between the rich and the poor people. In 1997, I started to read about Che Guevara and Malcolm X. The history of Che Guevara helps me to understand how important it is to fight against capitalism and what I have to do everywhere I go, and how to protect people at work.

Samuel Rubio is originally from Mexico.

Challenge to Learn English
Hayna, Blaine

Going to school is difficult because I'm very busy at home. I spend a lot of time doing housework. Shopping takes time, cooking takes time, cleaning takes times, and washing clothes takes time. I have six children and my youngest child is two. Sometimes my children get sick and I need to stay home with them. School is difficult for me because of speaking English, reading, and writing. English is new for me, but I have a plan to make it easier. I get up at 6:00 a.m. to get ready. My husband helps with breakfast. My older children get themselves ready. I try to stay healthy. When I succeed, I will be proud of myself.

Hayna is originally from Somalia.

Challenges with English
Nyatoni Ruach, Blaine

I moved from Sudan to the United States in July of 1999. I worked in Memphis, Tennessee cleaning bathrooms. People would say to me, "Excuse me," and I didn't understand English. I wanted to learn English so I could speak. It was sad. I didn't know yes and no. The English is difficult for me. In 2005, I started learning English. I learned the alphabet and some words. My husband had to go to the clinic with me because I didn't understand the doctor. I learned some things but I need to learn more. Right now I go to Metro North to learn more English. When I learn more English I will feel happy. My husband doesn't go to the clinic with me anymore because I can talk with my doctor. I want to be able to communicate with American people more than I am. My next step is to get my GED. I will feel happy when I learn things.

Nyatoni Ruach is originally from Sudan.

Seeing Different
Halima Osman, Owatonna

I came from Somalia during the civil war. When I came to the United States, I saw different things like weather, people, places, roads, and even big different buildings. For example, the weather is cooler and there is snow here, but in Somalia there is not a snow season. Next, the people are very different in the United States. People come from many different places, and there are different colors of people. There are also many different religions. Most of the time, everyone gets along well. Also, the government is helping people more in United States.

Halima Osman is originally from Baidoa, Somalia.

Lydia Perkins, Minneapolis

The Story of My Name
Nasro, Minneapolis

My name is Nasro and I am glad to have my name. Nasro means "helper." My mother gave me this name. I didn't know how she found my name. I didn't know the meaning of my name until last night when Heather told me to look it up on the Internet. I am proud of the meaning of my name. I always help people, old and young. My name describes my behavior. A lot of people asked me what my name means before. Now I am interested to find the meaning of my name so I can tell the people. Most of the people in Somalia don't know what their name means or how they can find it on the Internet. I want to teach other people in my culture how they can find the meaning of their name. It is my pleasure to have my name.

Everything Has Its Cost
Long Le, Woodbury

My family has been living in the United States for one year and six months. I'm from Viet Nam. In my country, I'm a Veterinarian with more than 20 years of experience. But my certification doesn't work here and I have many difficulties because our life has changed a lot.

Last year, I went to ABE class. My first ESL teachers, Gail and Dominique, taught me how to write my resume, look for a job, practice interviews, and many other things. Finally, I got a temporary job in a pie factory. That was a hard job! While I worked, the sweat made my shirt wet, but I worked like crazy and after three weeks the company hired me. Now I have become the best on my team.

Some of my new friends asked me, "Why didn't you stay in Viet Nam and get a lot of money?" "Why did you come to the US and get a hard job?" I just smile. I think, "Everything has its cost!" My family is my treasure. I hope for more safety for my treasure. I wished that my wife didn't have more stress every day, I wanted my children to go to the best schools and learn the best lessons. So my hard job is nothing! Everything has its cost.

Long Le is 46 years old and is originally from Viet Nam.

Money
TG Araya, Columbia Heights

If I want to buy something like a TV or a microwave, I will go to the website and I will check for a discount. If I find a good discount, I will buy something. I don't buy at the regular price. The most expensive thing I ever bought was a house. We paid a deposit of $121,000. That was too much for us. Also the loan term is the most expensive thing ever in my life. I wish to pay everything at one time and not for the rest of my life. But it takes time. Sometimes I don't think about my bills because I don't want stress in my life. I enjoy my garden. I will enjoy what I have, things that are easier.

My Role Models for My Life
Anonymous, Minneapolis

The role models for my life are my spiritual mentors. Since I was young, I was always seeking for something out of the ordinary, because I had a lot of questions about life, love, marriage, and God. Though my parents were very fervent Catholics, they couldn't provide the answers to these questions. They were so important to me. My priest, when I asked him, could only tell me that I'd get the answers when I died.

I was living in my country of Guadeloupe when my sister-in-law suggested that I move with them to France, where I could study and work. It was there, in Paris, that I saw written on pamphlets the same questions I'd had back home. I asked quickly, "How

can I have the answer to such serious questions?" That encounter led me to the man and woman who would make an incredible impact on my life, helping me to transform myself from someone very pessimistic to someone optimistic and hopeful with a sense of purpose and direction for my future.

Rev. Dr. Sun Myung Moon and his wife are my role models and mentors, not just because their contributions toward world peace by establishing God-centered families have impressed me, but because they've motivated me to find true love and happiness by learning to live for the sake of others. This is an art which needs to be taught, and learned, and practiced sincerely. Such a sacrificial spirit is what I feel our nation desperately needs at this time. They taught me how to discern good from evil, and showed me how to avoid becoming a prey to others even as I keep loving and caring for others. We are meant to use what we've been given for the sake of a greater purpose, lest we end up with empty hands in the next life. I've come to realize that just as love is invisible yet real, the spirit world is also very real.

Rev. Dr. Sun Myung Moon and his wife are my role models not just because they teach me how to live a life of integrity, but because they demonstrate the heart of a "True Parent," the heart of absolute true love which always desires to treat others even better than others have treated them, by living for the sake of others. I'm deeply grateful to have them as my mentors, my models, and my spiritual true parents.

Minnesota
Cecilia Garrido, Austin

Living in Minnesota it's an adventure for me, especially in winter with all the different sceneries that we can see in cold mornings. It could be from trees full of ice that look like they were glass trees or they could be all white full of light or heavy snow and everything looks just beautiful. I love winter as long as I don't have to drive. Spring is as beautiful when it looks like suddenly everything becomes green again. Summer is hot enough to enjoy walking or riding a bike around the lake, and watching how all the people enjoy the nice weather. I love fall as well, with all the beautiful colors that trees and plants get at this time of the year. In Austin, MN, the Nature Center is a beautiful place to go on every season of the year.

Learning in Neighborhood House
Shawn Hu, Saint Paul

In order to improve my English, I found the free English course in Neighborhood House on the internet, and applied to be a student by calling. The teacher of Neighborhood House agreed to my request and asked me take part in the English pretest to decide which level course suited me. In this way I became a student of the Intermediate class in Neighborhood House.

In Neighborhood House, the English class has a different schedule, you can select the suitable time for you to have the class. We have English class from 9:00am~11:00am or 11:30am~1:30pm, from Monday to Friday. In the class, the teachers are very responsible and have patience with each student no matter if their English is bad or better. In our class, the students came from different counties, such as Nepal, Mexico, Somalia, Cambodia, Thailand, Cuba, Namibia, Ethiopia, etc. The different students have their different native languages. Our class is just like a big international family. In our class everyone is learning English and trying their best to describe what they are thinking about, what they are wanting, what are their feeling in English. When we have questions to ask our teacher, the teacher always explains the question by different ways, by different expressions, different body actions, some pictures, drawing some graphics, etc. In the class, we have conversation with teacher and conversation with each other. The teachers guided us to do some English practice and to play games in English. Also in the Neighborhood House, there are many volunteers, including a retired teacher, a young student of university, some other persons, even some people with disabilities; they contribute their time and ability to help us. I really am thankful for their lovely actions.

In this way, we learned a lot of English topics which are closely related with life, including job, housing, health, banking, shopping, etc. I think learning English in Neighborhood House is interesting and enjoyable.

The most important thing is that through learning English, it can improve my communication ability, it can enhance my living capability in United States, it can help me blend in this new environment and new social, and help me to earn my own living.

My First Time Ice Skating
Nereo Linares, Minneapolis

My first time ice skating was fun and scary. I held all the time on to the wall. Three friends and I arrived at the rink, everything looked fun and a lot of people were skating at the rink. Some people were eating hot dogs, nachos, and pizzas at the tables.

We rented ice skates and put them on fast. Then my friends ran and gained momentum before stepping onto the ice, they got three rounds and I was still in the same place on the wall. I couldn't believe it was so difficult and my friends told me that it was easy and laughed at me, but what they said was not true.

The second time was also too difficult, but I could walk with a walker. Then I got a new job at the same place and skating is free to employees. Every day I practice for a half an hour during my break, two or three times a week and then I did it very well. One day they invited me again but this time they were surprised. They couldn't believe I could skate and that I was working there. Now I like to skate because I can do it very well and enjoy it.

Nereo Linares is 26 years old and is originally from Mexico.

Matt Horsch, Duluth

There Are Some Ways to Improve Your English
Vixay Yathortou, Minneapolis

Actually, everybody knows. English is very important to communicate in the world now. So how can you communicate if you don't understand English? That is a good question.

I have some ideas for you. First, you should study hard and don't be lazy to review the words. Second, you should open you mind like not to be shy to talk to people and try to make conversation when you meet them. Then you can watch movies that are translated to English. If possible, try not to speak your own language at home. Next try to find the words by yourself and if you need help you can use dictionary or ask friends what that is. After all, I think you can improve your English easily.

Field Trip
Anonymous, Woodbury

On Tuesday, October 12, 2010 was my kid's school field trip. That day I went with my kids to Axdahl's Garden Farm in Stillwater. Before we went, the teacher told us about farms, tractors, wagons, and pumpkins. We walked to the farm. When we arrived at the farm, we saw the animals. There were pigs, horses, goats, and the farmer gave us some animal food to feed the animals. We washed our hands after feeding the animals. Then the farmer gave us a hayride to the pumpkin patch. Before we went, the farmer said, "Can you help me remember which way to go when we come back." That was funny.

We saw many ghosts and scarecrow decorations hanging in the trees. We arrived at the pumpkin patch. We saw many pumpkins on the ground. I would have been surprised if I hadn't known before that a little tiny vine can grow big, big pumpkins. My kids asked me how the tiny vine could hold the pumpkin. Everyone got to pick one pumpkin. After that, we rode on the hayride to the cornfield. At the cornfield we couldn't see anything, because the corn stalks were very tall.

This was the best field trip. From this trip I learned how pumpkins become jack-o-lanterns. My kids learned how pumpkins grow from little tiny vine. My kids were so happy that they each got a pumpkin to bring home for Halloween. They couldn't wait to go home, to tell their dad about the fieldtrip. My kids also couldn't wait to go back to the farm.

How to Study
Hijazi, Coon Rapids

When I was in my country in Lebanon I went to study, but at the school we had to pay money every year, about 1,500 dollars for each student. My family had five children and they had to pay 7,500 dollars with the books and all supplies for each one. When I was 12 years old I stopped going to school. My family couldn't pay for school anymore. That was the reason why I stopped my education.

On March 3, 2001, I got married. I traveled with my husband and my son to the United States. We lived in Texas one year and we planned to move to Minnesota. I started studying at ESL school. I was in level one but when I started I couldn't speak, write, or read English or Arabic. I could read a little bit of Arabic.

I want to tell what the difference is between learning Arabic and English. The Arabic letters stick together but the English letters are separated from each other. The Arabic letters are written right to left. In English, left to right. They looked different for me. English is easier to learn than Arabic. The most difficult is to hear correct pronunciation of English words. I want my children to know both Arabic and English. I read Quran in Arabic to my children. I read both English and Arabic story books.

Hijazi is originally from Lebanon.

Things I Learned from Others
Martha Bol, Fridley

Learning is very important to improve your life. The first things I learned from my mom, most things, like being honest and having respect for others. The second, I learned from my teacher. She taught me a lot of information. One important thing I learned from my teacher was that she said, "Education is not race. Take your time, be ready to learn." Also, I learned from my friend when I came from Sudan to the United States of America. She gave me a good idea, to go to school and learn English. She also told me to take a permit test so she could teach me how to drive a car. She told me the important thing is to follow the rules in America and learn American culture so life will be easy for you and your family. I worked out ideas with my friend and I started to organize my life and my family. Now I drive and take my kids to soccer and also to the library. Having a friend or someone to share good ideas with helps you learn different things or different ideas. Being with a good friend will help your life a lot.

Martha Bol is originally from South Sudan.

Danger Night
Anonymous, Richfield

It was a cold night in December. I was home that night watching a movie when the phone rang. It was a phone call from my brother. He was working that night. He asked me to give him a ride. I noticed from my window that it was raining and the temperature was getting low. A few minutes later, I was going to pick up my brother. While I was walking out of my apartment toward my car, I almost fell down. I noticed the pavement from the parking lot was icy. I thought it was a really bad night to go out, but there was no way my brother was going to get back home. I started driving my car through the street. Suddenly, the stoplight turned red and I pressed the brake to stop my car. My tires didn't respond to stop. I was lucky there was no car passing through. I kept driving to get in the freeway. I hoped things were better. But when I entered the freeway, I realized the road was getting worse. It was a very slippery road. I saw a lot of accidents when I was driving; they were caused by the icy pavement. All cars were driving slowly. Finally, I got back home safe after driving three hours. Normally it took me about forty minutes to go and come back. It was a dangerous experience.

Reflections About "I Have a Dream" By Martin Luther King, Jr.
Marisa Thull-Vargas, Saint Cloud

The speech pronounced by Martin Luther King, Jr. was very encouraging. I think he was an authentic leader who believed and pursued his dream, to live in a country where everybody has basic civil rights. He said, "We must forever keep our struggle with dignity and discipline. We must not become violent. We must not distrust all white people, for many of our white brother's stand with us for freedom. We cannot walk alone." In my opinion, he demonstrated he wasn't a fanatic and radical person; he was a visionary leader who understood the importance of each singular person to win this battle. He fought for the civil rights of minorities, in that specific time, the Negro. Now, almost 50 years later minorities are living similar situations, especially the Latino minorities. Their rights aren't being respected. Many of them find themselves outsiders in their own country. They are living in poverty inside the richest country in the world. They are getting less pay for their jobs, and sometimes in general, society. The war for civil rights that Martin Luther King, Jr. started motivated many other people who continued fighting until the government recognized that they should change the Constitution. Martin Luther King, Jr. is an example to follow. As Latinos, now is our time to fight for our rights!

Marisa Thull-Vargas is 45 years old and is originally from Peru.

The Beauty of Mother Nature
Hector, Minneapolis

I really admire the beauty of Mother Nature. I really enjoy watching the sky when we have rainy days, a night when I can watch the stars, the sunrise, and so many different things that you can watch. I also really like to hear how the birds sing, breathe fresh air, watch the animals, bugs, plants, and so many other things. One day I was driving on highway 394 when I saw the sky and it rained on both sides of the highway. It was something amazing. You have to see this to enjoy it. One day when I was kid I saw the full moon. Then I saw a star going fast and disappear. I could spend a lot of time describing how beautiful it is to watch the sky. This is one of the things that I really admire.

In 2004 I worked at Golden Valley Country Club. It was very relaxing. Every morning, I enjoyed listening to the birds singing. Also when I mowed the grass, I saw them fly very close to me. They tried to eat bugs coming out of the grass. The workers at the golf course built small houses for them. Every season they come back to the same place. I don't know how, but there are too smart to be that small creatures.

The dog is probably my favorite animal. It is amazing to see how smart a dog can be. Everybody grows up with a dog, at home or in your neighborhood. What I most like about them is they are loyal, friendly, and don't care if you are not the best or perfect person they are always going to love you. I like elephants, lions, tigers, turtles, horses, bears, etc. In conclusion, what I really admire is this world is so beautiful and we are destroying some of them. Life is very short and there is no time to waste with another things. We are worried about so many problems when we have this beautiful world to enjoy it.

How a Woman Decides the Life That She Wants to Have
Lilia Contreras, Robbinsdale

There are a lot of women in the world with different ideas, statuses, countries, and ways to live. But here is my history, just one of thousands of histories of women, and my thoughts about how we have to choose our destinies or maybe just accept them.

First, I was a very good child. I was a good student, not the best, but a reliable student and that helped me to finish college. After college I decided to go to another country (the United States) and learn another language (English), but when I arrived in Los Angeles, I only stayed there for 10 days because I decided that it was not the life for me. So I returned to Mexico.

I started to work in a company, and I achieved all my career goals. I was an important person in the business. I helped to grow the company. And that was the most important thing for me. I was a business woman. I thought that material things were very important. I lived in the moment, spending time and money with friends in night clubs. Without a formal boyfriend, I thought that I was free and I was it. I criticized the women who left their lives to get married and have children. But I got pregnant, got married, and left my country, my work, my friends, and my night life, all in just six months.

Now that I am a wife and a mom, I have learned it is much harder to be a parent than to run a company, but it is much more important and more satisfying. I think that change is always good. We have to accept it and sometimes give ourselves the opportunity to have a different life. Even if we think that our life is perfect, it can always be better. But we have to fight hard with love and kindness and above all things, have faith and trust in our instincts. Believe in something, in God or whatever your ideas are, but believe and live with love. The material things are important for a good and comfortable life, but it is always more important to have somebody to love and spend time with.

And now I am the woman that I want to be, and if life gives me more time, I still have a lot of plans to do. Thank God for everything.

Lilia Contreras is originally from Mexico.

About My History
Feysal Maalin, Minneapolis

I came from Somalia in East Africa. I have been in the United State of America since 2007. When I came here, it was hard to begin my new life. I worried about finding a job. There were a number of obstacles before getting work. Then I decided to start school, because, I couldn't achieve with my lack of knowledge.

All the time, I believed an education is the key to everything.

In addition, I would like to share with you short story that happened to me.

It was 12:15. I came back from school. Always, I used to ride the bus from the school to home. I didn't know how to use the bus in Minnesota well. I got on the bus. I put money in the machine, but the bus went another direction. After while, I realized I was in the wrong place. I was a little confused with direction. I called my friend and I told him the address. I stayed. He told me, "Get off the bus and use opposite bus from there."

Feysal Maalin is 25 years old and is originally from Somalia.

How to Be an Excellent Student
Yer Ntxawm Vue, Fridley

Before I came to the United States I knew none of the letters in English. I was going to school. I was just like a newborn baby. I didn't know how to speak English, read, and write at all. The first week I went to school my teacher asked, "What is your name?" And I didn't know what she was saying to me. I thought she told me how to speak, but she didn't. She just asked what my name was. When she and any students asked me, "What is your name?" my answer back to them was, "What is your name?" They said, "No, what is your name?" with their finger pointed at me. I just said the same question back to them again. I had thought that was the right answer to say back, but it wasn't. After a few months, I knew what people tried to say. Each night I studied very hard to understand English until now.

Now I am able to speak English better. I also know how to read and write in English. Now I can help my children study, teach them how to do their homework, and meet with their teachers. Now I know how to answer any question when people ask anything about me. Now I have my diploma, and I also plan to go to college. I'll study harder to reach college one day soon I hope.

Education and Goals
Ayanle Yusuf, Minneapolis

I'm from Somalia. I was born and raised in capital of Somalia, Mogadishu. In my childhood, I was so obsessed about education because I believe education is the key of the world. Also, education is the power that could take you the point you need in this world. Fortunately, I got the opportunity to learn until high school in my native country. I knew how miraculous this chance was to me and also I knew how valuable education is. Even though I haven't reached the goals I need yet, I'm optimistic about my future.

Education is the power that could change your life. For example, if you graduate from college you might earn a better job and higher income. You can buy a home and you might do things you weren't able to do if you weren't educated.

Other reasons that education is better is that education is good for your children and your family. For example, if your kids are have hard homework then you can help them to answer and pass the test. And may your children earn a better grade.

Since I have vision impairment, education is a tool that I could use to enhance my ability and to distribute the individuals who need the most. There are a plenty of individuals living in my native country Somalia and they desperately need someone who at least provide them basic education.

So, in my goals I'm planning to get my GED in order to help 1) my family 2) to distribute my ability to the folks who deserve it like the Somalia disabled. My other goals is to not only distribute skills or education they need, but also to give them inspiration they need to succeed their life. Somali disabled, especially blind and low vision folks, are abundant and isolated from other society. They are not educated and in fact they didn't have opportunity to educate themselves. In Somalia in general, we don't have education for disabled folks to give

them the ability to be educated and gain more skills. Also, Somali people do not believe the disabled person can do any tasks

So, the education would change all that and will lead me and others who are disabled a bright future.

Ayanle Yusuf is originally from Somalia.

My Journey to Italy
Miguelito, Minneapolis

I want to talk about my trip to Italy in 1993. I remember that experience; it was really wonderful. I was living and working for about four years in Milan, Italy, while also taking classes in jewelry manufacturing.

At the beginning of my arrival in October 1993, my friends were waiting for me. They gave me a little trip inside Milan. The Duomo di Milano (Italian cathedral) is a place downtown were many people from different countries join to talk about their experiences coming from their countries. The food was delicious with different flavors, and their architecture was so interesting. My first day in Milan was so wonderful.

During my days in Milan, I met Father Barbieri, president of the organization Coopération Internationale. This is a nonprofit organization, which receives donations from different countries to help many poor people around the world, especially people from Africa. I was working close to him receiving donations from Italian people and giving food to the poor people living in Milan. People from Italy are very helpful and kind. They made me a comfortable life in Milan. I was living in a place with the Father Barbieri and many other immigrants from Africa. At the same time, I was taking classes in manufacturing jewelry, and I learned many strategies in how to do business.

After four years of living in beautiful Italy, I decided to return to my country, of course with some money in my pocket, to continue doing jewelry busi-

ness. I also kept working on my profession, which is mechanical engineering specializing in HVAC (Heating Ventilation and Air Condition), doing many commercial and private projects. It was so hard for me to choose what to do with my life, but after thinking about it, I decided to move to the U.S.A. in August 1999, without understanding any English. That is another story...

My Life in the U.S.
Bless Say, Saint Paul

On November 12 2008, I arrived in the U.S. When I arrived in Saint Paul, Minnesota, it was winter. I saw snow everywhere. I saw many trees except fir trees which have no leaves. I asked my niece if the trees have died since they didn't have any leaves. She told me that they have not died; their leaves come up after the winter. I wondered about that because in our land the trees that don't have any leaves are dead.

Everything was so different here. The first person who I met at MORE School was teacher Sheryl. She tested me before I started to study in ESL classes. She is social and friendly. She was my first friend in the U.S. In April 2009, I started studying English in teacher Nathan's class. He was my first teacher in the U.S. and very nice to the students. ESL classes have helped me a lot. Now, I still study at MORE School. MORE School is my first school in the U.S. After teacher Nathan quit teaching, teacher Denay and teacher Michelle continued teaching. All of the teachers at MORE School are kind, friendly and helpful. I love all of them very much.

May God bless all of the teachers in the U.S.

My Decision to Come to the United States
Huseyin Baral, Crystal

For me, it was a very hard decision to come to the United States because I already had work, family, and friends back in Turkey. I had to make the decision because I fell in love with an American woman in the Grand Bazaar where I was working and she was a tourist.

I had been working in the Grand Bazaar with 4000 shops in it. I was a manager in one of the shops there, designing and selling silk purses to people from all nations. I miss talking and doing business with them. I love my family and miss them a lot, too. We would come together often, talking to each other, making breakfast in the morning together from the same tray.

My friends from the Grand Bazaar and I would get together every Thursday to play soccer. We would also go to one of the traditional places where Turkish people go to relax. We would smoke water pipes and look at the colorful mosaic lamps and the carpets hanging on the wall. I had Sundays off and my friends and I would take a ferry out to Büyükada Island to swim and enjoy the view of the sea.

My girlfriend and I decided to apply for the fiancé visa. We had to wait seven months and prepare all the proof of our relationship. She came to Turkey for my interview at the American Embassy and finally we got the visa. We were so happy! After 14 hours of flying, I arrived in the United States.

We had our wedding at the Holiday Inn. Every-

one that we love was invited to our wedding. It was an amazing day! And now we are both hard at work in our busy life in America.

Huseyin Baral is originally from Turkey.

Dedication to a Teacher
Tsehai Getahun, Saint Paul

This essay is dedicated to an amazing woman who has changed many people's lives in just one year, especially mine. Her name is Heather Herman. She is caring, educated, and inspiring.

Heather is a caring and compassionate person. She would do everything she can in her power to help a student. No matter how many of us would go to her office and bombard her with questions or concerns, she's always made time to listen with a smile on her face. I remember going to her office many times wanting very much to quit but after talking to her I would be encouraged. Her sincere words and support compel me to continue.

Heather is a very educated woman and holds multiple degrees. For instance, she has a M.F.A. in Creative Writing at New Mexico State University, a M.A. in English Literature at Clemson University (with Honors), and B.S.J. in Journalism at the University of Kansas (with Honors). Despite of all her accomplishments, she is the most humble and modest person, as they say she is 'down to earth.' She's

Vue Xiong　　　　　　　　*Saint Paul*

not afraid or too proud to share her fears and struggles and that had a lot of impact on me. She is interested in new ways of learning and encourages students to give input and participate. She embraces and respects diversity and she has inspired and boosted my self-esteem and many other students.

For me, staying as long as I have is a success because in the past, I couldn't stay long enough to get my GED. I was a student here before Heather's arrival. There were great teachers and very helpful tutors but not as many students were graduating or passing the GED tests and many time students including me did not show up. Also some the teachers seemed very discouraged. But since Heather has started working even the teachers seem encouraged and perform better. Her lively spirit seems to help everyone and the school atmosphere. It is true.

I'm not where I want to be yet, but I'm not where I used to be. I have improved so much in many areas, most of all my attitude and learning the importance of being persistent no matter what life may bring. This is the greatest inspiration Heather gave to me. I'm fortunate to have met her and dedicate this essay to her. I wish you the best in everything you do. You are the best!

Make a Decision to Immigrate to the U.S.A.
Maxime Kabamba, Brooklyn Park

Many people around the world are attracted by the reputation of life in America and want to immigrate to the United States. Immigration is an important decision. A person has to consider not only the requirements of the immigration authorities (government), but also their own personal life. The first thing is to gather all the information on administrative requirements and then to learn as much as possible about where you want to go: the geography, climate, people, culture, economics, community feeling, purchasing power, language, etc.

After collecting all this available information, which usually can be found on the Internet or any other reliable source, a person must analyze and review

it. Is the collected information sufficient to give you a global view and define the path for you to follow? Can you achieve your immigration goal and will it satisfy your well-being? Will you have to make changes in your goal?

It should be noted that in the course of the process, the realities do not necessarily correspond to the plans; there may be adjustments to make and obstacles to overcome.

Maxime Kabamba is originally from Congo.

Knowledge Market
Ojulu Omot, Bayport

School is the most important thing in every human being's life. It is the market where each individual will go to get knowledge for free. In general, school is the place where all people will go to learn how to read, spell, write, and talk. In other ways, school is the bridge for a better new life.

If any person goes to school, he or she will be a different and better person form uneducated people. School will give him or her enough education according to their willingness to learn. Then the school will open their eyes to see the new things that they didn't see before. The school will make them think better and that will change their living style to have peace in their life.

To have good knowledge from school, we first need to have intelligent teachers who will understand the student's problems as well. If there are no intelligent teachers, the communication between students will be poor and that would stop the students from learning. The good school doesn't mean a big or small building, but strong, smart, and dedicated intelligent teachers. For example, if there were no devoted intelligent teachers the students will hate the school. Then their learning interest or ability will decrease.

To have good, important schools is not only dependent on the smart teachers alone. It needs willing, nice, hard working students who will be able to follow the teachers and school rules to learn. For example, to have a good school it needs students who are always equipped and ready to learn. That means the students who are ready, are carrying their school materials such as books, pens, pencils, rulers, and erasers. Equipped students are not enough to make a good school, but the clean classrooms that have clean tables and chairs.

In general, the school is the market of education, knowledge, and wisdom where the people will go to learn to get a better future. People go to school to get knowledge, so they will get good jobs that bring in enough money for their living. The school that has intelligent teachers always changes the students. This will bring the real peaceful living to the neighborhoods. School is the important, free knowledge market for both poor and rich people to go to learn the new things that they didn't know before.

Three Different Countries
Sahra, Saint Paul

Randall Ringo, Foley

I came from East Africa and I was born in 1985, in Mogadishu, Somalia. I remember when my country had a civil war. It began in 1991 and many people died because of killing by guns and hunger. Unluckily, my brother didn't survive the war in Somalia. So, the rest of my family escaped to Kenya. We came to Kenya and started everything new. It was a new life with a new language. Finally, we became refugees in Kenya. After a long wait in Kenya, we came to live in the United States of America.

Now I'm so happy because I'm learning English for the first time. When I came to America, I didn't know how to read and write in Somali or English and I didn't know math either. I went to high school in Minneapolis, Minnesota first. For two years, I had a very hard time understanding the teachers, but other than that, I was ok. All the students were from Somalia except for four students. The only problem that

I had was the Somali students were speaking Somali in the classes so, it made very difficult for the first two years. After that, I changed schools and I learned much better ever since. I finished four years in high school, but I didn't graduate. I was supposed to graduate in 2005. If I had gone back to school that summer, I think I would have gotten my diploma. After all, I wasn't smart enough to think about my education, but I realize now. I want to get my GED so I can fulfill my goals, what I liked to do most of the time. I always liked to help different people around the world, like the help I got from so many people in a different country, especially my teachers. I thank them from the bottom of my heart and God bless you all.

How My Life Changed
Maandeeq Osman, Rochester

After I arrived in America, my life changed. My life changed big time. For example, I had to grow up fast, find a job like everybody else, and become independent.

I came to this country when I was a teenager. I had no family to turn to. Life was tough and exciting. It was tough because it was a new place and new people. I was looking forward to a new place, therefore I had to grow up fast. Since I had never left home, I didn't have much experience. I always stayed with my family. But when I look back, the best thing to happen to me was when I came to America because America was always my dream place, and it was exciting when I came. Although I never thought I would be living in America one day, I never believed my dream would come true, but oh boy was I wrong, and the dream came true. I am very happy to be here and I am thankful for what I have. God bless America.

The next barrier in my life was it was very hard to find a job after I came to America because of the language barrier. Also, I didn't have transportation. When you don't speak the language it's really hard and frustrating to find a job. It's hard because you can't communicate with anyone. It's also hard because you can't ask questions or ask if they are hiring or not. I didn't have transportation and that complicated my life and my job search. Therefore, I went to school and studied English. After awhile I applied for a job, bought a car, and opened a checking account and savings account. I also went shopping, what girls do best, and I went on vacation to Washington DC. It was a lifetime vacation.

Finally, after I came to this country I had to become independent. First, I was scared and didn't know how to become independent, but I am very glad I was able to become independent. When I was back home I stayed home, didn't work much, and always asked my parents for what I needed and they provided it. They never complained when I asked them, especially my father. But when I came to America everything changed. I had to do for myself, otherwise there was no one else to do for me. But on the other hand, I was glad to be independent. I had to because my parents were not working as a result of the war in my country. So I was able to help them as much as I could. My parents are thankful for what I have done for them.

After I arrived in America, my life changed big time. I had to grow up fast, find a job, and become independent.

About Myself
Leyla Ahmed, Minneapolis

My name is Leyla Ahmed. I have personal stories about too many things. My stories are mixed, because some are very good experiences while others are too painful.

First, I was born in Mogadishu, Somalia. Then in the mid nineties I was separated from the rest of my family therefore, I spent most of my childhood with my grandmother at the border between Somalia and Kenya, which is one of our neighboring countries. I never had any kind of education in my young age so I felt upset and terrible.

Secondly in 2006, some of my family and I to moved in to U.S.A. I met some difficulties when I was new to this country such as language, weather, public transportation, and missing the rest of my family who are still in Africa. I attended several schools in Minneapolis, and I am currently going to the Southside Adult School in Minneapolis. I met many students from all over the world, which we share the same destiny, which is how we can get a higher education in this country.

Last, I got a baby daughter. She is so beautiful and good girl. My family and I are very proud of her. Her name is Sara and she is four and half years old. She goes to Head Start in Minneapolis. The rest of my family will be coming in United States of America one day.

Leyla Ahmed is 24 years old and is originally from Somalia.

English for a Job
Fauzia Shawich, Andover

I came to the United States March 3, 1999. I couldn't speak English. I was pregnant with my daughter Lena. After I had my daughter, I applied for a job at Mercy Hospital. I didn't get the job because I didn't speak English. Then I applied for a job at Head Start and I got it. I went to English classes at the Adult Learning Center so that I could communicate better with people surrounding me. I would like to thank you for helping me with speaking English.

Fauzia Shawich is originally from Nuba Mountains, Sudan.

My School Experience
Anonymous, Saint Louis Park

I was born in Oromiya, a region in Ethiopia. I have been here since 2009. I live Saint Louis Park. I finished high school back home but I didn't speak English. School was different than my previous country. The teachers didn't help students because almost 60 or

70 students in one classroom. It was difficult to help students for the teachers. Now I go to language school. Go to school not difficult for me because I went high school my previous country. In the U.S.A. teachers are very helpful and the students help each other too. My English is better than before. Now I understand English language but I need to learn more English. I wish to go to college when my English get better.

Just Want to Share My Story
Samita Hunter, Cloquet

First time I came to Minnesota was on November 5, 2004. I thought all the trees were dead. I wondered how people could survive around here as back two or three hundred years ago there was no electricity. The weather was very different from Thailand and the language, too. It is hard for me to communicate with people around here. I spoke English very little at that time. I attend ESL Class in Cloquet, Minnesota. I didn't have an experience about English before I came to Minnesota. I wanted to learn reading and writing. First time in class I did not do very well, however, time by time, day by day, my English is getting better.

The teacher is very helpful and constructive. I call this class "Everything Class" because the teacher can teach everything we want to learn. We have sewing in class and sometimes we learn to do quilting. Our teacher has a friend and tutor who know a lot about quilting, so she comes in and helps teach us about quilting to. They also teach us how to pick out material. They are very patient and helpful.

I have learned a lot from this class and I have enjoyed my classmates. Thank you to teacher Angela, her friend Sandy, and also to her supervisor. I appreciate very much what they have done for me.

The Change of the Seasons
Arinchaya Bayerl, Cloquet

The 24 hours on the plane was a very long journey for me. When I arrived it was spring in Minnesota, but the weather was still cold. This was only the beginning of my adventure. I feel nervous and excited at the same time. There are so many things to learn that I have never seen before.

I have never been in weather like this. How do people live in such a place that is so cold? The summer time began and I was very happy to see everything turn green, but this is still not the same as my home in Thailand. I touched the water in Lake Superior and wondered how people swim in water so cold. The summer was nice and my husband took me to many beautiful places.

Then came the season called fall. I have never seen the trees change color. In my country the trees never change like this. We took many pictures to send back to my family so that they might know what my new home was like. I thought this season was very beautiful until all of the leaves fell from the trees.

Then the winter came with so much snow and very cold like I have never seen before. This was the first time I had ever seen snow. Even as cold as it was, I thought it was very pretty. I imagined in my mind before that the winter would be like staying in a giant cooler and the snow would be like a giant ice drink in my country. In the winter everything was covered with snow. There were no colors, just white everywhere and dark. My husband told me that the winter lasts a long time. Now I am waiting for summer because the winter is too cold.

Hopes and Dreams

A Dream Come True
Haddas Abebe, Saint Paul

My name is Haddas Abebe. I am from Ethiopia. My mother died when I was born. My father never remarried but became a priest in the Ethiopian Orthodox Church. I had two older brothers. As a child I was a shepherdess. I watched the sheep while other children walked to school. When I was twelve, my father gave me in marriage to an older man. We had two sons and a daughter. During the civil war in Ethiopia, my father and my husband were killed. Then in 1986, my brother took me, his son, and my three children— ages 8, 12, and 14—to Rochester, MN, where we had a sponsor.

Life was very difficult because I didn't know any English and I couldn't read or write in my own language. I could only give my thumbprint for my name. I started to learn English by hearing people talk. I went to ESL school at different times but it was far and I didn't have transportation so in the cold weather I would stop. It was very difficult to raise my children, especially when my sons became teenagers.

My daughter married a very good man and moved to St. Paul. I became a citizen in 1997. I took driver's training and got my license. I moved to St. Paul in 2001 and my daughter helped me get an apartment. My neighbor told me about MORE Multicultural School and I started there in 2003. It was like my family especially with my classmates and my teacher. We wrote in our journals and I told her my story. Then one day she asked me if I wanted to try to get an adult high school diploma. I thought it was impossible but she pushed me and promised to get tutors at MORE to help me. So I started studying for my diploma in 2005. Now I am 59 years old and I will graduate in June. That will be a dream come true and the happiest day in my life. Thanks to my teachers for not giving up on me.

Haddas Abebe is from Ethiopia. As a child she was a shepherdess. She watched the sheep while other children walked to school. She was able to come to Minnesota in 1986 because of a sponsor. Her life has been difficult because she didn't know English. She started attending classes regularly in 2003. Now, at the age of 59, Haddas will receive her high school diploma in June. For her it will not only be a dream come true, but the happiest day of her life.

There Is Always Hope
Araceli Sánchez-Calderon, Minneapolis

Brittany was only 6 months old when the doctor told us, "Your baby has a tumor on her right kidney. She needs a surgery." I remember that my husband and I held our hands and started praying. It's difficult to believe, to have faith when you are in the middle of a problem.

I couldn't sleep that night. There she was, my little baby inside of that cold room in surgery. I was hopping, "Everything is going to be fine." After a few hours, Doctor came to us with a big smile on his face. He said, "Your baby is okay; surgery was successful." I started crying and thanking God for giving my daughter a second opportunity to live.

Now Brittany is 9 years old. She is a lovely, smart, talented girl. I learned that there is always hope if you can just believe.

Araceli Sánchez-Calderon is 27 years old and is originally from Mexico.

Untitled
Rukia O. Osman, Minneapolis

I came to the United States in 2008. I live in an apartment with my husband. I hope to visit my family back home and bring some of them here to the United States. Right now, I go to school to learn English. I am trying to study nursing. Hopefully, I will reach my goals.

My family lives in Diredawa, a large city in the eastern part of Ethiopia.

Rukia O. Osman is originally from Ethiopia.

My Life in America
Galina Pankova, Jordan

My name is Galina. I am from Kyrgyzstan. I have been living in the United States of America for about eleven months. My parents, two brothers, and four sisters live here. My friend lives in Kyrgyzstan. I miss her sometimes. I talk on the phone with her and tell her about my life in the United States.

I like studying English. I hope that I am able to find an interesting job for myself. Right now it is very difficult for me to find any job, because my English is not good. I like knitting, sewing, and making things with my hands. In the future, I want to go to college.

Galina Pankova is 40 years old and is originally from Kyrgyzstan.

Life in America
Mo Vang, Saint Paul

My name is Mo Vang. When I leave my country to America, it was on August 11, 2005. I left my family in Thailand and I came to America to live in Saint Paul. I went to school for two years now. My husband has a job for three years now. I look for a job, but I don't have a car. I want a job because I need money to buy a car.

I go to school to learn more English to better myself. I have three kids. I think my life in America is to learn and know English so I can find a good job. If I have a good job I can help my kids to be better. I want a better life for my family in America.

Mo Vang is 26 years old and is originally from Thailand.

Journey of My Life
A Lee, Saint Paul

My name is A Lee. I came to America three years ago. I am studying and learning English. I attend the Hmong Cultural Center. My goal is to finish school. I want to find a good job. I plan to open my own business in my life and I want to travel to different countries for one month. After I come back home, I want to visit my friends and my family.

Story About Myself
Williams, Minneapolis

I grew up with my parents on the farm far away from the city. I lived for many years on the farm working with my father. When I was fourteen years old, I went to work in the city, because I wanted to buy my own things. My first job was washing cars. I worked for three years washing cars. The pay was not good or the economy either. That is why I decided come to the United States.

Finally, I got to the United States in 2007. Now I have a better job and I am studying English. I am making my dreams came true. Now the only thing I wish for is to return with my family to my country. I hope someday my dreams will come true.

Williams is originally from Ecuador.

My Life in the U.S.
Xia Yang, Saint Paul

My name is Xia Yang. I am 30 years old. I came to America on April 3, 2010. I love America, but I don't like paying bills. In America, I learn and speak English. I don't have any kids in America. I want to change myself to be a kid again, so I can start learning English as I am growing up. Yes, I want to go back to visit my own country. I miss my mother, sisters and brothers in a village in the jungle. I always want to see them. I also want to hear the birds singing—it has a beautiful sound. Also, I miss the beautiful waterfall in my own country.

Xia Yang is 30 years old and is originally from Laos.

Changing My Star
Julio Olan, Minnetonka

We are living in a world where everyone has his or her own star. We are separated into categories. Some are in the limbo, others in the category of poor, middle class, and rich. And probably you are asking, "Who decided that?" Well, you'll have to go back into your ancestors' history and see what they did for you. Because you know, everything we plant, we or our loved ones, will harvest someday. It doesn't matter if it is good or bad; we'll get exactly that. It's the rule of life.

Maybe you are coming from a royal family— or probably not. But it doesn't matter anyway, because we are here— breathing the same air, living in the same world, walking in the same journey. Yes, it's the same journey that we shared; born, grow, get old, and finally die. It's the journey of life.

It's our time and opportunity to make the difference. Today more than ever, we have to start dreaming during the night and working hard with our own hands during the day, until we make sure to have enough for our own future or for our loved ones to come.

During these difficult times we are facing, where the economy is the priority of everyone, we have to go the extra mile, do our best, thank God for what we have and pray for what we need. I believe we can change our star by not being miserable, lazy, dishonest or corrupt but by being positive, honest, kind, truthful and hard workers.

I'm changing my star. I'm living in the country of opportunities, in the most powerful nation of the world. I'm living in the United States of America. I'm an immigrant as were the founders of this great nation. I have a wife and two little kids. I'm thinking for their future. I want their success. I want them to inherit my best. That's why I'm changing my star.

My name is Julio Olan. I'm from Tabasco, Mexico. I was born into a very poor family. I think we weren't at the poor level, we were worse than that. But, now is my turn and I will change that with the help of God.

May God bless you and the United States of America.

Julio Olan is 26 years old and is originally from Mexico..

Life in America
Abayneh Tekle, Cottage Grove

After I finish class I wait for my ride. Then I go home, change my clothes, rest for 20 minutes, eat a banana and an apple. After that I work out for one hour. Next, I take a shower and eat dinner with my wife, her aunt and her brother, which is the custom of Ethiopian culture. After dinner we discuss our day and watch TV. Around 8:30 we do our separate activities. I do homework, read, and study grammar on the computer. Finally, around 11:30 I go to bed and sleep.

Now I am looking for a part-time job. One day I will fulfill my dream to go to college to study physical therapy. Finally, my life is not something to complain about.

Abayneh Tekle is originally from Ethiopia.

Being a Mother Is Hard
Marisol Jacinto-Vázquez, Shakopee

In the United States a lot of opportunities are given to people. In 2010 I had a difficult time. I have three sons and I am a single mother. I do not have a driver's license, and sometimes have no babysitter. I don't understand English very well. I feel very frustrated because I do not have a driver's license, and I do not have family here. I feel I sacrifice my time with my children, because I need to work very hard to have enough money to pay the bills and provide something fun for my sons. I am going to Family Literacy to learn English, and to help my sons with their homework. It is very important for me to learn English so I can talk, write, and read with my sons.

Even though life is difficult, I stay here for the education and work opportunities.

Marisol Jacinto-Vázquez is originally from Mexico.

Untitled
Warsan Farah, Saint Paul

I have a question for you.

Are you trained for life? What I mean is that there are situations that do not go with our desires or the way we want them. Unfortunately, there are great adversities in life or problems that we'll never be able to solve. Therefore, my question is what do you do when there is no hope to control over your affliction?

I was sitting at the library enjoying reading while I was waiting an hour to start my class. All of a sudden, negative thoughts flooded me, and then my heart started rising. At that moment, I was disturbed. I started to think more and listen with my editor voice. I became vulnerable emotionally. I felt sad and angry and my eyes filled with water, but I managed to fight back. Then I walked clumsily and went to my home to make shelter for my poor self. While I was on my way back, a light bulb lit on my head and asked me this question "are you strong enough for life storms?" To hear that little voice reminds me if I was at night before the dawn. That enables me to calm down and tackle my thoughts back. That is why I am asking this question to you. I am sure I am not alone when it is raining.

Warsan Farah is originally from Somalia.

In the Future I Would Like to Find a Job for Me
Pang Vue Thao, Saint Paul

I was born in Laos in 1964. As a child, I loved to play soccer. I was in a school in Laos and I finished second grade. As a young boy, I helped my mom and dad with the garden. When I got older, I got married to my wife. Her name is Sia. We have nine children: five boys and four girls. As my children got older, I began to look for a better life; I decided to come to America. I came to the United States in 2002. Me and my wife had another child. Her name is Cindy Thao. We stay home to raise her. I decided to look for an education. Now I know how to speak and write English. In the future, I would like to find a job. After I find a job, I want to provide for my wife, daughter, and son. In the end, I believe that I am very lucky to come to America. America is the land of opportunity.

PangVue Thao is 47 years old and is originally from Laos.

My Life in the U.S.
Luis Zumba, Minneapolis

When I was in college in my country, I had the opportunity to come to the United States. That was very important decision because my future was in my country. I felt sad with everybody, my family, friends and my college especially thinking how my life will be different in other country. Always thinking about what will happen in the future. When I arrived here, the best was knowing people of different parts of world working hard trying to be better in their lives. Each person has different ideas and goals.

The other thing was laws in this country has are very strict and we need to link to it. It's like learning to live, to start again and know this country's ideas cultures, and rules. I think the changes to this world are going from sleeping to awakening. But I am here in the United States and live in Minnesota. I'm working and going to school trying learn English.

How My Life Changed
M. Barrios, Austin

When I came to the United States I was sixteen-years old. Like many other people I came to pursue my dreams. Before I started my trip I made a plan about what I wanted to do with my life in the United States. My plan was to work for three years and then go back to my home country. That sounds easy but the realism was different. First, I didn't find a good job, then I met a young man and we liked each other. After a year and a half we had a baby and four months after the birth we broke up. So before three years everything in my life has changed. All those changes happened about ten years ago. Now I am still living in the United States and I have been taking English classes for three years and my life is still changing. But these changes are good for me because now I can speak English. Also I can write and read too. So I think this is why God didn't let me go back to my country. Now I have a new dream, but this time I will work very hard to realize it and the destiny will not change it again. Over the years I have learned to never give up even in the most difficult situation.

My Dream
Iman Ahmed, Eden Prairie

When I was back home, I had a dream. My dream was to come to the U.S.A. When I went to the ambassador to get a visa, they gave me the visa. I was very happy. When I came to the U.S.A., the first thing I heard was "Welcome to America." I smiled. I was very happy because my dream had come true.

Iman Ahmed is originally from Sudan.

A Lot of Nerve
Anonymous, Minneapolis

Growing up, I was raised by my parents who were illiterate and never went to school. So I decided to be brave and do something they did not do when they were young. When I first came to the United States, many of my family members told me that I should find a job, but I have decided to be brave and do something that my parents did not have the opportunity to do, I went to school. I started going to high school. And it was very tough for me to compete with native English speakers. But, with many hours of hard work after school I found a way to survive and I was very happy to graduate within three years of starting high school.

The Unknown
Trena L. Sumrall, Minneapolis

When you're a child, you have big dreams and think you have all the time in the world. I wanted to do so much with my life, but I took a wrong turn on the road and kept going. When I met my husband, I started to dream again about the life I wanted with him and the accomplishments we would achieve together. My dreams did come true with my best friend. I got the family I always wanted, the kids, house, cats, dog, and a whole lot of love. Never did it come easy, with sleepless nights, tears, and the unknown of tomorrow's day. Remembering nothing is free is important. Your dreams are to work hard at it and keep your eyes on the prize. Happiness is always worth fighting for.

A Privileged Woman
Anita Licona, Eagan

I am an accomplished woman who has experienced life to the fullest. I am happily married to the best man alive. We have two beautiful children, a boy and a girl. I am so proud to be from a country that has the most beautiful flag in the world. I also feel proud because I live in a peaceful city in Minnesota. Eagan is a good place to live.

The school that my children attend teaches them so much and gives them a desire to learn more and more. Every day, I to learn new words or a new phrase. I'm proud of myself. Now I am more capable of being a contributing person in my community.

I am proud to be a part of such a great country that has made remarkable progress in its economy, technology, and education since its first settlers arrived. It says in the scriptures that unions are blessed. Therefore, as a union of states, this country is a blessed place. I am so grateful to be here and have the ability to provide my children with a good life.

Anita Licona is originally from Mexico.

Untitled
Warda Karama Sayid, Saint Louis Park

When I came to the United States I had a dream to become an office administrator, but I did not get a chance to finish my education. At the time I was a mother of 5. Now I'm trying to learn English and to work for my future. I hope one day I'll reach my goal. I want to be a better person.

My Dream
Helena, Minnetonka

I was born in Belarus. Belarus is a very beautiful country and it has very nice weather. At the age of 15 I decided that I wanted become a nurse. I started to study nursing and I worked 9 years in a hospital. Because of political and economical issues, my family and I left Belarus and moved to Israel. Israel is a small and hot country, but it's also a very beautiful place. I lived in Israel for 20 years. I started to study nursing again. And then I worked as one for 12 years in an intensive care unit. Because of the endless war between the Palestinians and the Israelis, my family and I decided to move yet again. And now I am in the United States.

I want to continue to be a nurse, but I don't speak English well. Now I study in the ESL class. I don't understand many words, especially past verbs, but I will study hard and I will speak, read, and write in English well. I will be a nurse in this amazing country. This is my dream.

Living in America
Anonymous, Hopkins

I have been living in America for 11 years. I like to live in Minnesota. I live with my wife and two of her children. We are happy to live in Minnesota because this is a good place to live. My children have social security and medical help. I'm happy to because I have a good job, but sometimes I feel I can't live here. I miss my family. They are all in Mexico.

Randall Ringo, Foley

East and West
Bashar Al Jalleeli, Maplewood

When I was a chap, I had a dream to see the West, because I lived in Middle East societies. I saw the western people in my father's office and I was interested in them. After that, when I was 13 years old I went to the United Kingdom in the summer for tourism. I was so interested in that country and those people. I saw many things that were different than my country. From that time I took the decision with myself to change my life. For 30 years I entertained that conception in my mind to make it real. At last I have a chance to change my life, and now I am in the United States to begin a new life with my family.

Bashar Al Jalleeli is 43 years old and is originally from Iraq.

Living in America
Shukri Mahamed, Eden Prairie

I like living in America. I live in an apartment. I drive a car to this school and sometimes I give my friends a ride. I live with my husband and my three children. They go to Prairie View Elementary school in Eden Prairie. We are happy. We play together. A house is not happy without children. Now I am learning English and also I want to get a GED diploma, if God says.

Shukri Mahamed is originally from Somalia.

One Thing
Rito Pérez Márquez, Minneapolis

There is one thing that means a lot to me, and that thing is getting the best education you can get. It is very hard, very stressful, but it is not impossible. It takes a lot of effort, a lot of work to get where you wish to get, but it is worth it.

If you think positive you can do it, like I said, it is not impossible. Education is something that will help you forever. It is something that we all need. It is a very important thing in life. Education has a big meaning that some people do not know, and to find that meaning we have to go to school.

School has helped me a lot, because since I started my life changed. At first it was hard, I didn't like it very much. I thought I wasn't going to make it but then I realized that school was a good thing. I started to like it more and more, and now I really like it.

I really want to get my high school diploma, but before I get it, I have to work as hard as I can. Once I get my diploma I will go to college to do or to get done with the things I have always wanted to do.

Goals
Tereual White, Minneapolis

If you try, you can finish what you started. Run to it and keep your head up. Someone sees you even if you don't think they do. Leap, dive, fly until you get what you want. There is no problem believing in what you want. Success is everywhere if you just look for it. Dreams can put you somewhere. Taking time to go through, I know is hard, but there is also success after doing it. Say your dreams are me and do it. You can say "can't" but say it while doing it.

The path you take becomes you. It doesn't matter how old you are, it doesn't have to stop there. Making something out of yourself is better than being a follower. Pick what's inside you. That will get you somewhere.

Vang Pao
Chue Thao, Minneapolis

In Laos I knew Vang Pao. He was a humanitarian. He and his people helped America. They had a war in Laos. They had war for a long time, but they didn't win the war. He and the Americans lost the war in Laos. He came with the American people to the United States. He also asked the Americans to bring Hmong people to the United States. Finally his dream came true.

My Nicest Gift
Iryna, Blaine

Everybody likes gifts. I do too. I have had a lot of gifts in my life—expensive and not very expensive. But for me, money, jewelry and different things are not important. More importantly for me are my health and my relationships with people. One of the nicest gifts in my life is my eyesight. I was born with bad eyesight. I really had a difficult time in my life. In school it was really hard because I couldn't see what was on the board. Outside, when the sun was bright, I couldn't see anything. In stores I couldn't see prices. It was so hard. I hoped for good eyesight. I prayed to Jesus. In my country, the doctors told me that they couldn't help me because I was born with this problem. But I believed that I would see well, and I would drive a car. When I moved to America, I went to an eye clinic. The doctors were not sure, but they said that we should try. I had two surgeries. I had this for free. My medical insurance covered it. I understand that somebody paid money so I could have insurance. I am really thankful for this. For me, this is gift—a great gift—the best gift in my life. I can drive now, and I can see well. I understand people who can't see. In future I am planning to help those people.

Iryna is originally from Belarus.

My Big Opportunity
Juan Escobar, Fridley

I came to the United States from El Salvador in 1998. Many people maybe do not know what part of the world El Salvador is in, but it is a small country in Central America. I came to the United States with the thought of working hard for only two years, but the time moved fast. The two years passed, and I changed my mind. After twelve years of working hard here, the opportunity came to study English in this country. Some people are surprised when I say, "I have lived in the United States for 12 years." But I came with other goals. Studying was not part of my thoughts. Now I think differently. Speaking English is important, but not only speaking, writing and reading are

the complements for growth in this country. Now I try to study hard every day because I do not know when my opportunity will be over.

Fear and Hope
Luis Moran, Bloomington

I came to the U.S. because there are more opportunities for people who want to work hard. This gives us a chance to help our families and have a better future. After that, I start thinking how different my life and family life can be for all. Now we wish to be together in this country.

The U.S. has all the opportunities to offer to the immigrants. Sadly, this way of life is at a crossroads with a dangerous way of thinking because the media is taking sides with people who don't like other people for different reasons, like language, religion, the color of your skin, and nationality. This is profiling people. The media is now aggressive about immigrants, talking about immigrants and the impact on the American way of life. They portray us immigrants as guilty of everything. They say immigrants are criminals and we are weakening this country. They say we came to take advantage and ruin all the prosperity created in the last 200 years.

I hope the freedom of speech isn't misused to propagate hate on the TV, radio, and newspapers. They are sowing seeds of mistrust and xenophobic history in this beautiful country. But I have hope because I see the majority of people in this country value people, love justice, freedom, and equality. They are kind and love the real soul of America. They got common sense to stand up and say we want our country back and have values to welcome people in need. They don't want the US to become a country of hate. We the people mean all the people, equal rights for all. This is the heart and soul of America. I hope this is enough to save us.

American history is an example of how simple people became great because they stood up in times of need, for example Washington, Lincoln, Roosevelt, Kennedy, Martin Luther King, and others who supported them in times of crisis. Now is the time to be like these people behind leaders or volunteers who want to have a better country.

I wrote this because the democracy was attacked by a gunman who shot and killed six people. This is important because one of the victims was a Congresswoman giving a speech at that time. I hope this doesn't happen again. This is sad, but I hope for the best for all the people living in the U.S., citizens or not.

Luis Moran is originally from Mexico.

I Am Thankful
Daw Nyo, Saint Paul

I am thankful for God and I am thankful for teachers. I am thankful for my life. I am thankful for my family because they pick me up at school every day. I am thankful for my school because they have kindness. I am thankful for God in my life because he counts me in 2011.

I am thankful for my daughter. I am the most grateful for her. She always gives me abundance in my life. Every weekend when she lived far away she visited me. There are so many stars up there but I know that she is my shining star.

Untitled
Paul, Minneapolis

Many people come to Unites States for an "American Dream." This just applies for many people outside of the U.S. But when you live here you can see reasons about why many people stay here, such as the American dream, refuge or for study.

My reason was for one more reason. I am here for my wife. I moved here when I met her in my country, Ecuador. No matter which reason is important to you, live here. Live here so that you can know about different cultures, languages, and religions.

If you have the opportunity to live here, enjoy this chance in your life.

Paul is originally from Ecuador.

About Myself
Shukri, Minneapolis

My name is Shukri. I was born in Somalia in 1990. At that time, my home country had a civil war. I don't remember but my mom told me what happened at that time. So, my family and I came to Kenya. I grew up in Kenya. When I was a child, I was planning to be a teacher. But when we came to Kenya, my mom and my dad did not have money for me to go school. So, I came to the United States and then I started at this school. When I get the GED, I will go to college and I will study my degree. When I finish my degree, I will be a teacher. So, my dream will come true one day.

Shukri is 20 years old and is originally from Somalia.

Multitask Informer
Donshay Mitchell, Minneapolis

I would say that this name, multitask informer, is about right for me because I've always been that person who loved to do more than one thing at one time, and tell the good news of the day to my friends and family. I want to run two businesses! For one is a clothing line with the best qualities and I want my very own City's Midnight Club. I must know with these types of goals there's going to be bumps in the road, in order for me to reach my achievements. There are many times in my life where I've gotten told I would never ever make it, but throughout all of those haters today I still stand as a mature adult.

Obtaining knowledge is the key to success. Yes, I know this for a fact because, me, I'm so willing and ready for whatever. Leadership would be another step in my handbook, seeing and watching followers is not good for us in America. To me following someone is a very hypnotizing influence. As citizens, we should always stand on our own two feet in power and in independence. Goals are what I'm always thinking about, things don't come easy. I'm here to earn my success. Intelligent, trustworthy and honest people that I have in my life encourage me to be the best I know I can be. Yes I will one day have my two businesses. Yes I will make it no matter what I have to do. And to say I will be rich soon, all it is—is to believe, trust and have faith.

Donshay Mitchell is 20 years old and is originally from Gary, Indiana.

Where I Want My Life to Lead Me
Gaudencio Cortés, Kensington

What do I want for my life? Good question. I have many answers. Let me share with you the most important things for me. Well, in this new year, I want to be a better person with my family, coworkers, friends, and neighbors, and help them with money and love. To the people around me, I want to be friendlier and to be patient. I would like to share some food with the poor and homeless people. They need care, too.

Many people around the world made wishes for this year, like me, but nobody thinks or makes a wish for the earth. I want to invite you to think about Mother Earth. We need to take care of her like a son because she is like a mother to us. She gives to us air, food, and water. In other words, she gives to us resources to live. Everyone needs to take care of the rivers, sea, trees, and glaciers. We need to leave something to our children, grandchildren, and to the future generations. If you and I did not take care of the Mother Earth, nobody of another world goes it to do. It is our responsibility to do it. If we do not take care of her we will all die pretty soon!

Finally, I want to build a house here or in my home country, as soon as possible, because I am old and the time flies faster. Let's work together, so we can do a lot of things like have respect for each other and peace. I know sometimes is hard but not impossible. We can do it. Our dreams can come true if we fight to the end. My best wishes to everyone in this year and looking forward.

Gaudencio Cortés is originally from Mexico.

Our Dream
Gloria Silva, Owatonna

Years ago, I left my hometown in Mexico. I also left behind family and friends just to follow my dream—a dream for a better life. Years from then, my dream is coming true. I have a better life. I have a nice job that I really enjoy. I have a beautiful child. My son, who is 13, also has a wonderful dream. He has always dreamed about being a doctor, because he can learn something new every day and help others. Just to look at his face I get very excited. That's my inspiration to keep working and make his dream come true. We both hope we can live our dreams and make this country a bigger and better nation.

My Achievement
Antoinette Smith Edgar, Saint Louis Park

My name is Antoinette Smith Edgar. I am from Liberia. I came to the United States on May 10, 2004. After 3 months, I got a job. My first pay was $300. When I saw the amount on the paycheck I was excited. I went to TCF bank and opened an account. When I cashed the check, I sent $100 to my parents in Liberia. Since then, I have been supporting my family. I love being in America, because it has helped me to become an independent woman. After a year, I got my second job with Speedway Super America, but I wasn't making enough money to live on. Then I decided to go to nursing assistant school. I got a certificate from the school. It helped me to work in the group homes, because I like to work with people with disabilities. Since then I have been working in the group homes. In 2010 I decided to go to college but my English was bad. I couldn't speak English well or pronounce well. Then I decided to attend ESL class to speak better English and pronounce, write, and read well. I have been attending for about five months now. I am doing well in speaking, reading, writing and pronouncing. Right now I am writing a story about my life in America. A year back, I didn't know how to type on a computer but today, I am on the computer typing. I extend my thanks and appreciation to the ESL teachers who taught me to reach this far.

About My Dream

Jeannette Mbiye, Saint Louis Park

I'm from Congo. I have been here 8 years. Now I have a dream. My dream is about the future. I love business. I would like to have a travel business and become a businesswoman. I would like to travel around the world, too. I hope my dream comes true.

As of now I have built a business of cooking services and the name of my business is Mima Bibi 243. We have already provided our services for three Congolese parties. They were all successes. People enjoyed the food. Now we are looking to expand our business to other American people.

Jeannette Mbiye is originally from Democratic Republic of Congo.

If I Won a Million Dollars

Katherine Hayes, Minneapolis,

Having a million dollars is a big thing, whether you win it through the lottery or any other game. If I won a million dollars, I could spend it in many ways.

First, I would pay off my bills. Next, I would give my children money, buy myself new clothes, and I would buy a new car. I would stay in my same place, but I would buy new things for my apartment. I would save my money. I wouldn't spend it all in the same place or at one time.

I would try to win more money the same way. I wouldn't spend my money foolishly. I would take a trip to an exotic island. These are the many things I would do if I won a million dollars.

Message for Egypt

Nancy Zakhary, Inver Grove Heights

Stop fighting each other. This country is your home. How can you burn? Please think before you do anything because if you listen to their words you will burn yourself.

And you have a choice between still Egypt safe and be the world's mother or you have another choice- to look at signs that say "No more pyramids." Hey Mubarak, I heard your people say that you have their money and they said you cannot save your own town.

Let's see they forgot everything what you did for Egypt. But don't worry. Some of us didn't forget you are our hero of the October War. Unfortunately, we have forgotten it now. So now they just see the bad side of you. But I want to tell you, "God will do the best thing He can for Egypt." I believe Mubarak did many good things for Egypt.

We are not a gracious world anymore. Don't cry Egypt. You do the best things for us. Don't cry about us. They restrain you. They don't know what they do. They don't understand you that much. I want to fight for you. I want to die for you. But don't worry; there are a lot of people that love you. These days will be done soon.

Egypt, I have a message for you. "Go in their dreams and tell them to stop fighting. Stop burning my land. This is mine and I let you to be born in it. If you cannot be save it, just leave it for who can protect it. I'm mad at them. Really mad at them, because now there is civil war between each other. I want to know who is responsible for the argument. I believe the people responsible are the Muslim Brotherhood. They want to break everything between us. They hate our civilization.

Nancy Zakhary is 21 years old and is originally from Egypt.

Index of Authors and Artists

D

Katherine Daley 27
Mohamed A Dawe 83
Alicia Daynuah 40
María De Jesus 67
Deevang 35
Deka 89
María De Los Angeles 28
Mauricio Ortiz Diaz 19
Lily Ding 76
Abdulqadir Dini 6
Mouna Driouch 92
Hana Duki 8
Amanda Dunning 88

E

Antoinette Smith Edgar 149
Hser Hser Eh 111
Pah Er 114
Chad Erickson 98
Yanet Escalante 80
Juan Escobar 147
Esperanza 5
Estefania 60

F

Deqa Dhagwel Hassan Farah 55
Fadumo Farah 104
Warsan Farah 142
Heather Farris 73
Flor 90
Shao Yan Fu 44

G

Gabriel 9
Alejandro Galicia 109
Galina 12
Muktar Ganno 88
Adriana García 69
Arlette García 43
Rosa García 13
Cecilia Garrido 126
Sergey Gavalov 34
Paw Gay 74
Ansar Gedi 104
Tsehai Getahun 134

Gia 3
Rosa Girón 22
Arlinda Gjiriti 23
María Godínez 12
Mauricio G. Villafuerte 36
Mr. Grbich 91
Dalia Gregorio Castro 31
Miguel Angel Guallpa 37
Kwon Lapreed Gullie 88
Sofia Gure 13
Til Gurung 71
Armando G. Cardenas 58
Imelda Gutiérrez 24
Luis Gutiérrez 40
Keshaun P. Guy 82
Belete Gwalu 50

H

Rizki Handarumsari 106
Michael Harris 97
Nestory S. Harusha 68
Katherine Hayes 150
Hayna 124
Hector 131
Jason Hegg 114
Helena 144
Hue Her 63
Pa Seng Her 20
Patricia Reyes Hernández 83
Anisa Hersi 2
Hibo 68
Hijazi 129
Chery Hlar 18
Hodan 65
Tommy D. Holloway, Jr. 83
Matt Horsch 128
Shawn Hu 127
Samita Hunter 138
Dora Hurtado 27

I

Florence Iketalu 46
Illiana Mestizo 26
Lydie Ilunga 41
Iryna 147
Joweriya Issa 15

J

Marisol Jacinto-Vázquez 142
Bashar Al Jalleeli 146
Abdullahi Jama 12
Javana 8
Davin M.S. Jenkins 87
Anab Jibril 69
Eridania John 60
Fonda Johnson 22
Juan Carlos 123
Chuol Juay 74
Juliana 72

K

Olga K 15
Sabrina K. 99
Maxime Kabamba 135
Pascal Kabamba 101
Miroslava Kapranov 45
Khadra 11
Zalina Khan 50
Ka Khang 77
Michael Gei Khaw 34
Lan Khuu 10
Anita Kimball 79
Belayneh Kirba 44
Jeanne Kisongo 114
Shannon Knight 94
Elizabeth Turmero Kovacs 47
U-sa Kruse 17
Jeff Kulah 89
Muhubo Kulbi 59
Abdi Hassan Kulmiye 119

L

Cenovia Lagunas 119
Kha Lam 56
Mariela Landi Bautista 32
Mary Lay 71
Long Le 125
A Lee 140
Edgar Lema 103
Etalem Lemu 53
Mark Lewis 84
Anita Licona 144
Michelle Lieske 111

S

D. S. 28
Liubovi S 7
Rebeca & Anthony S. 29
Bounthanh Saengtarahn 79
Safiya 15
Patricia Sagredo 35
Sahra 136
Yesica Avila Salazar 33
Nadia Saleem 73
Gosa Samu 49
Araceli Sánchez-Calderon 140
Jimmy Sanmartín 28
Ana Santos 100
Sara 73
Álvaro Barrios Sarmiento 93
Bless Say 133
Warda Karama Sayid 144
Mei Schilling 120
Soon Sellen 27
Hyekyung Seo 68
Sergei 7
Angela Seriram 61
Shahira 50
Azar Sharafshahi 85
Fauzia Shawich 137
Aisha Sheikh 117
Shukri 148
Than Shwe 20
Gloria Silva 149
Silviano 90
Gail Simpson 95
Antoinette Smith Edgar 149
Bradley Smith 94
Ramon Smith 87
R. Lawrence Smith 93
Moo Moo Soe 57
William Spence 41
Jodi Sperandio 18, 77
Joni Sperandio 29, 38
John Strle 83
Uniek Styles 75
Isabel Suazo 42, 75
Suleiman 120
Trena L. Sumrall 144
Htoo Swein 61
Sherry Synkiew 51

T

#214018 95
Lourdes T 3
Addis Taddese 9
Halima Talha 45
Getenet Tamerat 41
Shaun Tanzy 98
Abayneh Tekle 142
Lan Thanh 7
Chue Thao 146
Janessa Thao 61
Pang Vue Thao 142
See Thao 31
Youa Thao 87
Thol Thim 81
Nhia Thor 2
Marisa Thull-Vargas 130
Oo Thundarah 1
María Tigre 78
Hla Tin 56
Martín Torres Balderas 93
Miguel Torres 11
Elizabeth Tot 8
Diep Tran 10
Nga Tran 61
Mohamed Awal Traore 103
Helene M. Trebesch 86
Elizabeth Turmero Kovacs 47

U

Melissa Urbano 52

V

Chao Vang 121
Houa B. Vang 91
Mo Vang 140
See Vang 54
Zoua Her Vang 71
Fabiola Vázquez 26
Eliud Velázquez 49
Velez 33
Richard Vickerman 85*
Monika Villeda 25
Blia Vue 116
Kia Vue 57
Yer Ntxawm Vue 132

W

Raymond Waddell 104
Symone Walton 112
Ahmed Warsame 6
Faisa Abshir Warsame 58
Damen Washington Jr. 104
Yayneabeba Weldeyes 3
Selie P. White 6
Tereual White 146
Williams 141
Hilda Wilson 36
Princeton Witherspoon 85
Myriam Wolfson 9

X

Choe Xiong 47, 55
Kazang Xiong 64
Mao Xiong 20
Shoua Xiong 122
Vue Xiong 6, 40, 48, 134

Y

Muzamil Yahya 94
Blong Yang 19
Der Yang 59, 65
Houa Yang 14
Khoua Yang 21
Lia Yang 18
Neng Yia Yang 20
Phainee Yang 5
So Yang 19
Xia Yang 141
Vixay Yathortou 129
Kyunghee Yoon 120
Ayanle Yusuf 132
Farhiya Yusuf 12
Kiin Yusuf 11

Z

Nancy Zakhary 150
Zemaor 22
Luis Zumba 143